HUME'S PHILOSOPHY OF RELIGION

LIBRARY OF PHILOSOPHY AND RELIGION

General Editor: John Hick, H.G. Wood Professor of Theology
University of Birmingham

This new series of books will explore contemporary religious understandings of man and the universe. The books will be contributions to various aspects of the continuing dialogues between religion and philosophy, between scepticism and faith, and between the different religions and ideologies. The authors will represent a correspondingly wide range of viewpoints. Some of the books in the series will be written for the general educated public and others for a more specialised philosophical or theological readership.

Already published

William H. Austin
THE RELEVANCE OF NATURAL SCIENCE TO THEOLOGY
Paul Badham
CHRISTIAN BELIEFS ABOUT LIFE AFTER DEATH
Ramchandra Gandhi
THE AVAILABILITY OF RELIGIOUS IDEAS
J.C.A. Gaskin
HUME'S PHILOSOPHY OF RELIGION
Hywel D. Lewis
PERSONS AND LIFE AFTER DEATH
Hugo A. Meynell
AN INTRODUCTION TO THE PHILOSOPHY OF BERNARD LONERGAN
Dennis Nineham
THE USE AND ABUSE OF THE BIBLE
Bernard M.G. Reardon
HEGEL'S PHILOSOPHY OF RELIGION
John J. Shepherd
EXPERIENCE, INFERENCE AND GOD
Patrick Sherry
RELIGION, TRUTH AND LANGUAGE-GAMES
Robert Young
FREEDOM, RESPONSIBILITY AND GOD

Further titles in preparation

HUME'S PHILOSOPHY
OF RELIGION

J.C.A. Gaskin
Trinity College Dublin

First published 1978 by
THE MACMILLAN PRESS LTD
London and Basingstoke
Associated companies in Delhi
Dublin Hong Kong Johannesburg Lagos
Melbourne New York Singapore Tokyo

Typeset by
PIONEER GRAPHICS
Printed in Great Britain by
UNWIN BROTHERS LTD
London and Woking

British Library Cataloguing in Publication Data

Gaskin, J C A
    Hume's philosophy of religion — (Library of
    philosophy and religion)
    1. Hume, David — Theology
    I. Title II. Series
    200'.92'4   B1499.R/14/G3

ISBN 0-333-23587-8

TO

To a' the men, and women too,
   That dine wi' me and have no view
Of how the world should be put right,
   Or pulled to bits with virtuous spite;

To a' the friends that walked wi' me
   O'er heather hills where men are free,
And turning hame, when comes the night,
   Would talk by fires we kindled bright;

To a' who formed this book for print
   And gave me thoughtful help or hint;
To a' on whom I've long relied —
   These arguments are now inscribed.

                      J.C.A.G.

Contents

Preface

The plan and purpose of this book are stated in the last two pages of the introductory chapter. However it seems proper to emphasise at the very beginning that while I try to make clear that Hume's discussions of religion fit together in a coherent picture (a picture most conveniently described as his philosophy of religion), the discussions themselves are very diverse. This diversity has to be reflected in any work which is concerned with Hume's whole account of religion. In the present case it is indicated by division of the subject matter into parts as well as chapters. Part I (by far the longest) is almost entirely philosophical exposition and analysis of Hume's arguments. Part II is concerned with his remarks on revelation seen against their peculiarly illuminating contemporary background and with his highly original account of natural belief. Part III deals mostly with the origins and social effects of religion. The final chapter is of biographical and interpretive interest and its conclusions are developed from the earlier discussions.

On first mention I give Hume's major works their full titles. I subsequently refer to them by the abbreviated titles and in the editions specified on page xi. A word of explanation may be called for here. I have given references to Kemp Smith's edition of the *Dialogues* rather than to J.V. Price's much more recent edition (Oxford, 1976). My original reasons for this were that Kemp Smith's edition is everywhere readily available and that my typescript was complete before the appearance of Price's work. In view of Dr M.A. Stewart's detailed and very critical review of Price *(Philosophical Books,* May 1977) there seems, however, to be no justification for discontinuing use of Kemp Smith.

In quotations the punctuation and spelling of the originals have been retained. Quotations from the Bible are from the Authorised Version of King James. Apart from a personal aversion to many recent translations, my reason for using this edition is that for Hume, and for almost all who have written in the English language since the beginning of the seventeenth century, the Bible and the Authorised Version are identical.

One other convention should be noted. I write 'God' with a capital letter only when the personal deity of traditional Christianity is specifically intended. In all other *or ambiguous usages* a small letter is employed. My only exception to this convention is when the reference is to a deity with features common to the Judaic, Christian and Moslem religions. In such cases the capital is employed.

An earlier and very much shorter version of part of Chapter 2 appeared in *Religious Studies* in 1976. The first section of Chapter 7 is taken from an article of mine in *Hermathena* (1964); part of Chapter 8 is adapted from one in *Philosophy* (1974). There are also paragraphs in Chapters 9 and 10 drawn from an article in the *Journal of the History of Philosophy* (1976). I am grateful to the editors of these journals for permission to use this material.

My thanks are due, in large or small measure, to more kind friends and colleagues than I can name, but I am particularly indebted to Professor Antony Flew. His careful and critical reading of the first draft has saved me from many small errors and not a few large ones, and his interest has been a great encouragement to me. I would also like to thank Professor R.J. Butler for his comments on part of Chapter 5, Professor E.J. Furlong for reading the final typescript, and Dr David Berman for his invaluable help in correcting the proofs. I am also very indebted to Nancie O'Sullivan, whose patient and accurate typing and retyping of the manuscript made possible this book.

There are others, close friends and relatives, whose help one perhaps takes too much for granted. I trust they will feel thanked and remembered by whatever worth this book has.

J.C.A. Gaskin

Trinity College
Dublin

List of Abbreviations

Reference to Hume's major works and to certain other standard texts will be given by means of an abbreviation followed by a page number (and volume where necessary). The following abbreviations are used:

Dialogues   *Dialogues concerning Natural Religion*, edited by N. Kemp Smith, 2nd edition (Edinburgh, 1947), reprinted with the same pagination, New York 1947 (Library of Liberal Arts).

N.H.R.   *The Natural History of Religion*, edited by H.E. Root (London, 1956).

Enquiry   *An Enquiry concerning Human Understanding*. The first number given is the page in the edition by Selby-Bigge (Oxford, 1902; 3rd edition Oxford, 1975, with same pagination). The second number is the page in the edition by C.W. Hendel (New York, 1955). Quotations follow the text of the former which is itself a reprint of the 1777 edition.

Moral   *An Enquiry concerning the Principles of Morals*. The first
Enquiry   number given is the page in the Selby-Bigge edition as above. The second number is the page in Hendel's edition (New York, 1957).

Letters   *The Letters of David Hume*, edited by J.Y.T. Greig, two volumes (Oxford, 1932).

New Letters   *New Letters of David Hume*, edited by R. Klibansky and E.C. Mossner (Oxford, 1954).

History   *History of England*, eight volumes (London, 1778). This edition containes Hume's final corrections.

A Letter   *A Letter from a Gentleman*, edited by E.C. Mossner and J.V. Price (Edinburgh, 1967).

Treatise   *A Treatise of Human Nature*, edited by L.A. Selby-Bigge (Oxford, 1888).

Life   E.C. Mossner, *The Life of David Hume* (Edinburgh, 1954).

Other minor abbreviations will, I hope, be intelligible. Unusual editions of Hume's works, where used, will be specified in full. Essays by Hume will be referred to by their titles, and wherever possible will be quoted from *Essays and Treatises on Several Subjects,* two volumes (London, 1777).

1 Introduction: Hume on Religion

> [Hume] seems to me one of those philosophers that think to spin
> out Systems, out of their own brain, without regard to religion,
> antiquity or Tradition sacred or profane.
>
> The Chevalier Ramsay

(i) PUBLICATIONS AND CONTROVERSY

Hume wrote a great deal about religion, most of it critical. His earliest remarks
on the subject, which might have settled many biographical puzzles, were
destroyed by their author. Writing to Elliot of Minto in 1751 he remarks:

> tis not long ago that I burn'd an old Manuscript Book, wrote before I was
> twenty; which contain'd, Page after Page, the gradual Progress of my
> Thoughts on that head. It begun with an anxious Search after Arguments,
> to confirm the common Opinion: Doubts stole in, dissipated, return'd,
> were again dissipated, return'd again; and it was a perpetual Struggle of a
> restless Imagination against Inclination, perhaps against Reason *(Letters,*
> I, 154).[1]

But his 'Early Memoranda' — notes and paraphrases taken while reading
Cicero, Xenophon, Bayle and others — do survive,[2] and indicate Hume's
interest in religion even in the years which preceded the *Treatise of Human
Nature,* his first published work.

The *Treatise* (Books I and II appeared in 1739; Book III in 1740) is not
directly concerned with religion, although we do know that Hume removed
from it before publication a chapter on miracles and possibly other sections
(see below, p. 102) which he had reason to believe would provoke hostility
from Scottish ecclesiastics or involve him in religious controversy. A few brief
and apparently inoffensive references to the existence of god and to religion
remain, but with the exception of the section called 'Of the immateriality of
the soul' they occur only incidentally in sections dealing with other subjects.
Nevertheless these passages, together with the construction which was put
upon some of his arguments, were sufficient to start an outcry in 1745
during his candidature for the Professorship of Moral Philosophy at
Edinburgh University. As a result of this outcry another candidate was
successful. A modern reader might find it a little puzzling to know what
aspects of the *Treatise* could possibly cause offence, but fortunately an
answer is to be found in *A Letter from a Gentleman* which Hume hurried
into print to defend himself in 1745. A copy of this came to light in 1966

and has been reprinted in facsimile.[3] In it Hume defends himself on six 'charges' arising from his arguments in the *Treatise*. These are: (1) That he maintains 'the Folly of pretending to believe any Thing with Certainty'; (2) that his principles lead to 'downright Atheism, by denying the Doctrine of Causes and Effects'; (3) that his account of the idea of existence involves 'Errors concerning the very Being and Existence of God'; (4) that he commits errors 'concerning God's being the first Cause, and prime Mover of the Universe'; (5) 'He is chargable with denying the Immateriality of the Soul, and the Consequences flowing from this Denial'; (6) that he is chargeable with 'sapping the Foundations of Morality, by denying the natural and essential Difference betwixt Right and Wrong, Good and Evil, Justice and Injustice; making the Difference only artificial, and to arise from human Conventions and Compacts' (p. 17f). This is not the place to discuss whether these accusations can be justified on the basis of what is said in the *Treatise,* but it is certainly the case that several of them were given more substance by Hume's later publications beginning with the two *Enquiries*.

In *An Enquiry concerning Human Understanding* (1748) Hume rewrote and clarified some of the material contained in Book I of the *Treatise* as well as adding new sections and giving the whole a much more obvious and deliberate anti-metaphysical and anti-theological content. Problems relating to free will and responsibility, miracles, the argument from design, the meaning of theological statements, the character of scepticism and the possibility of excluding metaphysics out of the scheme of things are examined, sometimes at length. In *An Enquiry concerning the Principles of Morals* (1751) Hume developed an account of social morality which is in effect a well-qualified form of utilitarianism. The work is of interest to a study of his philosophy of religion not only because of its sharp asides at the expense of the clergy and the church, but because the moral philosophy which it contains makes no reference whatever to divine sanctions or authority: the connection between moral conduct and religious belief is portrayed as purely contingent. This contingent connection, according to Hume, shows itself in historical events, some of which he chronicled in his lengthy and successful *History of England* (published between 1754 and 1762).

The *History* is good 'philosophical history' in the manner followed by Robertson and Gibbon. That is to say it contains both an account of events and the author's enlightened comments upon them. This convention allows Hume opportunities to observe that the social and political manifestation of organised religion and of impassioned religious belief, as they have shown themselves in history, have almost always been bad. In another work, *The Natural History of Religion,* published in 1757 in the middle of writing the *History,* Hume generalises the lesson:

> What a noble privilege is it of human reason to attain the knowledge of the supreme Being; and, from the visible works of nature, be enabled to infer so sublime a principle as its supreme Creator? But turn the reverse of the

medal. Survey most nations and most ages. Examine the religious principles, which have, in fact, prevailed in the world. You will scarcely be persuaded, that they are any thing but sick men's dreams: . . . . Hear the verbal protestations of all men: Nothing so certain as their religious tenets. Examine their lives: You will scarcely think that they repose the smallest confidence in them (*N.H.R.*, 75).

The *N.H.R.* is the first of the two major works which Hume devoted exclusively to religion. In it he discusses the psychological and environmental causes which might have brought about belief in divine power independently of any good reasons for such belief. He concludes that fear of the unknown causes which control man's environment could, in primitive societies, lead to belief in malevolent or capricious powers. Only at a later stage in man's understanding of his environment do the regularities of nature suggest the activity of a single omnipotent god. Even then the ignorant man 'will tell you of the sudden and unexpected death of such a one: . . . . The excessive drought of this season: . . . . These he ascribes to the immediate operation of providence: And such events, as, with good reasoners, are the chief difficulties in admitting a supreme intelligence, are with him the sole arguments for it' (*N.H.R.*, 41).

When Andrew Millar, Hume's London publisher, first printed the *N.H.R.* he did so as one of *Five Dissertations*: the other four included the celebrated essays 'Of the Immortality of the Soul' and 'Of Suicide'. In the first of these Hume set out in aphoristic form most of the traditional and some original arguments to show that man does not have an immortal soul; in the second he argues that circumstances may arise which make suicide a moral duty notwithstanding the dictates of religion. Why these essays were never published is not precisely known, but it would seem that a copy got into the hands of the polemical and vindictive Warburton, and that Millar was warned by Warburton or his agents that the volume as it stood would provoke prosecution. All Hume tells us is that 'from my abundant Prudence I suppress'd [them] . . .' and that 'Mr Millar and I agreed to suppress them at common Charges . . .' (*Letters*, II, 253). He never again offered these essays to the public although he did leave a copy of the suppressed pages to his nephew with authority to print them if he thought fit. This copy is now in the National Library of Scotland. These essays are of interest since they contain opinions on matters relating to religion which are not mentioned elsewhere in Hume's published work.

During the 1750s Hume's literary reputation waxed great but did so against a background of very dangerous opposition from those who thought his writings a threat to both religion and morality. It is possible that Hume's experience in 1745 when he was rejected for the Chair of Moral Philosophy at Edinburgh determined him to act in the character he had been given. It is possible that maturity and the beginnings of success gave him the confidence to disregard the unanimous advice of his friends. It is certain that having been very cautious about what was included in the *Treatise* he suddenly became

relatively incautious about what went into the *Enquiries,* the *History,* the
N.H.R., and the miscellaneous essays (see, for example, his astonishingly
tactless footnote on the character of the clergy in 'Of National Characters').
But the boldness of his writings in the 1750s did not pass without adverse
effect. In 1752 the united opposition of the Glasgow clergy and the
influential Duke of Argyll prevented Hume from being given the Chair of
Logic at Glasgow University. Mossner comments 'So the academic infatuation
with respectable mediocrity once more triumphed; and, while Professor Clow
of Glasgow remains as insignificant as Professor Cleghorn of Edinburgh,
Scotland's most distinguished philosopher of the eighteenth century never
held a chair of philosophy' *(Life,* 250). True, and doubtless deplorable. But
at least it is to the credit of Scotland that the Great Infidel was *considered*
for both positions, a consideration he would scarcely have been granted at
either English university or in Dublin where Trail, the Bishop of Down and
Connor, begged him in 1765 not even to set foot since 'His Character as a
Philosopher is an object of Universal Disgust not to say Detestation in this
Country'. Even at home he was not entirely secure. Between 1755 and 1757
an attempt was made to excommunicate Hume from the Church of Scotland.
In 1757 semi-official pressure resulted in the suppression of the essays on
immortality and suicide, and in 1759 there was an outcry against the volumes
of the *History* dealing with the Tudors. Whether Hume became alarmed at
the intensity of this hostility or whether he respected the emphatic advice
of his friends is not known; but having written the first draft of his greatest
and most extensive work on religion in 1751, and having revised it twice, he
kept the manuscript unpublished until his death.

   The *Dialogues concerning Natural Religion* finally appreared in print in
1779, three years after Hume's death. They form a complement to the
discussion contained in the *N.H.R.* That work had dealt with the psychological causes of religious belief; the *Dialogues* examine some of the arguments
used to maintain that religious belief is reasonable and true. In the *Dialogues*
Hume discusses at length the argument from design, the problem of evil, the
character of religious scepticism, one version of the *a priori* arguments for
existence of god and the meaning of language used to make statements about
god's nature.

(ii)   THE OBJECT OF THE EXERCISE

From the foregoing it will be seen that Hume's discussion of religion is both
diverse and comprehensive. In the *Enquiry* and *Dialogues* he discusses the
reasons for religious belief. In the *N.H.R.* he examines the causes. In the *Moral
Enquiry* and in the *History* he traces the ethical and social effects of religion.
His critique of religion is in fact much more comprehensive than the best-
known of his philosophical works might suggest or apparently do suggest to
some philosophers. (See, for example, Warnock's uncharacteristically mis-

leading remark that some philosophical visions bear 'as with Hume, on morality perhaps but on religion not at all'.[6]) But the diversity has the disadvantage that most critics and commentators have been content with self-contained articles and piecemeal development of some particular item in Hume's account of religion without making any serious attempt to relate the item to the rest of his account.[7] Even recent books devoted to Hume on religion have a tendency to treat one aspect of his thought. R.H. Hurlbutt's *Hume, Newton and the Design Argument*[8] gives a scholarly account of the Newtonian origins of the particular type of design arguments which Hume attacks. A. Jeffner's *Butler and Hume on Religion* [9] contains a good exposition and comparative analysis of both Hume's and Butler's thought. [10]

My purpose is somewhat different. It is to bring Hume's various accounts of religion into a coherent picture in which it can be seen that his failure to find any convincing reasons for religious belief in the arguments of natural religion leads him first to consider religion's foundation in revelation, then to consider its possible status as a 'natural instinct', and finally to search for its causes in human nature. I shall try to show that Hume's conclusions about religion form a coherent whole and that his critique moves steadily towards one crucial conclusion with its consequences for personal religion and morality. This conclusion is that natural order may possibly take its origin from an intelligent being, but if it does then that being has no moral claim upon or interest in mankind. The attempt to give a comprehensive account of Hume's philosophy of religion will result in a book which is mostly philosophical discussion but which also contains such non-philosophical material as the history of a religious controversy and discussion of the moral and social effects of religion. I can only say that the diversity is in the original and that it is not possible to ignore it for the sake of a convenient homogeneity of treatment.

I begin with an examination of what Hume has to say about the reasons for belief in god.[11] In eighteenth-century thinking these reasons were regarded as twofold: the arguments of natural religion and the evidence which authenticated the Christian revelation. Of the former, by far the most prominent was the design argument.

Part 1 Natural Religion

2 Order and Design

The spacious firmament on high,
With all the blue etherial sky,
And spangled heav'ns, a shining frame,
Their great Original proclaim.
The unwearied sun from day to day
Does his Creator's power display,
And publishes to every land
The works of an almighty hand.

Addison

The occurrence of purpose or order in the natural world provides, in both
pagan and Christian traditions, by far the most widely used and generally
accepted ground for arguing from the world to the existence of an intelligent
and powerful designer-god. The argument, in various forms, is to be found in
Plato, Xenophon and Cicero; in Aquinas, Newton and Berkeley; and in almost
all eighteenth-century attempts to establish the reasonableness of religion.[1]
Paley's version of it was recommended reading for most undergraduates
throughout the nineteenth century. In the twentieth century the argument
still has its philosophical advocates and thrives in the reflections of scientists
who feel that their ability to describe the intricate working of the world
argues that it is in some way the product of an intelligence vastly greater than
but in some respects similar to the human. Thus Einstein is able to write the
scientist's 'religious feeling takes the form of a rapturous amazement at the
harmony of natural law, which reveals an intelligence of such superiority that,
compared with it, all the systematic thinking and acting of human beings is
an utterly insignificant reflection'.[2] It is the various forms of the design
argument, some of which still give rise to thinking of this sort, which Hume
subjects to searching and devastating criticism in Section XI of the *Enquiry*[3],
and throughout the *Dialogues*.

(i) THE STRUCTURE OF THE ARGUMENT

In eighteenth-century writers it is common to find such confidence in the
design argument that its conclusion is stated without discussion. The titles
'The Master Craftsman', 'The Divine Artificer', 'The Designer' or 'The Great
Architect of the Universe' are found as synonyms for 'god'. Even a careful
writer like Butler speaks of the argument as if its validity were too obvious to
need discussion '. . . the manifold appearance of design and final causes, in the
construction of the world, prove it to be the work of an intelligent mind . . .'[4]

But when a search is made for a definitive version of the argument it is hard
to find or devise one. In 1751, when he was working on the *Dialogues,* Hume
wrote complainingly to a friend: 'I cou'd wish that Cleanthes' Argument [the
design argument] could be so analys'd as to be render'd quite formal and
regular' *(Letters,* I, 155). The version which he eventually gave to Cleanthes
is this:

> The curious adapting of means to ends, throughout all nature, resembles
> exactly, though it much exceeds, the production of human contrivance; of
> human design, thought, wisdom and intelligence. Since therefore the effects
> resemble each other, we are led to infer, by all the rules of analogy, that
> the causes also resemble; and that the Author of nature is somewhat similar
> to the mind of man; though possessed of much larger faculties, propor-
> tioned to the grandeur of the work, which he has executed *(Dialogues,* 143).

John Stuart Mill suggested an equally careful and somewhat similar
formulation of the argument a century later:

> Certain qualities, it is alleged, are found to be characteristic of such things
> as are made by an intelligent mind for a purpose. The order of Nature, or
> some considerable parts of it, exhibit these qualities in a remarkable degree.
> We are entitled, from this great similarity in the effects, to infer similarity
> in the cause, and to believe that things which it is beyond the power of
> man to make, but which resemble the works of man in all but power,
> must also have been made by Intelligence, armed with a power greater
> than human.[5]

The design argument is thus an argument from analogy. It is also empirical
in the straightforward sense that it appeals to observed similarities between
artifacts and works of nature. In a recent attempt to express the formal pattern
of the argument (an attempt to which I shall return later) Professor R.G.
Swinburne writes:

> Our argument thus proves . . . . to exemplify a pattern common in scient-
> ific inference. As are caused by Bs. A*s are similar to As. Therfore – given
> that there is no more satisfactory explanation of the existence of A*s –
> they are produced by B*s similar to Bs. B*s are postulated to be similar
> in all respects to Bs except in so far as the dissimilarities between As and
> A*s force us to postulate a difference.[6]

Of these formulations, Mill's is the one which in itself most clearly suggests
that the design argument can appear in more than one form. His 'certain
qualities' can be either the *order* or the *purpose* to be found in the natural
world.

If *order* is taken as the feature of nature in stating the argument, then what I shall call the *regularity argument* results: for example, the orderly and regular workings of the solar system, like the orderly working of a traffic system, come about by the design of some rational agent. They are neither 'brute facts' incapable of further explanation nor are they attributable to 'chance'.

If *purpose* is the feature of nature used in stating the argument then what I shall call the *teleological argument* results: for example, the camera and the human eye have striking similarities of structure; the camera was made by an intelligent being for a purpose; therefore the purpose which the eye fulfils was also given it by an intelligent being. The analogy in this version of the design argument is almost always between natural objects and *things made to serve a purpose;* scarcely ever between the workings of the natural world and human *purposive actions.*

But the teleological argument is vulnerable to any scientific advance (such as Darwin's theory of natural selection) which might show that the appearances of purpose in nature are explainable by reference to the operation of laws which have no foresight of the ends to be achieved.[7] The regularity argument is not vulnerable in this way. It could be argued (as Philo argues with a slightly devious purpose in *Dialogues,* 165) that every advance in the natural sciences which displays another or more general law-governed aspect of the universe is further evidence in its support. The more successful the natural sciences become, the less plausible it looks to say 'all this came by chance alone' and the less intellectually satisfactory it is to say 'the regularities which science discovers are ultimate brute facts about the way things are'. As Swinburne and others have pointed out, the regularity argument offers an ultimate agent explanation of why things are as science finds them to be.

In much eighteenth-century writing the teleological argument is more prominent than the regularity argument. Thus Paley's classic statement of the design argument in 1802 is given almost exclusively in terms of examples which fit the teleological argument, and almost all writers in the preceding century pay considerable attention to the means—end adaption of the parts of plants and animals. But from this prominence of the teleological argument it does not follow either that eighteenth-century writers were unaware of the regularity argument or that Hume's criticisms have little modern interest because they are largely directed at the now abandoned teleological argument. Indeed they are not so directed. The subject of discussion in most of the *Dialogues* is the origin and significance of order, not the inference from purposive structures.

In Newton, perhaps the most considerable influence upon this area of eighteenth-century thought, both arguments are to be found. In the *Opticks,* Query 31, he writes '. . . the first contrivance of those very artificial parts of animals, the eyes, ears [etc] . . . can be the effects of nothing else than the wisdom and skill of a powerful and ever living Agent'. This is the attention to the purposes served by the parts of animals which was to become so typical of the teleological argument. But in the 'General Scholium' to the second edition of the *Principia* he lays emphasis on the system and order discernible in the universe: 'This most beautiful system of the sun, planets and comets could only proceed from the counsel and dominion of an intelligent and powerful being'. (It is this near awe at the cosmic observance of physical laws, not the purposes observable in living structures, which moved Addison in the hymn quoted as the motto to this chapter.) When Maclaurin was expounding Newton's system in 1748 he attributes to him what we tend to think of as a very twentieth-century version of the regularity argument: the version which sees god as the explanation of the laws of nature being what they are: 'It appeared to him [Newton] much more just and reasonable, to suppose that the whole chain of causes or the several *series* of them, should centre on him [god] as their source and foundation; and that the whole system appear depending on him the only independent cause.'[8] What is remarkable and in need of an agent explanation is the lawfulness and regularity of the universal system, not merely the occurrence of those parts of it which appear to fulfil some purpose.

In Hume, as in Newton, the design argument is sometimes formulated as the teleological argument, sometimes as the regularity argument, sometimes as a mixture of both. In Cleanthes' statement, already quoted from the beginning of the *Dialogues,* he speaks of 'the curious adapting of means to ends, throughout all nature' — a formula which appears to confine the discussion to the teleological argument. But in other places in the *Dialogues* Hume speaks of 'the order and arrangement of nature' and in the *Enquiry* he writes:

[The religious philosophers] paint, in the most magnificent colours, the order, beauty, and wise arrangement of the universe; and then ask, if such a glorious display of intelligence could proceed from the fortuitous concourse of atoms, or if chance could produce what the greatest genius can never sufficiently admire *(Enquiry,* 135: 145).

Elsewhere he again emphasises the *order* rather than the *purpose* to be found in nature:

Were men led into the apprehension of invisible, intelligent power by a contemplation of the works of nature, they could never possibly entertain any conception but of one single being, who bestowed existence and order on this vast machine, and adjusted all its parts, according to one regular plan or connected system. *(N.H.R.,* 26).

But although it is possible to show Hume attending to one or other of the sub-arguments in the design argument, or to both at the same time (e.g. *Dialogues,* 146: 'Order, arrangement or the adjustment of final causes. . .') It is apparent from his discussion that he does not generally distinguish or need to distinguish between the two. What he does is to provide criticisms of immense subtlety and penetration which either apply mainly to the regularity argument or to both the sub-arguments. These criticisms I shall now consider.

In what follows I shall take it that Hume in the *Dialogues* is any speaker who appears to be making a good philosophical point and I shall treat the *Enquiry* and the *Dialogues* as a continuous body of philosophical argument. I shall speak of the 'design argument' whenever it is unnecessary to distinguish between the two sub-arguments and, in order to keep clear of gratuitous and, at this stage, unimportant complications in the discussion, I shall take it that no feature of nature (purpose, order, fitness of means to ends, etc.) used to state the argument will analytically imply the activity of an agent. For example, if it is observed that nature is *orderly* this will not analytically imply the existence of an *orderer*.

Precisely how many criticisms of the design argument can be individuated in the *Dialogues* and the *Enquiry* depends upon how Hume's continuous flow of argument is sub-divided. For the purposes of discussion in this chapter, I have distinguished ten interrelated criticisms. They are set out in groups according to their influence upon the argument. The first imposes restrictions upon what could be concluded from the design argument if it were valid, the second is a special objection arising from Hume's account of causation, the third group is concerned with the quality of the analogy in the argument, and the last with alternative explanations of the order to be found in the natural world. The ten criticisms, (A) to (J), are as follows.

(ii)   RESTRICTIONS ON THE CONCLUSION

(A)   *If the gods are the cause of order in the universe, then they possess that degree of power, intelligence and benevolence which appears in their known effect (the world) and nothing more (Enquiry, 135: 145 et seq).*

Hume expresses the bones of this criticism in two sentences in the *Enquiry* which I shall denote P_1 and P_2.

P_1 When we infer any particular cause from an effect, we must proportion the one to the other, and can never be allowed to ascribe to the cause any qualities, but what are exactly sufficient to produce the effect *(Enquiry,* 136: 145).

P_2 If the cause be known *only* by the effect, we never ought to ascribe to it any qualities, beyond what are precisely requisite to produce the effect: Nor can we, by any rules of just reasoning, return back from the cause, and infer other effects from it, beyond those by which alone it is known to us *(Enquiry,* 136: 146; my italics).

Thus, for example, if we find in a junk shop a painting of an arcadian land-

scape, we can confidently conclude from what we have seen or heard about
the origin of paintings that its origin lies in the activity of an artist, and
from what we know about human beings we can infer that the artist had a
body temperature of approximately 98.4^{0} F. But from the arcadian land-
scape alone we cannot conclude that the artist was also an architect who kept
bees. In general, we can know more about a cause than that it is just sufficient to produce a given effect when we know from experience what kind of
thing the cause is. But in the case of arguing from the world to a god, we are
not, it is to be assumed, already familiar with what gods are like and, if our
inspection of the world suggests a designer of limited power who is indifferent to human welfare, we cannot then conclude that he is a god of infinite
power concerned with human good. It will be noticed that this consideration
does not attempt to invalidate the design argument. It only restricts its
conclusion to what can actually be inferred from the phenomena.

Swinburne (p. 207) comments here:

> the universal adoption of this celebrated principle [P_1] would lead to the
> abandonment of science. Any scientist who told us only that the cause of
> E had E-producing characteristics would not add an iota to our knowledge.
> Explanation of matters of facts consists in postulating on reasonable
> grounds that the cause of an effect has certain characteristics other then
> those sufficient to produce the effect.

But Hume would be in complete agreement with this as is shown, for example,
by his comments (*Dialogues*, 162–63) on the unsatisfactory character of
explanations which have recourse to faculties or occult qualities in accounting for effects.

The important question to settle is when am I in the *common* situation
(which Swinburne characterises) of knowing more about or being able to
postulate on reasonable grounds more about a cause than that it is just sufficient to produce a given effect, and when am I in the *special* situation (which
Hume states in P_2) of knowing the cause *only* through its effects? Hume's
answer is that I am in the special situation when the cause is the only one
of its kind as far as I can know. Thus when I infer the cause of something to
be a human agent I am in the common situation and I can at once infer other
human type activities in the cause because I know from experience what
humans are like and what they can do: 'man is a being, whom we know by
experience' (*Enquiry*, 143: 152) On the other hand with the cause of the
regularities in the world I am in the special situation. This cause is unique, as
far as I can know, and is known to us only from the given effect: 'The Deity
is known to us only by his productions, and is a single being in the universe,
not comprehended under any species or genus, from whose experienced
attributes or qualities, we can, by analogy, infer any attribute or quality in
him' (*Enquiry*, 143:153).

It will be noticed that Hume does not propose the universal adoption of the principle P_1 since it describes an inference pattern which is immediately qualified in his remarks by P_2. Swinburne's comment does not allow for this qualification. Hume is himself very much alive to the dangers of mixing up the common and the special situations. If you saw a half-finished house (*Enquiry*, 143: 151-2), would you not infer that it was a work of intelligent contrivance and that it would be completed? Likewise if you saw one human footprint in the sands would you not infer that there had been another? Why then when you see a world displaying very great signs of contrivance but falling short of perfection do you hesitate to infer that its cause is limitlessly good and powerful, or that the world is moving towards perfection? Because in the former case you know what finished houses are like, and that they are designed, and you know that human beings generally have two legs. This is the common situation. But in the latter case the degree of completeness of the world is not known by comparison with anything else like it and neither is the power and perfection of its cause. Gods are not beings known to us by experience. This is the special situation (which Hume underlines in a footnote which reiterates P_2; see *Enquiry*, 145: 154).

What the religious philosophers are tacitly assuming, as Hume points out, is that they *do* know more about God than the design argument could establish if it were valid. In particular they claim that God has moral attributes. Hume's general repsonse to this claim is a rhetorical challenge: 'I ask; who carried them into the celestial regions, who admitted them into the councils of the gods, who opened to them the book of fate, that they thus rashly affirm, that their deities have executed, or will execute, any purpose beyond what has actually appeared?' (*Enquiry*, 138: 147). The possible answer to this challenge, that the Christian revelation admitted the religious philosophers to the councils of God, will be considered in Chapter 7. At the moment what is being argued by Hume is that the design argument, if valid, does not itself establish that the designer has attributes beyond those which appear in the world. In particular it does not show that the designer has perfect moral attributes. Indeed the situation is worse.

(B)   *If the design argument is valid then the existence of natural evil in the world is evidence against god having the moral characteristics attributed to him in theistic religions (Dialogues, 193–213).*

What I here distinguish as a separate criticism of the design argument is clearly a particular and very important application of the first. Swinburne dismisses it: 'this does not affect the argument from design which, as Cleanthes admits, does not purport to show that the designer of the universe does have these characteristics'. I do not know where Cleanthes is supposed to admit this. The entire discussion in the *Dialogues* takes place within the agreed assumption that 'the question is not concerning the *being* but the *nature* of God' (*Dialogues*, 141; see also 128) and in Sections X and XI, where the problem of natural evil is being discussed, Cleanthes makes it very clear that he *does* wish to establish the moral attributes of the Deity from the observed character of the world: 'If you can make out the present point, and prove mankind to be unhappy or corrupted, there is an end at once of all religion. For to what purpose establish the natural attributes of the Deity, while the moral are still doubtful and uncertain?' (*Dialogues,* 199). Cleanthes' question is not merely rhetorical. It poses a vitally important restriction on the sort of conclusion which might be established by the design argument. There is a world of difference between an argument which might establish the moral character of the designer and an argument which leads to Philo's bleakly alien god: 'The true conclusion is, that the original source of all things is entirely indifferent to all these principles, and has no more regard to good above ill than to heat above cold' (*Dialogues,* 212). This is not the place to discuss the problem of evil.[9] Philo concedes that the problem of evil might be solvable: that the facts of the world might be shown to be *consistent* with the presumption of divine benevolence and omnipotence (especially if talk about infinite attributes is dropped). What he does not concede, and I do not see how such a concession could be defended, is that the facts of the world could themselves be used as *evidence* from which to infer divine benevolence and omnipotence. It is Hume's contention that the savage, predatory and wasteful economy of nature is alone sufficient to prevent us *inferring* the benevolence of the designing intelligence unless we give 'benevolence' a new meaning quite at variance with the normal. As Mill wrote more passionately: 'Not even on the most distorted and contracted theory of good which ever was framed by religious or philosophical fanaticism, can the government of Nature be made to resemble the work of a being at once good and omnipotent'.[10] Thus if the design argument indicates the existence of some gigantically intelligent and powerful agent, it also indicates the amoral character of that agent. If we argue from world to god, we arrive at 'nothing but the idea of a blind nature' (*Dialogues,* 211) or at a power which has 'no more regard to good above ill than to heat above cold'. As Philo and Demea both agree, the order of nature is not such as to provide *evidence* of the power *and* benevolence of its cause.

(C)   *If valid, the design argument could establish a number of conclusions incompatible with monotheism, namely, that the universe is (1) the product of a committee of designers, (2) a discarded experiment in universe making or the product of a second rate god, (3) a creation which has ever since been allowed to run on at its own devices.*

(1) 'A great number of men join in building a house or ship, in rearing a city, in framing a commonwealth: Why not several Deities combine in contriving and framing a world?' (*Dialogues,* 167). The standard reply to this sort of polytheistic argument is an appeal to Occam's Razor: don't multiply entities without need. The lack of any need in the case of the design argument is argued by Berkeley:'Further, is there not in natural productions and effects

a visible unity of counsel and design? Are not the rules fixed and immoveable? Do not the same laws of nature obtain throughout? The same in China and here, the same two thousand years ago and today?'[11] *(Alciphron,* fourth dialogue, §5).

Swinburne (p. 210) provides the identical objection in modern dress:

> If there were more than one deity responsible for the order of the Universe, we should expect to see characteristic marks of the handiwork of different deities in different parts of the Universe, just as we see different kinds of workmanship in the different houses of a city. We should expect to find an inverse square law of gravitation obeyed in one part of the Universe, and in another part a law which was just short of being an inverse square law . . .

Hume is aware that Occam's Razor poses an objection to polytheism and shortly after the passage already quoted he remarks: 'To multiply causes, without necessity, is indeed contrary to true philosophy: But this principle applies not to the present case.' Why? Because it is an open question whether all the attributes of deity are united in one subject. But this is not an entirely satisfactory answer. An open question between two alternatives is exactly the sort of situation where it *is* appropriate to close on the simpler alternative (in this case monotheism) by an appeal to Occam's Razor. The real dispute between Hume and Olding [12] on the one hand and Berkeley and Swinburne on the other is whether it is in fact an open question between monotheism and polytheism. Berkeley contends that monotheism is more reasonable because of the unity of natural law; Hume that polytheism is more reasonable because the analogy in the design argument works better (if it works at all) for polytheism than for monotheism. Most human artifacts result from corporate endeavours. Therefore most natural objects should result from the corporate endeavour of gods: 'This is only so much greater similarity to human affairs'.

The dispute, it appears to me, centres upon two distinct ways in which natural laws could be said to differ. It is true that different natural laws apply, for example, to planetary motions and the circulation of the blood and that these two areas cannot be subsumed under one more general law. It is false that natural laws differ in that they conflict with themselves – sometimes the inverse square law, sometimes an inverse cube law. Now critics of Hume's point about polytheism look for conflict of the latter type and fail to find any. Defenders point to differences of the former type and argue that such differences are typical of human artifacts in which many workers co-operate to an agreed end. Thus the electric system and the plumbing system in a house differ but do not (usually!) conflict, and the difference signifies the demarcation between different tradesmen. In like manner Hume could argue that electromagnetic theory and genetic theory signify the demarcation between different gods co-operating (possibly, as with humans, under a

master-builder) to an agreed end. The universe *could* be a Robinson Crusoe
effort by a solitary god. More probably, on the evidence of the design
analogy, it is either a co-operative effort by a commune of gods or a
sub-contracted job master-minded by a chief architect. It is this possibility
which gives Hume what justification he has for rejecting the obvious
application of Occam's Razor in favour of monotheism in this context. It
is apparent from elsewhere in his writings that Hume in his own person does
not advocate polytheism. He never speaks in its favour as a personal belief
in any private statement and in the *N.H.R.*, although he speaks of it as the
original religion of mankind (*N.H.R.*, 23) and as perfectly natural and
reasonable (p. 54) providing we confine our attention to 'the footsteps of
invisible power in the various and contrary events of human life' (p. 27), he
also says, more than once and with sincerity as far as I can judge:

> For though, to persons of a certain turn of mind, it may not appear
> altogether absurd, that several independent beings, endowed with superior
> wisdom, might conspire in the contrivance and execution of one regular
> plan; yet is this a merely arbitary supposition, which, even if allowed possible
> must be confessed neither to be supported by probability nor necessity.
> All things in the universe are evidently of a piece. Every thing is adjusted
> to every thing. One design prevails throughout the whole. And this uni-
> formity leads the mind to acknowledge one author (*N.H.R.*, 26).

Hume's argument about polytheism given to Philo in the *Dialogues*
should thus be understood as a way of damaging the design argument — it
gives polytheism a rational possibility — not as an affirmation of his own
beliefs.

(2) 'Many worlds might have been botched and bungled, throughout an
eternity, ere this system was struck out: Much labour lost: Many fruitless
trials made . . .' (*Dialogues,* 167). 'This world, for ought he knows, is very
faulty and imperfect, compared to a superior standard; and was only the
first rude essay of some infant deity, who afterwards abandoned it, ashamed
of his lame performance; it is the work only of some dependent, inferior
Deity; and is the object of derision to his superiors' (*Dialogues,* 169).
   These are two of the several unacceptable possibilities which Hume points
out *could* be true on the basis of the ambiguous evidence provided by the
design argument. Both are appeals to his more general thesis that since we
have no experience of the creation of worlds (*Dialogues,* 148 etc.), or of any
world other than the one given, we are not entitled to express any judgement
about its merits: we literally have no standard to judge that this is the best
of all possible worlds, therefore it *could* be a botched effort etc. But this
thesis is somewhat less clear-cut as an objection to the design argument than
it appears at first sight. The word 'World' can, among other things, mean
either 'the earth or a region of it' or 'the universe or a part of it'. If the

former is intended by Hume then it is now false that we have no standard of comparison whereby we can judge the excellence of the earth. As Hume himself asks 'Is not the moon another earth? . . . Is not Venus another earth?' (*Dialogues*, 150) and by the standard of these, now relatively well-known 'earths', we can confidently pronounce our earth a veritable Eden in the solar desert. But if, as seems likely, Hume intends 'world' to mean 'the universe' then it is unavoidably true that we cannot find a standard whereby to judge its merits. Indeed it is logically impossible to judge the merits of all there is by the standard of something else. This means, as Hume points out, that we cannot say this *must* be the best of all possible universes. It is logically possible that by the standard of something we cannot experience the universe we have could appear 'botched and bungled'. Hume's point is not that these logical possibilities (a botched and bungled universe, the best of all possible universes etc.) have an equiprobability based on equal positive evidence, but that the design argument leaves us with no good reason to choose one possibility rather than another. They are equiprobable through our complete ignorance, an ignorance which the design argument does nothing to alleviate.

(3) The world 'is the production of old age and dotage in some super-annuated Deity; and ever since his death, has run on at adventures, from the first impulse and active force which it received from him . . .' (*Dialogues*, 169).

This is not just another in the list of logically possible universes which our ignorance leaves as equiprobable. What Hume is now pointing out (rightly I think) is that, given the universe we actually have, it could be the production of a Christian-type, immanent God who created and continues to sustain it all, or it could be the production of a deist god who made it and thereafter left it alone. In terms of the design argument the universe could be like a watch created *and* lovingly sustained by the master watchmaker; or it could be like a watch, constructed, wound up and then left to go on forever or until it breaks up with age. The importance of this ambiguity is that if the Christian theist appeals to the design argument then, even if it is valid, its conclusion is perfectly non-committal about whether the creator is immanent or not.The evidence for his immanence and his sustaining activity (highly suspect to Hume — see Chapter 7) has to be imported from elsewhere.

(iii)   THE UNIQUE CAUSE OBJECTION

(D)   *It is only when two species of objects are found to be constantly conjoined, that we can infer the one from the other; and were an effect presented, which was entirely singular, and could not be comprehended under any known species, I do not see, that we could form any conjecture or inference at all concerning its cause (Enquiry, 148: 156; see also Dialogues, 149).*

This one of the few occasions in his critique of religion when Hume appeals to a thesis drawn from his own philosophy, in this case to his analysis of the causal relationship between objects. According to Hume (and this part of his analysis is not obviously objectionable) if we call x the cause of y then we have observed that x and y are contiguous, successive with respect to time and have 'constant conjunction in all past instances' (*Treatise*, 87). His contentious psychological analysis of the necessary connection we attribute to established causal relations need not concern us in this context. The vital point is his contention that for a cause—effect relation to hold between objects we must have experience of the cause and effect being frequently conjoined, that is, being 'two *species* of objects' (*Dialogues*, 149): 'Contiguity and succession are not sufficient to make us pronounce any two objects to be cause and effect, unless we perceive, that these two relations are preserv'd in several instances' (*Treatise*, 87). If this is so, then Hume's objection to the design argument is unavoidable. The argument treats the universe as a unique object and it is not possible to infer anything about the cause of a *unique* object. 'To ascertain this reasoning, it were requisite, that we had experience of the origin of worlds' (*Dialogues*, 150), that is, in more than one instance. We have of course no experience of the origin of worlds, let alone in more than one instance.

In the conclusion to his careful assessment of the design argument, McPherson rejects Hume's claim that argument to a supreme designer is rendered impossible by the uniqueness of the universe.[13] Swinburne too rejects the claim: 'cosmologists are reaching very well-tested scientific conclusions about the Universe as a whole, as are physical anthropologists about the origins of our human race, even though it is the only human race of which we have knowledge and perhaps the only human race there is' (p. 208). Flew, on the other hand, remarks:

> Hume's second insight is to recognise that, although it is experience which provides our only possible standard for deciding any question of fact, it must from the very nature of the case be impossible for this authority to give us any decision, or even any guidance, about the Origin of the Universe itself. For if the question of its 'external' Origin — as opposed to any questions about its 'internal' development — is indeed a genuine question of fact, it is certainly one about which we can have no evidence at all. [14]

The principal question at issue is this: given that in *most* cases causal relations are established from the constant conjunction of two species of objects, what should be concluded about those few cases in which a causal connection appears to be scientifically established by investigation of an effect which is unique as far as we know? Swinburne offers two such instances: the origin of the human race, and cosmologists' conclusions about the universe as a whole. But neither of these are instances of the same kind of thing as conclusions about the divine cause of the universe. They are both instances of what Flew calls 'internal' development whereas the divine cause

of all there is would be an 'external' cause. This distinction between external
origin and internal development — which Flew does not characterise in
general terms — is as follows. A statement about the internal development
of the universe, even if it contains or appears to contain statements about the
origin of unique collections of objects such as men or all there is, is arrived at
by extrapolation from known regularities which are themselves derived
from repeated or repeatable observations. A statement about its external
origin is not arrived at in this way. Thus although the human race may be the
only human race there is, its genetic and/or evolutionary origin is a special
case of genetic and evolutionary regularities which apply to many species.
Again, the cosmologists' conclusions about the origin of the universe as a
whole must at some point depend upon extrapolation from known sceintific
regularities, for example, upon the speed of light or the calculated rate of
expansion of the observable universe. I say 'must' because if they do not,
then any one hypothesis, big bang, continuous creation of matter or whatever,
will not, for scientists, be disputably different from any other hypothesis. In
this way, although the universe is a unique object, the scientists' accounts of
its origins are generated from within it by extrapolation of regularities which
are far from unique. This is what distinguishes a seriously presented
scientific cosmology from a (seriously presented) mythological or religious
account of the origin of the universe. The latter is given in terms of an
'external' cause — god, the great spider etc. — which *does* make the universe
a unique effect in just that sense which entitled Hume to distinguish it as
'Not comprehended under any known species' and to conclude that we cannot
'form any conjecture or inference at all concerning its cause'. What Hume is
saying, surely correctly in this context, is that the design argument, because
it leads to a divine *external object* as the cause of the universe, employs the
experience-based internal causal relation in a meaningless way. Of course *if*
the analogy in the argument to an agent cause is sufficiently good *then* the
divine creation of a unique object would in a sense be comprehended under a
causal species, namely, human acts resulting in artifacts. But, according to
Hume, the analogy is not good and in *this* circumstance the objection that the
universe is a unique object not subject to meaningful application of external
causal explanation comes into play.

It could however be argued [15] that uniqueness is relative to description
and that anything can be made unique under a sufficiently detailed description. Hence uniqueness cannot be a ground for saying that the causal relation
does not apply since, if it were, the causal relation would never apply. A
possible reply would be as follows. There seems to be an intuitively obvious
difference between speaking of the uniqueness of the universe where 'universe'
is understood as meaning 'the total of all there is', and speaking of the uniqueness of an individuated object such as the pen in my hand as I write these
words now. This individual pen, I may say, is one of a species known by
experience: the concept 'pen' is satisified by many instances. But the universe
as it is understood in a sentence such as 'the universe (the total of all there is)

is caused by god's creative act' *could not* be satisfied by more than one instance. Thus the force of Hume's contention that we could not form any inference at all concerning an object not 'comprehended under any known species' rests heavily upon the words *'known species'*. The 'known' has to be 'known by experience' and the 'species' has to be 'class of objects known by experience to contain more than one member'. In this sense the universe could not be a known species and is unique in the peculiar way which makes it nonsense to talk of its external cause.

(iv)   WEAKNESS IN THE ANALOGY

(E)   *The analogy between those objects known to proceed from design and any natural object is too weak and remote to suggest similar causes.* (This argument appears both in the *Enquiry* and in many locations in the *Dialogues*.)

In the article to which I have already referred, Swinburne concedes that 'if there is a weakness in the argument it is here that it is to be found' but he refuses to assess the weakness since it is perhaps more a task 'for the preacher and the poet than for the philosopher' (Swinburne, 211).[16] But this will not do in the context of Swinburne's generalisation that Hume's criticisms are 'bad criticisms of the argument in any form'. The central and most strongly urged criticism which Hume presents is that the analogy is hopelessly weak and in assessing the design argument it seems quite artificial to ignore this criticism.

Swinburne's scheme for the sort of analogical argument which the design argument exemplified (quoted above, p. 10) may be stated thus:

As *are caused* by Bs
A*s *are similar to* As
Therefore A*s *are caused* by B*s

Where B*s are similar to Bs 'except in so far as the dissimilarities between As and A*s force us to postulate a difference' between B*s and Bs (Swinburne, 205). Thus: artifacts are caused by human agents: natural objects are similar to artifacts; therefore natural objects are caused by non-human agent(s) similar to human agents except in so far as the dissimilarities between artifacts and natural objects force us to postulate a difference.

My difficulty with this otherwise very useful formulation is that the statement 'A*s are similar to As' omits reference to the main element characteristic of argument by analogy. 'How good an analogy is there'? we ask, meaning: 'how close a similarity is there between the objects compared'? Swinburne does of course allow for this question in his concluding qualification: B*s *are similar to* Bs 'except in so far as the dissimilarities between As and A*s force us to postulate a difference', a qualification which he emphasises in his reply article p. 198 (see note 16). But analogical arguments are not usually set up by conceding similarity and then noting differences after the conclusion has been reached. They are set up by establishing explicit points of similarity in the analogy and countered by disputing whether the similarities hold, are of sufficient importance, or are negated by dissimilarities. Thus it would seem desirable that the scheme for analogical argument should at least allow the points of similarity between the objects to be stated: objects are similar *with respect to certain features* which have to be specified if the similarity is challenged. A way in which this could be done in Swinburne's schema is as follows:

As *are caused by* Bs
A*s *are similar to* As *in features* $x_1, x_2 \ldots, \ldots x_n$
Therefore A*s *are caused by* B*s

where B*s are as similar to Bs as the number and/or relative scale of x_1 to x_n allow us to suppose. Thus the analogy would be weak if either n were a very small number or if the scale of any particular x found in association with A*s were very different from the scale of the same x found in association with As. Thus both a beetle and a man can move from one place to another. But this single feature of similarity, given also the vastly different scale and complexity of its occurrence, is unlikely to be used in an analogy to show that beetles, like men, also enjoy music. It might be objected here that a beetle and a man are also *different* with respect to certain features y_1 to y_n and this constitutes an anti-analogy which further weakens the analogical force of such few similar features as can be found. Thus in formulating a full schema for analogical argument allowance should be made for stating differences between A*s and As. This is true. But I am reluctant to introduce this additional complexity for present purposes since most of Hume's objections to the analogy in the design argument do not depend upon it. This is because his points turn upon weakness in the similarities not upon the presence of dissimilarities. This same concern with strength and weakness in the positive analogy rather than with the anti-analogy shows itself in Hume's general comments on the character of analogical argument:

> Where the causes are entirely similar, the analogy is perfect, and the inference, drawn from it, is regarded as certain and conclusive [that is, it becomes an inductive conclusion] . . . But where the objects have not so exact a similarity, the analogy is less perfect, and the inference is less conclusive; though still it has some force, in proportion to the degree of similarity and resemblance (*Enquiry*, 104: 112; see also *Treatise*, 147).

Now it is Hume's frequent and emphatically repeated contention that the degree of similarity between artifacts and natural objects is exceedingly slight *both* with respect to the number of features they have in common *and* with respect to the scale of these features. 'The dissimilitude is so striking, that the utmost you can here pretend to is a guess, a conjecture, a presumption concerning a similar cause (*Dialogues,* 144). And again: 'All the new discoveries in astronomy, which prove the immense grandeur and magnificence of the works of nature . . . become so many objections, by removing the effect still farther from all resemblance to the effects of human art and contrivance' (*Dialogues,* 165)

Put in this way the criticism needs neither defence nor elaboration. Anything whatever man-made is exceedingly unlike the universe at large; so unlike that Hume is moved to suggest that the cause of the universe must be beyond understanding by any possible analogy: 'But this method of reasoning [from analogy] can never have place with regard to a Being, so remote and incomprehensible, who bears much less analogy to any other being in the universe than the sun to a waxen taper' (*Enquiry,* 146: 155). But it could be argued that the analogy is not between artifacts and the universe at large. In the teleological argument the analogy is between the purpose to be found in both natural objects and artifacts, and in the regularity argument it is between the order to be found in both. Thus the design argument should read 'Artifacts are caused by human agents. Natural objects are similar to artifacts in displaying the features of order and/or purpose. Therefore natural objects are caused by non-human agents *etc.*'. But this, as Hume points out, is to make the analogy incredibly weak. The features of similarity named are only two (or one if we assume that the theory of natural selection has devalued the teleological argument) and the scale on which the feature(s) occur in artifacts and natural objects is almost ludicrously different: 'Admirable conclusion! Stone, wood, brick, iron, brass have not, at this time, in this minute globe of earth, an order or arrangement without human art and contrivance: Therefore the universe could not originally attain its order and arrangement, without something similar to human art' (*Dialogues,* 149).

It is, however, sometimes argued that the particular feature chosen in the regularity argument is one which experience gives us special reason to believe is closely related to the activity of an agent cause. The point was originally made, with reference to the teleological argument and with great clarity, by J. S. Mill:

> The circumstances in which it is alleged that the world resembles the works of man are not circumstances taken at random, but are particular instances of a circumstance which experience shows to have a real connection with an intelligent origin, the fact of conspiring to an end [or, presumably, in the regularity argument, the fact of order — J.G.]. The argument therefore is not one of mere analogy. As mere analogy it has its weight, but it is more than analogy. It surpasses analogy exactly as induction surpasses it. It is an inductive argument.[17]

The appeal, according to Mill, is not to a bad inductive argument: the number of cases in which we know order to derive from an agent cause *versus* the much greater number of cases in which we observe order and have to infer an agent cause. The appeal is to one highly significant feature of similarity where on one side of the analogy we know that the feature *always* arises from an agent cause. Hume is aware of this move and I make his answer into a separate criticism of the analogy in the design argument.

(F) *'Order, arrangement, or the adjustment of final causes is not, of itself, any proof of design; but only so far as it has been experienced to proceed from that principle' (Dialogues,* 146).

Hume speaks of *order* and *final causes* or purposes. In the present instance his objection is thus directed at both the regularity and the teleological arguments. In my discussion I largely ignore the teleological argument. This is because (a) in the *Dialogues* the context of the remarks is concerned with discussion of the origin of order and no further reference is made to purpose; and (b) Hume has no need to try to show that purpose in nature is not specially related to an agent cause (a difficult thing to do if purpose in nature is admitted) since he has an argument (see below p. 36) to explain the appearances of purpose as the consequence of non-purposive regularities. It may seem obvious that the design argument is an empirical argument and that it would be destroyed if forced into a form of cosmological argument by asserting *a priori* that 'order can only arise from an agent cause'. But Hume is here also denying that as a matter of fact order is always and intrinsically related to an agent cause. There is nothing which specially relates order to an agent. Is this true? Yes, for the reasons (1) to (3) which follow. These are suggested by what Hume says but I develop them in each case.

(1) We can observe that the cause of order is the activity of an agent only in a minute percentage of the examples of order which are known to us: 'Here we may remark, that the operation of one very small part of nature, to wit man, upon another very small part, to wit that inanimate matter lying within his reach, is the rule by which Cleanthes judges of the origin of the whole' *(Dialogues,* 176).
But as it stands this ridicule of Cleanthes' case is not decisive. It *is* sometimes possible to argue from a small sample. What is found to be a property of one sample of hydrogen in a laboratory, in the absence of any evidence to the contrary, will be presumed to be a property of all samples of hydrogen wherever found. On the other hand, if I know of one grove of trees that it has been deliberately planted this does not give me grounds for asserting that all groves of trees have been deliberately planted. When does a sample give grounds for an assertion about a whole population?
The hydrogen in the laboratory was a sample taken at random of a stuff which we have no reason to think of as other than homogeneous. What is true of it (in the absence of evidence to the contrary) would be true of *any*

sample. The grove of trees on the other hand was a particular grove known to be planted and we know that groves of trees are sometimes planted and sometimes grow up by themselves; therefore the known origin of a particular grove gives us no guidance about the origin of any other grove. But this is precisely the case with the origin of order. We know, and our knowledge has the same grounds as with the grove of trees, that order is sometimes found and sometimes imposed by man, and the known agent origin of order in a few particular cases does not give grounds for a pronouncement concerning the origin of order in general. But, it may be said, this still fails to grasp Mill's point. In *all* cases in which we *can* explain the origin of order (or, in the teleological argument, the adaption of means to ends) its origin is found in the actions of an intelligent agent. This is a plain inductive argument of the same sort as finding — suppose that we were to find this — that *all* groves of trees *whose origin we know* are deliberately planted, and therefore concluding that the origin of all groves of trees is deliberate planting. But it is not the same sort of argument. It is not the same because in talking about explaining 'the origin of order' an undiscussed assumption is being made that when we have traced the origin of order to the activity of an intelligent agent we have explained it in a way in which we have not satisfactorily explained it if it is traced to the operation of some high-level natural law. Thus it is tacitly accepted that while the origin of order in a railway system is satisfactorily explained by the activity of its intelligent designers, the order in the solar system is not satisfactorily explained by the Newtonian laws of motion (or some refinement of them). This tacit assumption is not acceptable. While it may be argued at length that one of the two explanations of order (agent or natural law) should be regarded as ultimate, this cannot be assumed at the start just to give preference to agent explanation any more than a behaviourist psychologist could assume at the start that because all the orderly events we 'properly' explain are a manifestation of laws of nature, therefore any 'proper' explanation of human agent activity must relate it to laws of nature. The plain appearance of things (which may of course be modified on investigation) is that there are two sorts of order in the world: that which is brought about by intelligent agents and that which is described by natural laws. It is this well-substantiated appearance of things which makes it reasonable for Hume to conclude that 'order, arrangement, or the adjustment of final causes is not, of itself, any proof of design; but only so far as it has been experienced to proceed from that principle'

(2) In a space-age film which otherwise stretches the credulity (and the patience) of its audience to the maximum, everyone is instantly supposed to recognise (and does recognise) that a large regularly shaped metal oblong emitting powerful radio signals and found beneath the surface of the moon is an artifact, not part of the order of nature. If order is supposed to be intrinsically, and always as a matter of fact, related to an agent cause, how is it that this distinction between artifacts and natural objects is so readily appreciated? What is it about agent-imposed order which distinguishes it

from the given or naturally occurring order? *First,* agent imposed order is recognised in objects which in structure and/or function are the same as or closely similar to objects we know from experience to be agent-ordered. The structural considerations which are important will include size (the order in sub-microscopic structures is never agent-given, nor is the order in cosmic systems) and regularity of shape (flat polished surfaces, regular geometrical shapes etc. are seldom — crystalline structures excepted — found in natural objects). The functional consideration of greatest importance will be the appearance of being endowed with a purpose. But as Jacques Monod points out in his very interesting discussion of these points in Chapter I of *Chance and Necessity* [18] the appearance of purpose is not in itself sufficient to distinguish between living beings and the artifacts produced by their activity. An additional observation has to be made: 'that the macroscopic structure of an artifact results from the application to its constituent materials of forces *exterior* to the object itself' whereas 'the source of the information expressed in the structure of a living being is *always* another, structurally identical, object'. *Secondly,* agent imposed order is recognised in objects which have both a macroscopic structural organisation and are either unique like a particular garden design or only repetitive (like a given make of motor car) in locally limited ways where the repetition cannot be explained by the operation of natural laws. Thus, for example, systems of concentric ring marks on flat boulders are usually attributed to intelligent agents since they are found only in localities where there have been human settlements and there is no known law of nature which could explain their occurrence. In contrast, cup holes are found in rock formations throughout the world, and in almost all geological strata, and they have a natural explanation in the action of water over long ages rocking a small stone or pebble.

Examples may of course be constructed in which the distinctions between artifact and natural object may be difficult to apply: an astronaut scatters on the moon a handful of identical sugar crystals, a handful of ball-bearings and a handful of dead but perfectly preserved ants. Later an intelligence knowing nothing of man and his ways discovers these three groups of objects. He rapidly decides the sugar crystals are natural objects because their internal structure is expressed in their shape in a way with which he is familiar as an expert on the laws of nature. But having neither anything like ball-bearings nor insects in his world he mistakenly concludes that both the ball-bearings and the ants are artifacts: he needs to see the bearings and the ants functioning before he can distinguish between the order *imposed* on the material of the artifact and the order given from within the material of the living natural object. Furthermore he would have to be familiar with reproductive living systems. In a more mundane context: is an oddly shaped stone man-made or water eroded? But these occasional theoretical or practical difficulties neither render the distinction between the order in artifacts and the order in natural objects generally unworkable nor show that we should not try to apply them.

That we do use and are entitled to use criteria of this kind for distinguishing between the sort of order characteristic of artifacts and the different sort of order characteristic of natural objects sheds light on the confusion in the Shakespeare plays argument. The order in nature, it is sometimes said, could no more have occurred without an agent as cause than the intelligible order in the plays of Shakespeare could have occurred without an intelligent author. But this neglects the difference between the *kinds* of order found in a play and in nature. The plays of Shakespeare are uniquely sophisticated examples drawn from a group of objects (intelligible writings) which in our experience *always* derive from agent intelligence and which display individuality and purpose. (This is what made the writings on Belshazzar's wall so significant – *Daniel,* Chapter 5.) On the other hand, the order, or multiplicity of orders, in the natural world is the repetitive, infinitely extended, nonpurposeful, sub-microscopic or cosmic order which is never found in artifacts and which is never mistaken for them. So different is the order in nature from the order associated with agent intelligence that on the exceedingly rare occasions when nature does seem to display agent intelligence the occasion is dignified as a miracle.

(3) Finally, according to Hume, we have no reason to suppose that order is intrinsically and always given by an agent since we can observe in the universe other things than rational agents which bestow order: 'A tree bestows order and organization on that tree which springs from it, without knowing the order: an animal, in the same manner, on its offspring . . . And instances of this kind are even more frequent in the world, than those of order, which arise from reason and contrivance' *(Dialogues,* 179).

Because of this it is, according to Hume, as reasonable (or as implausible) to account for the origin of natural order by reference to vegetation or generation as to account for it by reference to an intelligent agent. Recent commentators have for the most part been rather critical of this argument. Thus McPherson observes that Philo is wide of the mark when he chides: 'The world, say I, resembles an animal, therefore it is an animal, therefore it arose from generation' *(Dialogues,* 180). Swinburne too objects that 'as analogous processes to explain regularities of succession, generation or vegetation will not do, because they only produce regularities of copresence – and those through the operation of regularities of succession outside their control' (p. 210). More generally Pearl argues that there is a significant difference between the origin of artifacts from design and the origin of vegetables and animals from 'vegetation' and 'generation':

> In the case of design, materials which are in a nonorderly state are transformed into an orderly system; but in the case of vegetation or generation, this is not the case. What we find instead is a process by which organized bodies generate other organized bodies. There is no genesis of order here, but rather its transmission from one body to another. Generation and vegetation are themselves orderly processes which the argument from design tries to account for . . . The point, I am trying to make, is that

vegetation and generation, unlike design, do not provide explanations for the existence of orderly systems and processes but are, in fact, themselves illustrations of that very order which requires explanation.[19]

But it appears to me that these objections do not take full account of Hume's intentions in Part VII of the *Dialogues*. He is saying that experience does not show order to be *specially* associated with the productions of an intelligent agent. It does not show this because order is also associated in our experience with vegetation and generation and 'Judging by our limited and imperfect experience, generation has some privileges above reason: For we see every day the latter arise from the former, never the former from the latter' *(Dialogues, 180)*.

The crux of the matter is contained in Pearl's phrase 'the genesis of order'. What is to count as a satisfactory genesis of order? Hume's point is that, as far as our experience instructs us, reason, generation and vegetation all provide a genesis of *some* examples of order and we have no occasion to elevate reason above the rest 'otherwise than by proving *a priori,* both that order is, from its nature, inseparably attached to thought, and that it can never, of itself, or from original unknown principles, belong to matter' *(Dialogues, 179)*. The critics' point is that vegetation and generation only provide a genesis of orderly structures, not of the orderly processes which give rise to these structures. Rational agents on the other hand are sometimes responsible for orderly processes. The question is not as Hume tries to make it — whether order could belong to matter *per se* — but whether orderly processes are explained by agent causes in a way in which they are not explained by vegetable causes. Do agents produce orderly *processes* as distinct from *structures?* The answer is equivocal. If I design and set in operation an automatic production line for canning peas then the genesis of the process is given by reference to me as an agent. But is the production line a process akin to the process of animal generation in such a way that my agent explanation of the former suggests a possible agent explanation of the latter? I think not. The rational agents within our experience are *never* responsible for processes akin to the processes displayed in the regular workings of natural laws. The difference between what one oak tree does producing another oak and what a man does designing a production line is not simply between producing structures and producing processes. The difference is that the oak tree behaves in accordance with natural processes over which it has no control while the man consciously and deliberately employs natural processes for his own purpose in the production of railway engines, atomic bombs and processed peas. In neither case is there ground for saying *this* provides a logically superior explanation of order which should be given preference in the explanation of the most fundamental natural processes themselves. To do this, as Hume points out, one would have to prove *a priori* that order could not belong to matter *per se*; to do this would be to establish some sort of cosmological argument.

In summary: The general analogy between the works of nature and human artifacts is very weak. The similarities are few and where they exist the differences of scale on the two sides of the analogy further devalue the argument. When reference is made to the particular feature of order it is found: that experience does not show that order always or even frequently has an agent origin; that the order in artifacts is recognisably of a different sort from the order in nature; and that the attempt to account for the order in nature by reference to an intelligent agent is little better than the arbitrary attempt to account for the same order by reference to generation or vegetation. But there is still another difficulty in the analogy.

(G)　*The balance of the analogy in the design argument between anthropomorphism and incomprehensible remoteness is difficult to maintain (Dialogues, 156-160, 165-168 et al.)*

There are two intersecting arguments here. Both set out to show that if valid the design argument leads to a deity unacceptably different from that worshipped in normal monotheistic religions. But what sort of deity is 'normally worshipped'? Swinburne remarks that 'For the activity of a god to account for the regularities [in nature] he must be free, rational, and very powerful' (p. 209). As far as it goes this description seems to be at least compatible with normal theism. A few years ago it would have been super-fluous to mention its most obvious corollary: that the deity is an *agent*. The design argument is null and void from the start unless the god is taken to be an agent, as he is always taken to be in theistic religions, some of the more rarified eccentricities of modern theologians only excepted. If then the theist takes his god to be an agent who is at least free, rational and very powerful, he cannot, according to Hume, rationally ground his belief in such a god upon an argument which wavers between the extremes of ludicrous anthropomorphism on the one hand and incomprehensible remoteness on the other. Let us consider anthropomorphism first.

The first move for Hume is to admit that the analogy in the design argument between the order in artifacts and the order in natural objects leads us to an agent in some respects similar to man as the cause of order in natural objects. It is then asked *how similar* and the answer is *similar at least in reason*. The only sort of rational agents we know are men (and possibly certain domestic cats). Therefore the deity must have a mind like the human (*Dialogues*, 166) since we cannot understand what else could count as a mind. But since the only rational agents we know also have either two or four legs, then the deity must have two or four legs and so on: 'And why not become a perfect anthropomorphite? Why not assert the Deity or Deities to be corporeal and to have eyes, a nose, mouth, ears, etc? Epicurus maintained, that no man had ever seen reason but in a human figure; therefore the gods must have a human figure' (*Dialogues*, 168). Swinburne comments that this sort of argument makes Hume guilty of what he calls the supersimilarity fallacy:

You argue by analogy from similarity of effects of human actions to other events to similarity of causes, men and a god. But the more seriously we are to take this argument, the more we must say that the god is like man, and so we are forced to become a 'perfect anthropomorphite'. The more human properties we attribute to the god, the more ridiculous does the conclusion become, and we eventually reach a stage when the whole argument can be laughed off. The error is to postulate similarities in causes in respects in which difference between effects suggests that causes are also different. I will call this error the supersimilarity fallacy (which produces death by the lack of a thousand qualifications.)[20]

Thus in foisting anthropomorphism upon the design argument, Hume postulates more similarity between man and the cause of order in nature than is justified when the differences between artifacts and natural objects are fully noted. Now while this is a just comment upon what Hume does, surely the strength of his ridicule is that when and in as far as it suits his purposes this development of the similarity between god and man beyond what the design argument might establish if it were valid is precisely what the *theist* does. He is, for example, particularly inclined to argue to moral attributes which are recognisably similar to moral attributes in man and which do not appear to be manifest in the effect – the creation – which we have[21]. But 'explanation of matters of fact consist in postulating on reasonable grounds that the cause of an effect has certain characteristics other than those sufficient to produce the effect' (Swinburne, 207). Agreed, with the qualifications above (p. 14). But if this is so, it will be a little difficult to know at exactly what point it becomes *unreasonable* to postulate a similarity between god and man which is anything more than just that degree of reason and power which is displayed in the effect we have, a similarity which is pro- bably an insufficient account of the theist's god. However, let us accept that it is unnecessary for the theist to indulge the supersimilarity fallacy and therefore unfair for Hume to foist anthropomorphism upon those who hold the design argument. The other side of the coin is an excessive remoteness between man and the origin of natural order.

The first move, as with the anthropomorphism argument, is to argue that 'like effects prove like causes' and that 'the liker the effects are, which are seen, and the liker the causes, which are inferred, the stronger the argument' (*Dialogues,* 165). The second move is to accept the regularity argument, give it all the strength with which a Newton or an Einstein would invest it, and then point out that the deity thus discovered is a being so remote and incomprehensible that he 'bears much less analogy to any other being in the universe than the sun to a waxen taper' (*Enquiry*, 146: 155). 'The discoveries by microscopes, as they open a new universe in miniature, are still objections, according to you; arguments according to me. The farther we push our researches of this kind, we are still led to infer the universal cause of All to be vastly different from mankind, or from any object of human experience and observation' (*Dialogues*, 166. The same point is made on the previous page with reference to astronomical discoveries). Unlike Hume's teasing attempt to foist excessive anthropomorphism upon users of the design argument, the suggestion that the regularity argument, the most powerful and enduring version of the design argument, would lead to a deity incomprehensibly different and remote from mankind, is probably made with entire sincerity. The contention that argument has come into a fairy land 'when it leads to conclusions so extraordinary, and so remote from common life and experience' (*Enquiry*, 72: 83) is a frequently repeated refrain in Hume's philosophical writings. But the particular fairy land reached in the regularity argument presents a very real difficulty to the theist. That which is arrived at, the 'universal cause of All', may be a sufficiently free, powerful and rational agent to cause All, but is this agent in any way comprehensibly similar to the rational agents of which we actually have experience? Can the conclusion of the regularity argument and the God whom the theist speaks of as having moral and personal concern, and to whom he prays, be *identified* with each other? The answer which Hume appears[22] to give to the former question (he does not explicitly discuss the latter) is that talk of power, reason and freedom in such an agent as the cause of All is incomprehensibly far removed from the experienced situations in which such words as 'power', 'reason' and 'freedom' get their meaning.

> At least, if it appear more pious and respectful (as it really is) still to retain these terms [thought or reason], when we mention the supreme Being, we ought to acknowledge, that their meaning, in that case, is totally incomprehensible; and that the infirmities of our nature do not permit us to reach any ideas, which in the least correspond to the ineffable sublimity of the divine attributes (*Dialogues*, 157. Philo speaking).

The difficulty with total incomprehensibility of the deity is that the theist cannot accept it:

> The Deity, I can readily allow, possesses many powers and attributes, of which we can have no comprehension: But if our ideas, so far as they go, be not just and adequate, and correspondent to his real nature, I know not what there is in this subject worth insisting on. Is the name, without any meaning, of such mighty importance? Or how do you Mystics, who maintain the absolute incomprehensibility of the Deity, differ from sceptics or atheists who assert that the first cause of All is unknown and unintelligible (*Dialogues*, 158, Cleanthes speaking).[23]

But Cleanthes' refusal to accept the incomprehensibility of the deity allows Philo to develop the forked objections to the design argument we have just been considering. On the one hand, if the theist insists upon the closeness of the analogy between deity and man in order to preserve the comprehensi-

bility of (some) of the divine attributes then he is easily led into anthropomorphism. This is both unacceptable in itself *and* incompatible with the
strongest version of the design argument: that which seeks the cause of all
natural order. On the other hand, if the theist relies upon the regularity
argument he arrives at a cause of all order whose remoteness and incomprehensibility are unacceptable to him, both because of what else he wishes to
say about his God, and because they make mysticism and scepticism
indistinguishable. This tension between personal God and ineffable Majesty
pervades Christianity. Hume was perhaps the first significant philosopher
to point out that it also pervades the design argument as it could be used by a
Christian: according to that argument the cause of order in the universe bears
less resemblance to man than the sun to a waxen taper.

(v) **POSSIBLE SOURCES OF ORDER**

(H) *If an intelligent agent is required to explain the order in nature then the
intelligent agent will in turn need to be explained (Dialogues, 160-4).
But if we stop at the agent explanation, and go no farther; why go so far?
Why not stop at the material world? How can we satisfy ourselves without
going on in infinitum? And after all, what satisfaction is there in that infinite
progress? (Dialogues, 161: Philo speaking).*

An answer is given by Cleanthes: 'Even in common life, if I assign a cause
for any event; is it any objection, Philo, that I cannot assign the cause of that
cause, and answer every new question, which may incessantly be started?'
(*Dialogues,* 163). Philo agrees, with qualification, that it is not an objection
if a cause cannot itself be explained (an example of such a cause might be
gravitation):

> Naturalists indeed very justly explain particular effects by more general
> causes: though these general causes themselves should remain in the end
> totally inexplicable: But they never surely thought it satisfactory to
> explain a particular effect by a particular cause, which was no more to be
> accounted for than the effect itself (*Dialogues,* 164).

The qualification in the word 'particular' needs emphasis. An explanation is
good and need not itself be explained *provided* the explanation is more general
than, or known apart from, the thing which it purports to explain. Swinburne
misses the significance of this qualification in his counter example:

> The existence of molecules with their characteristic behaviour was 'no
> more to be accounted for' than observable phenomena, but the postulation
> of their existence gave a neat and simple explanation of a whole host of
> chemical and physical phenomena, and that was the justification for
> postulating their existence (Swinburne, 208).

Precisely! The postulated existence of molecules explained *more* than a particular observable effect. *More* is known about molecules than that they explain, say, why water is produced by burning hydrogen. But it is Hume's contention that the postulation of an agent cause to explain why the order in nature is what it is (or is there at all) is a postulation which does *not* explain. Such an explanation is no more general than the order in nature itself: 'No new fact can ever be inferred from the religious hypothesis; no event foreseen or foretold; no reward or punishment expected or dreaded, beyond what is already known by practice and observation' (*Enquiry*, 146: 155). Nor is the operation of an agent intelligence intrinsically any better understood or less in need of explanation than the order in nature:

> To say, that the different ideas, which compose the reason of the supreme Being, fall into order, of themselves, and by their own nature, is really to talk without any precise meaning. If it has a meaning, I would fain know, why it is not as good sense to say, that the parts of the material world fall into order, of themselves, and by their own nature? (*Dialogues*, 162).

'It were, therefore, wise in us, to limit all our enquiries to the present world, without looking farther' is Philo's typically Humean conclusion.

But it is the contention of Swinburne (p. 204) and others that we have alternatives. Either we can take the regular workings of the universe as brute facts, ultimately unexplainable by reference to anything. Or we can explain the regular workings of the universe by reference to 'the rational choice of a free agent'. Of these alternatives Swinburne prefers the latter because 'we can explain some few regularities of succession as produced by rational agents and the other regularities cannot be explained except in this way'. Hume would seem to prefer the former because no more general understanding of the universe is achieved by postulating an agent as its cause. But the preference for an agent explanation may be an anthropocentric prejudice. In what sense is the rational choice of a free agent an ultimate explanation, while behaviour in accordance with some high order principle of nature (e.g. gravitational attraction) is a mere brute fact or a less than ultimate explanation? There certainly are things in the universe — for example the framed copy of the *Oxford Almanack* for 1750 which hangs on the wall in front of my desk now — which lack a sufficient explanation if mention is not made of the rational choices of a free agent (mine in this instance). But I do not see in what way, for example, the regular workings of the solar system lack a sufficient explanation if they are not referred to the free choice of a rational agent. What is supposed to be insufficient in the Newtonian story given with suitable footnotes by Einstein etc? If the answer is 'the existence of the regularities themselves' then the answer may be retorted back on agent explanation in the way Hume suggests. What lacks a sufficient explanation in the account of the almanack on the wall is the wholly unexplained existence of this odd corner of nature called 'the free choice of a rational agent'. *That* is in itself no better understood than the brute fact order in nature and if, as Hume remarks, we are to give a preference to one sort of order above the other it had better be to the brute fact order which we observe giving rise to rational agents. It is the orderly process of animal generation which gives rise to reason, not the other way about.[24] (See *Dialogues,* 180.)

(I)   '*I esteem none more plausible than that which ascribes an eternal, inherent principle of order to the world*' *(Dialogues,* 174).

Philo professes to adopt this suggestion as the most plausible among a group of theories which he rejects, namely, those which depend upon the principle 'What we see in the parts, we may infer in the whole'. But in the present instance his rejection is less than complete. He observes that 'all the changes and corruptions, of which we have ever had experience, are but passages from one state of order to another: nor can matter ever rest in total deformity and confusion' . . . 'How could things have been as they are, were there not an original, inherent principle of order somewhere, in thought or in matter?' He adds 'Chance has no place, on any hypothesis, sceptical or religious. Every thing is surely governed by steady inviolable laws' (ibid.).

Philo's suggestions contain both a confusion and an insight. Let us note the confusion first. It arises from his use of 'chance' as a synonym for the phrase 'total deformity and confusion'. Very briefly: there are at least two degrees of order known to us. There is the mechanistic order in systems of a conveniently observable size in which the fixing of parameters at one time enables the state of the system at any other time to be calculated. One of the most obvious examples is the solar system. In such a system neither 'chance' nor 'total disorder' have any place. But there is also the much more widely found statistical order in which the concept of chance, or randomness, has a place, while that of total disorder has not. This is the sort of order in which the predictable outcome is the statistical resultant of a collective in which the individual events, frequently unobservable, are, or are taken to be, chance or random results. For example, the uniform pressure upon the surface of a gas jar is the statistical resultant of the random movements of molecules contained within it. Total disorder, on the other hand, would give no predictable result of any sort: the gas jar might just as well dissolve or become a hedgehog or *anything*. Now the confusion which starts in Philo's reference to matter in total 'deformity and confusion' can be made clearer. While we could perhaps formulate a concept of 'total disorder' and then agree that it was not satisfied by anything in nature (which is what Philo wants to do), this agreement would *not* imply that in nature 'chance has no place' nor would it imply that 'every thing is surely governed by steady inviolable laws'. Philo reaches these two conclusions by assuming that the notion of mechanical order must apply to the random events which make up statistical order. This assumption is made possible by illicitly conflating the notion of 'chance' with that of 'total disorder' and then ruling out the former on the grounds that the latter is never found in nature.

The insight is in opening up the possibility that in the design argument we arrive ultimately, not at an object — a being or agent who has attributes — but at what Hume calls a 'general cause' or *'principle'*. Hume's account of 'ultimate springs and principles' (very different from, and frequently obscured by, his better-known account of causally related objects) has to do with the natures which objects have in virtue of which they can be observed to be causally related. He gives as a list of such principles: 'Elasticity, gravity, cohesion of parts, communication of motion by impulse' (*Enquiry,* 30 : 45). Another list is provided by Philo (*Dialogues,* 178). But of course if the design argument does lead to an 'original, inherent principle of order' this would make the argument quite useless to religion. Such a principle could no more be good or compassionate than gravity could be angry or greedy. Indeed, as Philo points out, to arrive at such a general principle is not even very satisfactory for the sceptic. It is just to acknowledge that order does somehow inhere in nature and we can *all* agree to that. But Philo makes one more attempt to account for the order itself. It is a suggestion of astonishing intellectual daring and foresight.

(J)   *'Is there a system, an order, an œconomy of things, by which matter can preserve that perpetual agitation, which seems essential to it, and yet maintain a constancy in the forms, which it produces?' (Dialogues,* 183).

Hume's answer is that there is such an economy, both in general in the order of the inanimate universe (which provides the starting point for the regularity argument) and in particular in the order of living organisms (which provides a starting point for the teleological argument). In his discussion in Part VIII of the *Dialogues* Hume makes the latter a particular case of the former but since the subsequent development of the theory of evolution has given the particular case a strength and content which the generalisation still lacks, I shall consider the particular case first.

Philo's argument is this. If matter is finite in quantity but exists in infinite time, then there will be a chaos, 'till finite, though innumerable revolutions produce at last some forms, whose parts and organs are so adjusted as to support the forms amidst a continued succession of matter' (*Dialogues,* 184). In Hume's unamended manuscript the following paragraph then occurs without the two additional paragraphs which now intervene:

It is in vain, therefore, to insist upon the uses of the parts in animals and vegetables, and in their curious adjustment to each other. I would fain know how an animal could subsist, unless its parts were so adjusted? Do we not find, that it immediately perishes whenever this adjustment ceases, and that its matter corrupting tries some new form? (*Dialogues,* 185).

From the idea that a living organism would not remain in existence as a living organism unless its parts were working in such a way as to preserve it there is only a small step to the idea of natural selection: that organisms, individuals and species, ill-adapted to their surroundings do not survive. Now both the theory of natural selection and Hume's anticipation of it have two consequences for the design argument. In the first place they provide an explanation for the structural order in living organisms. The order need not be related to the activities of an agent but could be the outcome of random variations occurring in conditions which have the effect of selecting some of the variations for preservation. In the second place the teleological argument is fatally weakened. If the appearance of purpose, the apparent adjustment of means to ends in animate nature, is only the satisfying of conditions which have to be satisfied if the organism is to survive, then the analogy in the teleological argument between human purposive contrivances and the seemingly purposive parts of nature altogether disappears.

An objection to all this is that what we can *now* see as a daring anticipation by Hume of the very well-evidenced theory of natural selection was *for him* merely a logical possibility. As Pearl remarks 'The possibility, if it is to undermine the design argument, must be grounded like the design argument on experience' (op. cit. p. 287). Now while it is obvious that Hume did not have at hand collected data of the sort Darwin provided in 1859, nevertheless he does present his suggestion as grounded on experience: 'Do we not find . . .' etc. The experience is of individuals, not species, but it is experience all the same. But the significance of Hume's suggestion lies not so much in the evidence with which he could support it as in the way in which it stands on its head traditional thinking about purpose in nature. The *same* evidence which could be read, for example, as 'how wonderfully the circulation of the blood is contrived in order to feed and warm the human body' could *also* be read 'the human body exists in its present form only because and as long as there is circulation of the blood'. The first reading, from which the teleological argument gathers all its strength, is no *better* grounded on experience than the second reading. They are both possible ways of interpreting experience. The particular contribution of the theory of natural selection has been to give enormously greater scope and content to the second reading. But this does not show that Hume's suggestion was not, in its time, a brilliant insight into the possible nature of things, nor does it show that because Hume preceded Darwin, therefore the design argument at the time Hume wrote was better grounded in experience than the non-teleological possibility he suggests. Design and natural adaption were of equal status as far as experience could decide since they were both ways of interpreting the same experience. This equality is in itself sufficient to upset the exclusive claims of design as a way of accounting for the order, in particular the purposive structure, of living things.

The case of order in living things is however just a special application of a more general thesis which Hume introduces as a possible way of accounting for the existence of order in the universe at large. His general thesis is that the present world actually is a system in which enduring order has arisen out of chaos,[25] and in which relatively permanent forms are produced by the undirected movements of a vast but finite quantity of matter operating over a limitless period of time: 'The continual motion of matter, therefore, in less than infinite transpositions, must produce this œconomy or order; and by its very nature, that order, when once established, supports itself, for many ages, if not to eternity' (Dialogues, 185).

In an article on the Dialogues, G. J. Nathan remarks that this is Philo again 'merely repeating the principle of internal causes of order' under 'the guise of presenting a particular system of cosmology'.[26] Philo certainly is again saying that 'the beginning of motion [or, presumably, order – J.G.] in matter itself is as conceivable a priori as its communication from mind and intelligence' but he is not 'merely' saying this. He is also saying how 'unguided matter' could develop the order we observe:

> Thus the universe goes on for many ages in a continued succession of chaos and disorder. But is it not possible that it may settle at last, so as not to lose its motion and active force (for that we have supposed inherent in it), yet so as to preserve an uniformity of appearance, amidst the continual motion and fluctuation of its parts? This we find to be the case with the universe at present. Every individual is perpetually changing, and every part of every individual, and yet the whole remains, in appearance, the same. May we not hope for such a position, or rather be assured of it, from the eternal revolutions of unguided matter, and may not this account for all the appearing wisdom and contrivance which is in the universe? (Dialogues, 184).

There are two difficulties here. In the first place, if the universe continued for ages in chaos and disorder, why should it ever 'settle at last' into the regular appearances there now are? This difficulty does not occur if the account of order is confined to the origin of settled structures – fixed objects like the moon or a lump of meteoric iron or a living organism. These could, and almost certainly have, come about from 'void and formless' matter formed and reformed in the sort of processes described in fundamental chemical and physical laws. But the difficulty becomes acute if we ask of the processes themselves how they could have evolved out of a state in which there was neither mechanical nor statistical order. However in Part VIII of the Dialogues Hume seems to be thinking not of a world of total disorder, but of one comprising matter behaving in accordance with fundamental physical laws though having no fixed or semi-permanent structures. I say this because he speaks of 'a continued succession of matter', of 'the eternal revolutions of unguided matter', of 'a perpetual revolution or motion of parts' and he always contrasts this with permanent forms rather than attributes to it absolute lawlessness. In this weak interpretation, his hypothesis would account for the development of structures but not for the regular processes or 'principles' which produce them.

The second difficulty is that if Hume is, after all, suggesting a genesis of the *processes* which give rise to the structures we have, then there should, according to his theory, be evidence that at some remote time the most general laws of nature known to us did not hold, or held with a different range of application than they have now. As far as I know there is no such evidence. Hume's account of the origin of order is then either wrong or else it should be understood in the weaker version I suggested above; namely as an account of orderly structures, in particular 'those very artificial parts of animals', not of orderly processes. These will be either inherent in the nature of matter as such or must be accounted for by the creative activity of an intelligent agent in the manner of the regularity argument. As Hume remarks 'The beginning of motion in matter itself is as conceivable *a priori* as its communication from mind and intelligence' and faced with these alternatives the only reasonable resource is 'a total suspense of judgement'.

*   *   *

There is at least one other criticism of the design argument implicit in much of what Hume says. It is that 'Our experience, so imperfect in itself, and so limited both in extent and duration, can afford us no probable conjecture concerning the whole of things' (*Dialogues,* 177). This final objection to the design argument is far wider in its aim than the present mark. It is one of Hume's most general and most persistently urged arguments that there are areas of traditional thinking 'of divinity or school metaphysics, for instance' in which a proper appraisal of human understanding will show that the whole subject matter is as nearly incomprehensible as makes no difference: 'We are got into a fairy land, long ere we have reached the last steps in our theory; and *there* we have no reason to trust our common methods of argument, or to think that our usual analogies and probabilities have any authority. Our line is too short to fathom such immense abysses' (*Enquiry,* 72 : 83). Because this objection is so general and applies just as much to the ontological argument or to theology in general as to the design argument in particular, I shall reserve it for discussion in a later chapter.

Consideration of these eleven interrelated objections to the design argument does not exhaust Hume's criticisms but it does indicate all the main areas in which his remarkably thorough critique is developed. Sir Leslie Stephen has observed that the *Dialogues* were the first sustained criticism of the design argument in any language. Their present-day importance is clearly indicated by the continuous flow of articles and books which take Hume's criticisms on their philosophical merits rather than merely as episodes in the history of ideas. But the curious thing about the influence of the *Dialogues* is not the interest which has developed since Kemp Smith's edition in 1935 but the lack of any obvious interest before then. In the late eighteenth century they seem to have passed largely

unnoticed and when Paley wrote his almost canonical exposition of the
design argument in 1802 he did so without reference to them. Even Mill
in the *Three Essays on Religion* seems to be scarcely aware how close he is
to treading in some of Hume's footsteps and Leslie Stephen, although
recognising the importance of the *Dialogues,* seems to think of them as
effective and yet somehow in the background. It may have been that at first
Hume's analytic critique was too far in advance of the thought of his time
to be readily discussed and then, later on, too unfashionable to be
acknowledged. In the early years of the present century the *Dialogues*
were out of print most of the time and that alone may account for their
neglect. Be that as it may the neglect is a thing of the past and no one is now
likely to repeat T. E. Jessop's opinion that the *Dialogues* are dated and done
with.[27]

Do Hume's criticisms invalidate the design argument? If a traditional
theistic conclusion (that there is a single, vastly powerful agent, possessing
moral and intellectual qualities) is drawn from it, then Hume's objection
that we cannot infer a moral designer from a non-moral design is very
damaging indeed. I shall discuss the implications of this particular objection
in the next chapter. If a similar conclusion is drawn, but omitting reference
to moral qualities, then his objections are slightly less clear-cut. Their effect
is cumulative, in particular his erosion of the plausibility of the analogy.
At the very least he has fragmented a once brief and dominant argument
into a large number of minute philosophical discussions, few of which seem
capable of decisive resolution either way. In this process he has damaged
beyond repair the argument as an easy way to rational belief in anything
the religious man might want to call god.[28]

I shall return in Chapters 8 and 10 to the estimate Hume puts upon his
own critique of the design argument, and to the question whether he
assents to some sort of vestigial argument — not really the design argument
at all — which merely concludes that there is a principle of order in the
world. But now I turn to the converse of the design argument: to
the problem of evil.

3 Evil, Freedom and the Religious Hypothesis

> I returned, and saw under the sun, that the race
> is not to the swift, nor the battle to the strong,
> neither yet bread to the wise, nor yet riches to
> men of understanding, nor yet favour to men of skill;
> but time and chance happeneth to them all.
>
> *Ecclesiastes*, IX

Hume's main discussion of what is usually termed the problem of evil (or the problem of suffering) is in Parts X and XI of the *Dialogues* and in Section XI of the *Enquiry*. Section VIII of the *Enquiry* contains some remarks on freedom and necessity which are relevant to what, following Flew and Plantinga, I shall call the 'Free Will Defence'. But these form an argument in their own right and I shall deal with them separately in the final section of this chapter.

Hume's main argument is that the existence of various forms of evil in the world places a highly significant restriction upon the inference which can be drawn from the order in the world to the character of the orderer. I shall call this the inference problem of evil. It is for Hume just a special case of the general illegitimacy (already discussed, see above p. 14f) of inferring more power, more goodness — more anything — in the cause than is actually manifest in the effect, the Universe itself. But as so often in Hume's critical discussion of sensitive religious positions his overt discussion of a 'philosophical' problem lightly conceals his real discussion of a crucial religious issue. In the present case his discussion of the inference problem of evil barely conceals what he has to say about the much more vexing aspect of evil which simply is the traditional problem of evil: the problem of showing that the evil appearances of the world are *consistent* with the existence of a god whom we already believe, from a mistaken estimation of the design argument or on other grounds, to be limitlessly powerful and good.

In this chapter I shall consider first the problem of evil as an objection to the design argument (the inference problem); secondly evil as an objection to belief in a benevolent and powerful god however such belief is arrived at (the consistency problem). I shall conclude with a look at Hume's contribution to the Free Will Defence.

(i)   THE INFERENCE PROBLEM OF EVIL

It seems probable that to a disinterested observer the existence of evil in the
world would merely suggest a restricted inference: if an agent could be
inferred from the phenomena then no moral characteristics could be inferred
in the agent. But of course the inference from world to god is seldom
disinterested. It is biased by preconceived ideas about what god is or should
be like. One of the most dominant of these is the idea that god has moral
qualities. He is concerned with the good, or so we suppose, and evil forms
no part of him. Now Hume's position is simply that of the disinterested
observer. The position is argued with great confidence by Philo in the
Dialogues and again, more briefly, by the sceptical friend in *Enquiry* XI.
The position is that the design argument does not establish the existence of
a god with moral characteristics: 'there is no view of human life, or of the
conditions of mankind, from which, without the greatest violence, we can
infer the moral attributes' (*Dialogues*, 202). But if this is so, then to the
theist the design argument will be of much reduced value. He may even sense,
as I think Hume intends, that if the phenomena of the world do not allow us
to infer the existence of a god who is morally concerned with the world, then
the phenomena may well be actually inconsistent with the existence of any
such god. In other words, if evil restricts the inference in the design
argument it may also restrict what sort of god there could be.

   The crux of Hume's position rests upon showing — what to many people
is only too painfully obvious — that evil of one sort or another does exist in
the world in sufficient measure to obstruct the inference to an omnipotent
and benevolent god. Thus the first half of Part X of the *Dialogues* is
occupied by Philo and Demea pointing out just how much misery there is in
the world. There is in abundance both *natural evil* (or 'physical evil' as
Hume is inclined to call it), in other words, evil brought upon us by nature
quite apart from our own actions or omissions, and *moral evil*, or evil
brought upon ourselves by our own actions or omissions. Men are tormented
by diseases and insanity. There is perpetual war amongst all living creatures
which embitters life. Storms destroy. War, famine and pestilence maim and
kill. At worst our lives are nasty, brutish and short; at best we never reach
contentment or true felicity: 'All the goods of life united would not make a
very happy man: But all the ills united would make a wretch indeed'.
According to Hume, but in this he misrepresents Leibniz (see below, p. 49f),
Leibniz and Dr King (*De Origine Mali*, 1702) alone have denied the reality of
evil but their theories are unacceptable to suffering humanity (and, Hume
could have added, lack 'all force for anyone who is not convinced that
God's existence can be firmly established despite actual evil'[1]). Cleanthes
demurs a little at the exaggeration of misery: 'I can observe something like
what you mention in some others'. But his protest is brushed aside: He is a
fortunate man indeed to be able merely to 'observe' it in others. The first
half of Section X culminates in Philo's classic statement of the problems of evil:

And is it possible . . . that after all these reflections, and infinitely more, which might be suggested, you can still persevere in your anthropomorphism, and assert the moral attributes of the Deity, his justice, benevolence, mercy, and rectitude, to be of the same nature with these virtues in human creatures? His power we allow infinite: Whatever he wills is executed: But neither man nor any other animal are happy: Therefore he does not will their happiness. His wisdom is infinite: He is never mistaken in choosing the means to any end: But the course of nature tends not to human or animal felicity: Therefore it is not established for that purpose . . . In what respect, then, do his benevolence and mercy resemble the benevolence and mercy of men?

Epicurus's old questions are yet unanswered. Is he willing to prevent evil, but not able? then he is impotent. Is he able, but not willing? then he is malevolent. Is he both able and willing? whence then evil? (*Dialogues*, 98).

The application of this to the inference problem is obvious and is stated no less than four times by Philo in the course of *Dialogues* X and XI, and once by the sceptical friend in *Enquiry* XI. If a man is 'not antecedently convinced of a supreme intelligence, benevolent, and powerful, but is left to gather such a belief from the appearance of things' then he will never infer perfect power and benevolence in the cause. But — an escape clause for the consistency problem — if a man already takes for granted the absolute power and benevolence of the cause then it is not *impossible* that in some way the appearance of things may be shown to be consistent with such an assumption: 'however consistent the world may be, allowing certain suppositions and conjectures, with the idea of such a Deity, it can never afford us an inference concerning his existence. The consistency is not absolutely denied, only the inference' (*Dialogues*, 205).

This observation, I think most people would agree, is correct. But Cleanthes does try the only obvious way of disputing it:

The only method of supporting divine benevolence . . . is to deny absolutely the misery and wickedness of man. Your representations are exaggerated: Your melancholy views mostly fictitious: your inferences contrary to fact and experience. Health is more common than sickness: Pleasure than pain: Happiness than misery (*Dialogues*, 200).

But as Philo is quick to point out, even if his representations are exaggerated, the mere *preponderance* of health over sickness is not sufficient to let us infer *infinite* power and wisdom and goodness in the designer. For that inference *all* apparent evil would have in reality to be an illusion or a misunderstanding by us of what is necessary for the best possible world and we have no reason to believe, as disinterested observers, that evil is an illusion or is necessary in the world. But supposing, as Cleanthes suggests at the beginning of part

XI, we drop all talk about infinite attributes which 'savour more of panegyric than philosophy' and talk instead of *'admirable, excellent, superlatively great, wise* and *holy'* (*Dialogues*, 203). Surely 'a satisfactory account may then be given of natural and moral evil'? Philo's reply is again that a disinterested observer would not infer from the given world even a limited but very great degree of benevolence in the cause. But why not?

Suppose that our cosmic isolation from any other possible habitable world were less absolute than it is. Suppose that a moon of Jupiter were found to be a world entirely similar to New Zealand before colonisation, save that it contained no men-like creatures. Would not the human space traveller find it very good indeed? And if he later discovered that some few individuals among the species which he found or implanted upon this fertile Ganymede perished miserably in occasional tempests or plagues, would he not *still* say that his new discovered world was very good for such creatures as men? And if he followed the design argument to its conclusion would he not infer a benevolent intention, great power and wisdom, in the designer of Ganymede? There are at least two difficulties with these agreeable speculations. In the first place, by parity of reasoning, they invite questions about the benevolence or otherwise of the intentions of the designer when he (or it) produced those vastly greater areas of the known universe which are alien to human or any other sort of life (even the Earth contains a Sahara and a Gobi desert). It is only by concentrating attention upon a very partial selection of worlds and then ignoring parts of those worlds that benevolence can be *inferred* in the designer. In the second place, it could be argued, from this scarcity of habitable worlds we should not infer that the designer is occasionally benevolent enough to permit life. Instead we should infer that the Earth (and Ganymede) have achieved one of those cosmically unusual states in which the existence of living things is possible.

These states are allowed for by the designer, if there is one, but are of no particular concern to him (or it) and the individuals in any species which happen to evolve are likewise of no concern. Thus, although to someone already believing that the designer has a moral interest in mankind the numbers of uninhabitable planets will provide no positive evidence against this belief, Philo's conclusion that the original cause, *as inferred from the phenomena,* is non-moral (that is, lacks any concern with or interest in the existence, let alone the happiness, of men) is the correct inference from a non-selective and impartial view of the universe. The original cause 'has no more regard to good above ill than to heat above cold, or to drought above moisture':

> There may *four* hypotheses be framed concerning the first causes of the universe: *that* they are endowed with perfect goodness, *that* they have perfect malice, *that* they are opposite and have both goodness and malice, *that* they have neither goodness nor malice. Mixed phenomena can never prove the two former unmixed principles. And the uniformity and

steadiness of general laws seem to oppose the third. The fourth, therefore, seems by far the most probable (*Dialogues*, 212).

But the most probable inference from the phenomena (and I now take it that Hume's fourth possibility is the most probable) is the one which is most radically different from the assumption of virtually all religious belief, namely, the assumption that the gods are *concerned* with the affairs of men. If the cause or causes of the universe are in no way bothered about the existence, let alone the good or ill, of living things in general and of men in particular, then these causes are not the gods which religions have worshipped. The only favourable thing to be said for theism by way of the design argument would then be that the very modest inference which the design argument does permit, although amounting to vastly less than a theistic god, is not actually inconsistent with the existence of a theistic god. Or is it?

Since the inference from the phenomena is to a non-moral cause, if the cause is alleged to be limitlessly or even very very powerful and good, then the appearance will be that the phenomena are inconsistent with this. Consider a parallel example. There is a large and representative collection of paintings by one Fiasco. Nothing is known about Fiasco except that he painted all the pictures in the collection. The collection contains no dominant group of subjects. There are portraits, still lifes, Arcadian land-scapes, street scenes, well-known buildings, seascapes, mythological subjects, biblical scenes etc. The most straightforward inference from the collection is that Fiasco was very catholic in his taste and painted whatever took his fancy. But a certain group of critics believe, on the basis of an unsubstan-tiated anecdote, that the only subjects Fiasco really took any delight in painting were seascapes. Now the fact that the paintings are of many subjects and that seascapes form an insignificant proportion of the whole is *prima facie* evidence that the critics are wrong. At least it is much simpler, much less intellectual fuss, to accept the obvious inference from the pictures — that Fiasco did not particularly care what he painted — than to contort and complicate the inference in order to accommodate the critic's belief. Now although Hume, through Philo, repeatedly allows the *possibility* that the phenomena of the world could be shown to be consistent with the existence of an intelligent, good and powerful god if we already have other grounds for believing in such a god, he also implies that the search for such consistency (like trying to interpret the artist's manifest indifference to subject matter as a real preference for seascapes) is an intellectual fuss which the more obvious inference to a non-moral cause renders quite unnecessary. The point is put most vigorously in the *Enquiry*, 139: 148.

> But still I ask; Why take these attributes [power and benevolence] for granted, or why ascribe to the cause any qualities but what actually appear in the effect? Why torture your brain to justify the course of nature

upon suppositions, which, for ought you know, may be entirely imaginary, and of which there are to be found no traces in the course of nature?

The answer to the second question is of course that traditional religious beliefs have seldom been regarded as merely suppositions or hypotheses which form one 'method of accounting for the visible phenomena of the universe'. To those who hold them, religious beliefs form an ultimate metaphysic of existence. Those who torture their brains to reconcile the facts of evil in the world with the existence of a good and powerful god do so because their belief in such a god is strong enough to withstand the *prima facie* simplicity and force of the inference that the original source of all things does not care an iota about any individual living thing or even about life as opposed to non-life in the universe.

(ii)   THE CONSISTENCY PROBLEM OF EVIL

The consistency problem of evil, for someone who believes in the existence of a powerful and loving god (whether these attributes are supposed to be infinite or very great does not matter for the moment), is just the problem of evil itself: the problem of accounting for the existence in the world of moral and physical evil which should apparently have no place in the creation of such a god: 'Why is there any misery at all in the world? Not by chance surely. From some cause then. Is it from the intention of the Deity? But he is perfectly benevolent. Is it contrary to his intention? But he is almighty' (*Dialogues*, 201). Philo adds that 'nothing can shake the solidity of this reasoning, so short, so clear, so decisive'. But if someone already claims to know — to be sure and to have a right to be sure — that a god exists who is powerful and concerned with living things — then for him some view of the world (not necessarily any which Hume considers) *must* shake Philo's reasoning. The mixed phenomena of the world *must* be consistent with the existence of a good and powerful god. But Hume nowhere allows the legitimacy of such claims to knowledge of god — knowledge which could be strong enough to overrule the problem of evil without solving it. The most he allows is confident belief in a god which the believer struggles to reconcile with the apparently contrary phenomena of the world. Some of the possible moves in this struggle for reconciliation attract Hume's comments. These moves are:

(A)   *The Porch Argument: that distributive justice is executed elsewhere and anon*

The argument is touched upon by the 'sceptical friend' in *Enquiry* XI only to be quickly dismissed:

Are there any marks of a distributive justice in the world? If you answer
in the affirmative, I conclude, that, since justice here exerts itself, it is
satisfied. If you reply in the negative, I conclude, that you have then no
reason to ascribe justice, in our sense of it, to the gods. If you hold a
medium between affirmation and negation, by saying, that the justice
of the gods, at present, exerts itself in part, but not in its full extent;
I answer, that you have no reason to give it any particular extent, but
only so far as you can see it, *at present,* exert itself (*Enquiry,* 141f : 150f).

The contention is not that life *could not* be 'a porch which leads to a greater
and vastly different building' but that no evidence exists to show that it is.
To attempt to reconcile the ways of god to man in this manner is mere
possibility and hypothesis (cf. *Dialogues,* 200). Hume leaves the argument
here. The suggested reconciliation is entirely speculative. But it is worse than
that. It is no reconciliation at all. If one person organises or condones a
brutal assault upon another person, the evil of that assault is never justified,
although it may be atoned for, by the aggressor organising the ultimate
felicity of the sufferer. This situation is not altered if we attribute
omnipotence or omniscience to the aggressor; indeed it is made worse. The
human person may be excused by sickness or ignorance. But the divine person
knows what he is about and no deficiency in him obliged *him* to construct
a faulty porch to his great building. This was something he chose and such a
choice would be inconsistent with *our* ideas of moral excellence.

In *Dialogues,* 199, Demea makes a suggestion to account for natural evil
which is in part similar to the Porch Argument but which turns out to be
something much more interesting.

(B)   *The General Laws Argument: that evil results from the observance of*
general laws in the universe

This world is but a point in comparison of the universe: This life but a
moment in comparison of eternity. The present evil phenomena, therefore,
are rectified in other regions, and in some future period of existence.
And the eyes of men, being then opened to larger views of things, see
the whole connection of general laws, and trace, with adoration, the
benevolence and rectitude of the Deity, through all the mazes and
intricacies of his providence (*Dialogues,* 199).

The point is made more succinctly in the *Enquiry.* 'The obstinate and
intractable qualities of matter, we are told, or the observance of general
laws, or some such reason, is the sole cause, which controlled the power and
benevolence of Jupiter, and obliged him to create mankind and every
sensible creature so imperfect and so unhappy' (*Enquiry,* 139 : 148). In
both contexts the argument elicits the same reply. *If* we already believe that
god is both vastly powerful and completely good then 'such conjectures
[as the observance of general laws] may, perhaps, be admitted as plausible

solutions to the ill phenomena'. But, Hume replies (*Enquiry,* 139: 148), such a belief about god's nature lacks sufficient independent justification for us to need to clutch at the operation of general laws as a possible way of protecting the belief. But this reply will not quite do. Those who believe in a powerful and good god usually hold (whether justly or unjustly does not matter at the moment) either that they do have sufficient independent evidence for their belief or that no evidence is needed. The real question is then: given the belief in such a god, could the good resulting from the observance of general laws account for the evil which sometimes results from their operation in particular circumstances?

In *Dialogues* XI Philo considers four circumstances upon which the occurrence of evil depends: 'none of them appear to human reason in the least degree, necessary or unavoidable'. One of these is 'the conducting of the world by general laws' (*Dialogues,* 206). Philo has two suggestions. The first is that the deity might conduct everything by particular volitions, preventing evil and producing good in all cases. The second is that the deity might at least turn to good effect all issues which we now call chance.

Professor John Hick describes the world which would result from Philo's first suggestion: 'In such a world, animal organisms would not have to learn to move about circumspectly, because all serious hazards would be obviated by a complex system of avoidance or transformation. . . .'[2]

Hume too is aware of the oddity of such a world: 'the course of nature would be perpetually broken, and no man could employ his reason in the conduct of life'. But would this really matter? Hick points out that at least it would make a great deal of difference. Evolutionary selection would become impossible. Exact sciences could never be formulated. Effort and strife against difficulty would be obviated. The world would be very different, but would it be worse? Hick's answer, which I accept, is that such a world would be worse from the point of view of the characteristically Christian notion of good: 'the kind of goodness which according to Christian faith, God desires in His creatures, could not in fact be created except through a long process of creaturely experience in response to challenges and disciplines of various kinds' (op. cit., p. 344). But even if we accept that the kind of goodness which the Christian God desires is the best possible kind of goodness, Hick's point does not touch Philo's second suggestion for the remedy of evils which result from the operation of general laws:

> Health and sickness, calm and tempest, with an infinite number of other accidents, whose causes are unknown and variable, have a great influence both on the fortunes of particular persons and on the prosperity of public societies: And indeed all human life, in a manner, depends on such accidents. A Being, therefore, who knows the secret springs of the universe, might easily, by particular volitions, turn all these accidents to the good of mankind, and render the whole world happy, without discovering himself in any operation (*Dialogues,* 206).

It does not appear to me that if the deity were to decide chance events in favour of the good and against evil that this would in any important or even noticeable way upset the structure of the world we know or produce a race of lotus-eaters; but it *would* make the world a lot safer to live in. The rotten building would still fall down but at a moment when no one was in it. The flu virus would still mutate but not to produce a new and deadly infection. The defective sperm would still exist but would fail to reach the ovary. There seems to be no reason why a benevolent god armed with great power and wisdom could not do these things and yet still leave a world in which the Christian ideal of good was possible. In order to dismiss Philo's second suggestion it would have to be established that every evil accident is unavoidably necessary in order to maintain, on the one hand, our knowledge of the sciences, and on the other hand, the possibility of the good life as understood by Christians. I do not see how such a position could possibly be established. Hick's comment on Philo's second suggestion is that 'evils are exceptional only in relation to other evils which are routine', *therefore*, however many evil chances are made good, others would remain (op. cit., p. 363). But this should not present any difficulty for the deity. The precise points at which chance outcomes should be directed by divine benevolence is a problem of discrimination and judgement, not a logical antinomy which it would be irrational to expect divine wisdom to solve.

(C) *The Optimum World Argument: that evil (moral and physical) is a logically necessary component in the best of all possible worlds*

> There are many philosophers who, after an exact scrutiny of all the phenomena of nature, conclude, that the WHOLE, considered as one system, is, in every period of its existence, ordered with perfect benevolence; and that the utmost possible happiness will, in the end, result to all created beings, without any mixture of positive or absolute ill or misery. Every physical ill, say they, makes an essential part of this benevolent system, and could not possibly be removed, even by the Deity himself, considered as a wise agent, without giving entrance to greater ill, or excluding greater good, which will result from it (*Enquiry,* 101: 109f).

This argument is much closer to part of Leibniz' position than the denial of the reality of suffering which Hume attributes to him in *Dialogues,* 194 (see above p. 42). Hume's reply is that when the argument is confronted by real suffering it is simply not acceptable as an explanation of the suffering. It may please a speculative man placed in ease and security but would 'more irritate than appease' a man subject to some painful disease or other apparently unnecessary physical evil. The same consideration, according to Hume, applies to moral evil. There is no practical plausibility in saying that 'everything is right with regard to the *whole,* and that the qualities, which disturb society, are, in the main, as beneficial, and are as suitable to the primary intention of nature as those which more directly promote its happiness and welfare' (*Enquiry,* 100 : 111).

There can be little doubt that in these remarks Hume has put his finger on the objection which in fact leads very many people to reject the Optimum World Argument out of hand. The rejection is not for logically coherent reasons but from the heart. Job, we feel, would dismiss Dr Pangloss as a fool who had no comprehension of what real suffering is, and Job would be right to dismiss Dr Pangloss in this way.

But let us consider the logical force of the Optimum World Argument rather than its existential implausibility. It appears to be Nelson Pike's position that logically the argument cracks the consistency problem of evil.[3] The core of the relevant part of Pike's position is this: Within a theology which takes the existence of an omnipotent and benevolent god as given, the existence of evil in the world *must* be consistent with the existence of such a god. Now 'If instances of suffering were necessary components of the best of all possible worlds [as Pike argues they could be — *J.G.*], then an omnipotent and omniscient being would have a morally sufficient reason for permitting instances of suffering'. But the *possibility* that evil is a necessary component in the best of possible worlds is enough to satisfy the theological demand that god's existence must be consistent with the fact of evil. It is no longer true that the existence of god and the facts of evil are logically incompatible since it is possible that the best of possible worlds should contain evil and that the world we live in is just such a world.

The crucial assumption of this theodicy is that instances of suffering could be logically indispensable components in the best of all possible worlds. Philo, as Pike points out, simply takes it for granted that this assumption is contradictory and hence that it cannot be used as a defence of Judaic or Christian theism. But Philo is over-hasty. On investigation the assumption is found to be logically possible and thus a *possible* defence of theistic belief. But admitting that the Optimum World Argument is a *possible* defence of theistic belief does not make it a plausible or valuable defence. To be that, it would have to be shown that the system we actually have is the best possible system and that it is one which in fact exemplifies the logical possibility of having evil as a necessary part of it. These things cannot readily be done for the very good reason that we have no understanding of what it would be to do them. The point is this. We cannot know how the system we have compares with the best of all possible systems. Being finite men, not omniscient gods, we have no idea what the best of all possible systems would be like. We do not even know what would count as a 'possible' system and we do not know what the word 'best' is the superlative of in such a context. Best for whom? For what? With respect to what? All we can intelligibly do, in theory or practice, is to examine the system we have and make such improvements as we can. For in the system we have it certainly does not *look* as though every evil is necessary and the successes of medicine, it might be argued, have already shown that *not* every evil is necessary. So the crucial assumption in the Optimum World Argument turns out not to be contradictory, but to be unusable because the language in which it is expressed has no relation to the only world we know. In short, the meaning of the phrase 'best of all possible worlds' is so obscure that no reliable argument can be formulated to show that it is (or is not) logically possible that the world we have is the best of all possible worlds. We do not even get as far as Demea's slightly less high-flown theodicy to which Cleanthes objects: 'To establish one hypothesis upon another is building entirely in the air; and the utmost we ever attain, by these conjectures and fictions, is to ascertain the bare possibility of our opinion; but never can we, upon such terms, establish its reality' (*Dialogues,* 200).

(D)   *That no better world than the present could be imagined or devised*

This way of dealing with the consistency problem of evil altogether escapes the logical and linguistic perplexities of the Optimum World Argument. It simply offers a challenge to devise a world better than the one we have. Hume takes up this challenge in *Dialogues* XI. He points out that there are four circumstances which produce most of the evil in the world and these do not appear to be necessary circumstances.

One is the mechanism of animal creation 'by which pains, as well as pleasures, are employed to excite all creatures to action, and make them vigilant in the great work of self-preservation' (*Dialogues,* 205). Why, Hume asks, could not men have been so constructed as to be activated exclusively by pursuit of pleasure rather than by pursuit of pleasure *and* avoidance of pain.

Professor Hick (op. cit., p. 339) finds a flaw in this suggestion. Since 'pleasant' and 'unpleasant' are the limits of a continuous hedonic scale, abolishing the unpleasant would merely remove the bottom half of the existing scale, re-establishing the new 'unpleasant' at what had been the middle of the old scale. The continuation of such a process would either abolish all contrast in the scale as new 'unpleasants' were successively removed, or would reduce to a semantic recommendation 'that we describe the unpleasant as a lower degree of the pleasant'.

While this is a fair objection to any suggestion that the unpleasant should be abolished, it does not appear to me a conclusive objection to what Hume is actually suggesting. He is suggesting that the particular sensation called 'pain', which makes up *some* of the unpleasant experiences on the hedonic scale, should be abolished. He is also recommending that, in situations in which pain would have been felt, a diminution of pleasure should be experienced instead. Now this is not to say that the unpleasant should be abolished nor does it imply a shortening of the hedonic scale (for example, acute thirst may well be more unpleasant than acute pain). Plenty of unpleasant experiences would be left: pinching and crushing kinesthetic sensations, blinding light, heat and cold which fall short of causing pain, thirst, hunger, the need to urinate or get out of a stuffy atmosphere into fresh air. What is more, Hume might say, if the human need for water can be adequately regulated by the (at first) mildly unpleasant sense of thirst, why cannot the human need to visit a dentist be regulated by an itching in the tooth rather than by raging toothache. And why, if pain *must* be retained in some warning systems, should it so often remain or become blazing agony when all possible corrective action has been taken?[4] Hume's suggestion is not 'I wish no living thing to experience unpleasantness' but rather, with Shelley, 'I wish no living thing to suffer pain', a sentiment which it would not seem unreasonable to expect a powerful and benevolent god to share and act upon.

Another circumstance of the world which produces great and, according to Hume, unnecessary ill, is the conducting of the world by general laws. As he remarks, the mere capacity to feel pain (the first circumstance) would not matter if the world had been so constituted that the capacity was very seldom activated. I have already considered what Hume has to say about this and offered some comments on Hick's reply. In summary: a world ruled by particular benevolent volitions of the deity would be different from the present world in ways which might well appear unattractive to most men and which would be unacceptable to Christians; but this objection does not seem to hold against a world in which evil chances were turned to the good by divine volitions.

The *third* circumstance is 'the great frugality with which all powers and faculties are distributed to every particular being' (*Dialogues*, 207f). The complaint is general but Hume gives a particular illustration of it. How much better life would be if men were 'endowed with a greater propensity to industry and labour'. I am in full agreement with Hick's objection here: 'If all men were endowed with, let us say, twice as much industry and perseverance as at present, this would mean not only that good men would work twice as hard for good ends but also that evil men would work twice as hard for evil ends. And the resulting state of the world would be proportionately the same' (op. cit., p. 365). And an objection of this character would apply not only to Hume's rather dour preference for industry and labour but to the amplification of almost any faculty or combination of faculties possessed by men. The result would not be more secure or happy men, but more powerful men; *physical* evil might be fractionally diminished but at the cost of an enormous potential increase in *moral* evil.

But it is the final circumstance which provides Hume with an almost un-answerable occasion for suggesting that benevolence armed with great power could have produced a better world:

> It must be acknowledged, that there are few parts of the universe
> which seem not to serve some purpose, and whose removal would
> not produce a visible defect and disorder in the whole. But at the same time,
> it must be observed, that none of these parts or principles, however useful,
> are so accurately adjusted, as to keep precisely within those bounds in

which their utility consists. . . . The irregularity is never, perhaps, so great as to destroy any species; but it is often sufficient to involve the individuals in ruin and misery (*Dialogues,* 209f).

The sort of thing Hume is thinking of is the wind which becomes a destroying tempest, the rain which becomes a flood, the heat which becomes a drought, the multiplying cell which breaks free of its proper bounds and becomes a cancer. These things, and many others like them, cause an immense amount of individual suffering and death and there appears to be no reason why they should ever have been allowed into the contrivance of the universe.

Hick's concession at this point to a view which can hardly be congenial to him is very generous: '. . . when such things happen we can see no gain to the soul, whether of the victim or of others, but on the contrary only a ruthlessly destructive process which is utterly inimical to human values'. He then considers and rejects the traditional view that nature is corrupted by the fallen angels (op. cit., pp. 367-368) before concluding:

> Our 'solution', then, to this baffling problem of excessive and undeserved suffering is a frank appeal to the positive value of mystery. Such suffering remains unjust and inexplicable, haphazard and cruelly excessive. The mystery of dysteleological suffering is a real mystery, impenetrable to the rationalizing human mind (op. cit. p. 371).

At an earlier point in his discussion of evil Philo appears to advocate a somewhat similar conclusion: 'How then does the divine benevolence display iteself, in the sense of you anthropomorphites? None but we mystics, as you were pleased to call us, can account for this strange mixture of phenomena, by deriving it from attributes infinitely perfect, but incomprehensible' (*Dialogues,* 199; see also and compare the reference to 'sublime mysteries' in *Enquiry,* 103 : 111). But the intention here is very different from Hick's. *His* intention is to commend the mystery as a thing of religious worth in itself: the suffering may be a part of the divine process of soul-making; mystery as such may be part of this process. *Hume's* intention is to argue that we should not find an inconsistency between the fact of evil in the world and the nature we suppose god to have because we do not know what nature god has. God's attributes are incomprehensible. With Hick, the mystery is the fact of evil. With Hume, the mystery is the nature of god. But of course from the point of view of Christian theism Hume's location of the mystery will not do. It shoots out the baby with the bath water (the gently tongue-in-cheek tone of the passage indicates Hume was well aware of this). There is no problem of evil for 'we mystics' because 'we' have refused to say that god is good and *that* refusal is more distasteful to the Christian theist than a frank acknowledgement that he cannot account for the evil which his compassionate God permits in the world.

Of Hume's four circumstances which produce evil in the world — and in

each case he is clearly thinking about physical evil — the abolition of pain
as an activating mechanism for the preservation of living species seems, at least
in part, possible. Total government of the world by particular benevolent
volitions of the deity would produce a world of beings unattractively like
Tennyson's lotus-eaters, and quite unlike the men we know, but benevolent
direction of evil chances would have no such obvious disadvantages. An
increased capacity in man for industry (or whatever) would be no improve-
ment at all and might well prove a disaster. But circumscribing nature at the
points where orderly processes appear to break down or become overwrought
would greatly mitigate suffering without producing any apparent compensating
disadvantage. Thus it does seem possible to devise a world more agreeable to
mankind than the world we have, and if it is possible to devise such a world,
the question remains: if god is benevolent and powerful, how is it that the
world contains the physical evil it does?

Although Hume does not accept any of the four 'solutions' to the problem
of evil that we have been considering, and although he twice presents the
problem in a very categorical form (*Dialogues,* 198 and 201) — 'Nothing can
shake the solidity of this reasoning' — it does not seem to be part of his final
purpose to argue the absolute or logical incompatibility between the facts of
evil in the world and the existence of a very good and very powerful god.
On the one hand he shows, conclusively I think, that a benevolent god
cannot be inferred from the phenomena. On the other hand he argues that
the facts of physical evil make the existence of such a god very improbable.
His existence is *improbable* because the simplest and most obvious construction which can be put upon the phenomena is inconsistent with it. But his
existence remains *possible* because there may yet be some way (so far
undiscovered) of showing how god's benevolence could be consistent with
the facts of evil. The case is similar to that of Fiasco the painter with his
supposed predilection for seascapes. It is possible but, in the face of the
evidence, implausible to say that his only real love was painting seascapes.
Likewise it is possible, but highly implausible, to say that god is vastly
powerful and wholly good. In each case the implausibility tells against the
assumption which generates the implausibility. The critics are therefore
probably wrong in attending to the unsubstantiated anecdote about Fiasco and
the sea. The theologians are probably wrong in accepting god's omnipotence
and benevolence as axiomatic.

(iii)   THE FREE WILL PROBLEM

So far Hume's discussion of evil has been largely confined to physical evil.
But in Section VIII of the *Enquiry,* after he has been discussing the meaning
which can be given to 'freedom' and 'necessity' as these terms are applied to
human agents, he suddenly presents a theological dilemma which results from
his conclusions and which is highly relevant to one possible explanation of
the existence of moral evil. The explanation in question is the one which says

that a good and powerful god permits evil of the sort introduced into the world by the free actions of men (everything from the mischief of tipping rubbish in public places to the infamies of a Stalin can be included) because *not* to permit this would so circumscribe the freedom of men as to reduce them to mere automata quite different from the free moral agents they are at present. Following recent convention, let us call this the Free Will Defence. Now Hume's arguments in Section VIII give rise to two answers to the Free Will Defence. One is the answer he himself suggests in the theological coda to the chapter. The other is the answer which Flew and Mackie developed independently in 1955 and which has given rise to a protracted controversy in the journals.[5]

Hume's argument in Section VIII is that men are free or have liberty of action in the sense that 'liberty' is taken to mean '*a power of acting or not acting, according to the determinations of the will;* that is, if we choose to remain at rest, we may; if we choose to move, we also may' (*Enquiry*, 95: 104). In this sense a man has freedom or liberty if he is not subject to constraint. But a man is also subject to necessity, or is determined in his actions, in the only sense Hume ever allows for 'necessity', namely, 'the constant *conjunction* of similar objects, and the consequent *inference* from one to the other'. Thus it is generally true among men that similar motives produce similar actions and it is true of individual men that each acts according to his character. Such action in character is voluntary action for which a man is responsible and morally accountable. Random or motiveless action on the other hand is the involuntary work of a lunatic, not of a responsible agent. Thus, according to Hume, a normal man in normal conditions is both free *and* determined since Hume attaches a sense to these terms which makes them compatible. It will be noticed that in effect Hume debars talk about freedom of the will and directs us to talk instead about freedom of actions. The point is underlined in a footnote: 'We feel, that our actions are subject to our will, on most occasions; and imagine we feel, that the will itself is subject to nothing' (*Enquiry*, 94n: 103n). But the will just *is* our character with its motives, store of information etc.

Flew's attack on the Free Will Defence begins by defining a free action as an action which follows from the character of the agent and is free from external constraint (op. cit. p. 150). He then points out that acting freely in this sense is not merely compatible with being caused to act in the way in which one does act but actually presupposes that our actions are causally related to our characters. If they were not so related our actions would be random not free. But this being so it would seem that god could have made us in such a way that we always freely choose to do the right thing. Hence the Free Will Defence is broken-backed.[6]

The similarity between Hume's account of liberty and the account which Flew gives in developing his argument is too obvious for comment. But there is nothing to show that Hume ever noticed that his account of liberty and necessity could be applied to the Free Will Defence in the way Flew (and

Mackie) were to apply it, nor do his remarks anticipate in any interesting way the controversy which followed from the Flew-Mackie argument. But Hume does follow up in detail another and equally important answer to the Free Will Defence. This is the theological dilemma with which Section VIII concludes Hume presents it, with an affectation of self-depreciating modesty, as an objection to his own account of liberty and necessity. But it is much more than that. It is a crucial impasse in the traditional Christian account of God's character and foreknowledge:

> if voluntary actions be subjected to the same laws of necessity with the operations of matter, there is a continued chain of necessary causes, pre-ordained and pre-determined, reaching from the original cause of all to every single volition of every human creature. . . . The ultimate Author of all our volitions is the Creator of the world, who first bestowed motion on this immense machine, and placed all beings in that particular position whence every subsequent event, by an inevitable necessity, must result (*Enquiry*, 99 : 108).

But, it might be objected, this is denying the fundamental (and reasonable) assumption of the Free Will Defence that we have in fact got free will. The illicit denial is then being used as a means of foisting responsibility for our actions onto god. Nothing of the sort! Hume is simply pointing out that if we *are* free in the sense required for moral responsibility, in other words, if we act in character and without external constraint, then the moral responsibility transfers to him in whom we live and move and have our being because *he* set in motion the necessary causes which give us the characters he foresaw we would have. Hume appears to develop the problem from his own theory but it occurs in most Christian theology and was particularly clearly seen by Calvin. From it the dilemma follows:

> *First,* that, if human actions can be traced up, by a necessary chain, to the Deity [i.e. 'He foresaw, he ordained, he intended all those actions of men which we so rashly pronounce criminal'], they can never be criminal; on account of the infinite perfection of that Being from whom they are derived, and who can intend nothing but what is altogether good and laudable. Or, *Secondly,* if they be criminal, we must retract the attribute of perfection, which we ascribe to the Deity, and must acknowledge him to be the ultimate author of guilt and moral turpitude in all his creatures (*Enquiry*, 104 : 109).

Hume answers the first horn of the dilemma firmly. Even if some philosophers (Hume only cites the Stoics but in a similar context in the *Dialogues* Leibniz is mentioned by name) do adopt what I have called the Optimum World Argument, this will not induce us to regard either physical or moral evil as things which should properly be viewed as goods. Evil is what it is and no speculative system of philosophy will make us think otherwise. So it is no use saying that if god is responsible for what appears as evil it must really be good

But Hume does not reject the second horn of the dilemma with the same vigour. Indeed he does not reject it at all. He simply says it is not possible 'to explain distinctly, how the Deity can be the immediate cause of all the actions of men, without being the author of sin and moral turpitude. These are mysteries, which mere natural and unassisted reason is very unfit to handle' (*Enquiry*, 104 : 111). Flew has pointed out[7] that earlier commentators have almost entirely failed to spot that Hume is not sincerely attempting to resolve the dilemma he presents. Flew himself describes the reference to 'sublime mysteries' as 'a smirking genuflexion of piety' and I do not doubt it is just that. But the significant point is surely that Hume's lack of enthusiasm for resolving the dilemma as a whole is biased against one horn of it. He *does* reject the suggestion that evil acts are not really evil. He does *not* reject the possibility that 'we must retract the attribute of perfection, which we ascribe to the Deity' and this possibility is just the one which Philo positively advocates in the *Dialogues*. When Philo winds up his argument towards the end of Part XI he contends vigorously and at length (p. 211f) that all the appearances point to an original cause which is blind to all moral or personal concern with living things: 'The true conclusion is, that the original source of all things is entirely indifferent to all these principles, and has no more regard to good above ill than to heat above cold, or to drought above moisture, or to light above heavy'. Nelson Pike (op. cit.) comments here: 'Philo claims that *there is* an 'original Source of all things' and that this source is indifferent with respect to matters of good and evil. He pretends to be inferring this conclusion from observed data. This represents a departure from Philo's much professed skepticism in the *Dialogues*'. Pike goes on to say that 'the point is not, I think, that Philo's new hypothesis is true, or even probable' but that Cleanthes' hypothesis (of a benevolent god) is very improbable. I agree that Cleanthes' hypothesis is improbable and that Philo is saying so, but I can see no evidence at all in the *Dialogues* or in any other Hume text to show either that the inference to a non-moral original source of things is inconsistent with Philo's scepticism or that he does not really mean what he says when he speaks of 'the true conclusion' from the observed data. I shall argue at length in Chapter 8 that Hume never sets out to disprove the existence of god, and in Chapter 10 that the issue in the *Dialogues* concerns the nature, not the being of god. But at the moment it is sufficient to observe that Philo's inference to a non-moral origin of things simply makes an explicit affirmation of the horn of the theological dilemma which Hume significantly fails to reject in the *Enquiry*. His position would then be that the Free Will Defence is broken-backed, not merely because it could entangle God in man's moral depravity, but because if the regress of determining causes goes back to anything then it goes back to a non-moral original source (which could be called 'god' if we feel so disposed).

*   *   *

Hume does not argue that there is a logical incompatibility between the belief in an omnipotent and perfectly good god and the facts of evil in the world. He says, on the one hand, that the facts of the world could never be used to infer the existence of such a god, and, on the other hand, that the facts of the world make the existence of such a god highly improbable. He considers and rejects four possible ways of reconciling the goodness of god with the facts of natural evil, and he rejects one possible way of reconciling the goodness of god with moral evil. If he concludes anything about the nature of god, then his conclusion is that god — the origin of things we may dimly and uncertainly discern — has no moral nature. This is the appearance of things and, as we shall see in subsequent chapters, Hume is unable to find any rational ground for any other belief about the *nature* of god. But the claim is sometimes made that our knowledge of the *existence* of god is not the dim discerning of some possible origin of natural order but the *a priori* knowledge that all contingent things have their being in a necessarily existent being. I shall now examine Hume's total rejection of this claim.

4 Being and Necessity

> *Mr Panscope:* You seem desirous, by the futile process of
> analytical dialectics, to subvert the pyramidal structure
> of synthetically deduced opinions, which have withstood
> the secular revolutions of physiological disquisition, and
> which I maintain to be transcendentally self-evident,
> categorically certain and syllogistically demonstrable.
> *Squire Headlong:* Bravo! Pass the bottle. The very best
> speech that ever was made.
> *Mr Escot:* It has only the slight disadvantage of being
> unintelligible.
>
> Peacock, *Headlong Hall*

There is no evidence to show that Hume had ever read Anselm's *Proslogion*
or was aware of the 'single formula which needs no other to prove itself
but itself alone' by means of which Anselm claimed to demonstrate the
existence of God (a demonstration which since Kant has been known as the
ontological argument). Nor is there evidence to suggest that Hume had any
first-hand knowledge of those authoritative versions of the cosmological
argument which form the first three of Aquinas' 'Five Ways'. Nor, although
he did know[1] Descartes' *Meditations,* does Hume's statement of what he makes
Demea call 'that simple and sublime argument *a priori'* (in Part IX of the
Dialogues) appear to owe anything very much to Descartes. Thus two major
statements of the *a priori* arguments for the existence of god were in all
probability unknown to Hume, and one, although known and criticised in
the *Treatise* (see below), does not form part of the *a priori* argument he
sets out in the *Dialogues*. The one he actually discusses in the *Dialogues*
appears to be a paraphrase of that set out by Samuel Clarke in the first of the
Boyle Lectures for 1704.[2] It is an argument which begins and goes most of
the way as the cosmological argument and then absorbs into its conclusion a
notion which is essential to the ontological argument, namely that of a being
whose non-existence would be self-contradictory. Hume's statement of this
hybrid argument is as follows:

> Whatever exists must have a cause or reason of its existence; it being
> absolutely impossible for any thing to produce itself, or be the cause of its
> own existence. In mounting up, therefore, from effects to causes, we
> must either go on tracing an infinite succession, without any ultimate
> cause at all or must at last have recourse to some ultimate cause, that is
> necessarily existent: . . . [the first supposition provides no reason why
> the whole chain of causes is what it is or is at all] . . . What was it, then,
> which determined something to exist rather than nothing, and bestowed

being on a particular possibility, exclusive of the rest? *External causes,* there are supposed to be none. *Chance* is a word without a meaning. Was it *nothing*? But that can never produce any thing. We must, therefore, have recourse to a necessarily existent Being, who carries the REASON of his existence in himself; and who cannot be supposed not to exist without an express contradiction. There is consequently such a Being, that is, there is a Deity *(Dialogues, 188f).*

I shall call this Clarke's *a priori* argument. (This may seem a bit unkind to Clarke since it is really Hume's version — possibly coloured by Leibniz, see note 2 — of Clarke's argument. But Clarke's own wording is diffuse and his discussion builds up over twenty or so pages. Hume's is terse and captures all Clarke's essential points.) Hume's total rejection of it occupies only four pages in the *Dialogues* and a few lines elsewhere in his work and it would be foolish to look in his remarks for the complexity and subtlety of a great deal of modern discussion of the ontological and cosmological arguments. Nevertheless what he has to say does contain in outline three seminal objections to the *a priori* arguments, objections which have appeared again and again in discussion and which continue to appear. The first concerns the notion of a necessarily existent being; the second that of a sufficient reason; the third the notion of existence as it alters or does not alter our conception of an object. I shall devote one section of this chapter to each of these in turn.

(i)   NECESSARY BEINGS

Hume's first and 'decisive' objection to Clarke's hybrid *a priori* argument is in form an objection to any argument (such as Descartes' in *Meditations* IV and V) which sets out to deduce the existence of a thing from the thing's necessary existence:

> I shall begin with observing, that there is an evident absurdity in pretending to demonstrate a matter of fact, or to prove it by any arguments *a priori.* Nothing is demonstrable, unless the contrary implies a contradiction. Nothing, that is distinctly conceivable, implies a contradiction. Whatever we [can distinctly] conceive as existent, we can also conceive as non-existent. There is no Being [i.e. thing we can distinctly conceive as existent], therefore, whose non-existence implies a contradiction. Consequently there is no Being [i.e. as before], whose existence is demonstrable *(Dialogues, 189).*

In the paragraph which follows this it becomes clear that Hume regards 'necessary' and 'demonstrable' as interchangeable words and his final conclusion is that the words 'necessary existence' or 'demonstrable existence' have no meaning.

With pedantic explication (indicated above in square brackets) of the terms used, Hume's argument is formally valid. The faults, if any are to be found, must therefore lie in the premises or in the rather bland assumption that there is an 'evident absurdity' in demonstrating a matter of fact. Although such an assumption is fundamental to virtually all empiricist epistemology, it is not quite so evident that it can be taken without explanation. Hume's explanation is in the *Treatise* and, more succinctly, in the *Enquiry* 25f: 40f and 163f: 171f.

The fundamental epistemological distinction, which I shall follow Flew in calling 'Hume's Fork' and from which the assumption is drawn, is between 'relations of ideas' or 'demonstrations' and 'matters of fact'. The former 'are discoverable by the mere operation of thought, without dependence on what is anywhere existent in the universe'; the latter are only discoverable by experience of the way things are. The former comprise the propositions of pure mathematics and, we would add, of formal logic; the latter comprise all statements about the way the world works and all statements about what things do or do not exist. The negation of any correct demonstration is contradictory and cannot be clearly conceived. The negation of any true matter of fact is merely false, not contradictory, and can be conceived as clearly as the true state of affairs: *'That the sun will not rise to-morrow* is no less intelligible a proposition, and implies no more contradiction, than the affirmation, *that it will rise'*. The same with statements of existence: 'that Caesar, or the angel Gabriel, or any being never existed may be a false proposition, but still is perfectly conceivable and implies no contradiction' (*Enquiry*, 25 : 40 and 164 : 172).

Now from this it is quite clear that the conclusion 'there is no being whose existence is demonstrable' is already built into Hume's epistemology. The possibility that any thing could necessarily or demonstrably exist is ruled out at source by Hume's Fork. But Clarke might reply that he is questioning this epistemology. There is at least one being, god, whose non-existence would be contradictory. *He* necessarily exists. The epistemology which rules this out could be an arbitrary stipulation. If so, then it can be disregarded. Alternatively the epistemology could be a generalisation about types of knowledge. In this case god is an exception, possibly the only exception, to the generalisation.

The sheer weight of authority and usage in favour of something like Hume's distinction between demonstrations and matters of fact is in itself sufficient to shed the gravest doubts on the suggestion that the distinction is arbitrary. If it is arbitrary the onus of showing it to be so must rest entirely upon those who maintain such an unconventional position. On what grounds could it be said to be arbitrary? What should be put in its place? How else than by means of such a distinction could we advise people of the silliness of trying to prove by pure mathematics that there is a yew hedge in my garden or of trying to establish Taylor's Theorem by careful observation of the segments of a chocolate cake? It is just not feasible to say that the demonstration/

matter-of-fact dichotomy is arbitrary. But one *exceptional* being whose existence is necessary is an altogether different matter since exceptions need not challenge the *general* appropriateness of the epistemology. The possibility of such an exception has been canvassed in several different ways. Let us consider some of these.

(1) To begin with, the existential propositions in mathematics, it is said, are necessarily true; therefore the entities whose existence they assert necessarily exist. If an exception to empiricist epistemology can be made in order to admit these, why not a like exception to admit the necessary existence of the Supreme Being? But, *per contra,* whatever sort of existence a mathematical entity might be supposed to have, the existence of the Supreme Being can hardly be similar. The one depends upon human convenience, convention and stipulation; the other (supposedly) is absolutely independent and self-subsistent. The existence of a mathematical entity, one is tempted to say, could no more be like the existence of the Supreme Being than a quaternion could be like a smut on the chimneypiece. Moreover it seems to be in keeping with the intentions of Hume's epistemology *not* to include among matters of fact — since these are specified by reference to experience — those somewhat esoteric existential statements which occur, for example, in mathematics: note, for example, that he speaks twice in the *Enquiry* Section IV of 'real existence and matter of fact'. Thus, whatever grounds there may be for asserting 'there is a prime number between 13 and 29', appeals to observation and experience are not among them. But perhaps, someone will insist, god's existence *is* just like this — in no way related to observation and experience — and therefore not subject to the categorical prohibition on necessary existence among matter of fact existences. But if this is insisted upon it will permit god's necessary existence only at the expense of giving up what makes god's existence the most gigantic matter of fact we can apprehend. The devotee of the ontological argument cannot have it both ways. He cannot give to god the conventionalist necessity of an entity in a logical system *and* avoid the triviality of such conventions. He cannot make god's existence necessary in this sense and at the same time preserve his god's awesome consequence in all matters of fact.

(2) Another way in which the necessary existence of the Supreme Being could be understood is as the existence of a Being which always has existed and never will go out of existence. In this sense the elements or atoms spoken of in Lucretius[3] are necessary. If they exist, then they have always existed and always will exist. But use of the word 'necessary' (or Hume's homologue for it, 'demonstrable') to mean 'always existed and always will exist' is exceedingly misleading since *P necessarily exists* will no longer entail *P exists*. That is to say, if god necessarily exists in the sense that he always existed and always will exist it is still an open question whether he does in fact exist — whether there is anything satisfying the concept of necessary existence thus understood — and for the *a priori* arguments this question cannot be left open. The converse

entailment does of course hold. If god, as spoken of in the great theistic
religions, does in fact exist, doubtless he always has and always will exist.
But this is an elucidation, not an *a priori* demonstration, of what is
believed.

(3) Again, God's existence is 'factually' necessary, it is sometimes said,
while Hume's rejection of necessary existence for things refers to logical
necessity. The notion of factual necessity is one which has been much
canvassed in its own right apart from arguments for the existence of god.
Suffice to say in the present context that accounts of factual necessity, as
applied to the existence of an entity, always seem to appeal to notions
like 'uncaused', 'independent' or 'eternal' and, as before, it remains an open
question whether *in fact* there exists anything which is factually necessary
in the sense specified and, if there is, whether that thing could be identified
with god.

(4) Finally, as Jerome Shaffer points out[4] there are tautologous existential
statements other than those considered above. Examples are: 'Fictitious
objects do not exist'; 'Members of extinct species existed once but no longer
exist'. But these, it appears to me, are not of the same kind as the statement
'god exists'. Their wording analytically entails the non-existence of their
subject class and no one need be worried by or question this obvious entailment. It is as straightforward as the tautology in 'non-existent wasps do not
exist'. I therefore find Shaffer's position somewhat strange when he remarks:
'Just as the tautology, "Fictitious objects do not exist", leaves open the
question whether there are any fictitious objects, so the tautology "God
exists" leaves open the question whether there is a God' (op. cit., p. 240).
I would have thought that the first tautology does *not* leave open any question
about the existence of fictitious objects just because 'do not exist' is a
repetition of the sense of the word 'fictitious': the tautology shows that to
assert the existence of fictitious objects would be self-contradictory. But the
second (alleged) tautology *does* leave open questions about the existence of
god since the meaning of the word 'exists' does not analytically repeat the
meaning of the word 'god': to assert that god does not exist may be false, but
it is not self-contradictory (unless the assertion is reduced to a triviality
by stipulative redefinition of the words employed).

These four, together with the suggestion that god's existence is necessary
by contrast with the contingency of all other things (see next section), do not
provide an exhaustive survey of the ways in which Hume's Fork might be
defied in the interest of giving meaning to the phrase 'necessary existence'.
But they do seem to indicate that there is no very obvious or overwhelmingly
powerful reason to admit the sort of necessary existence which the Deity
might be supposed to have as an exception to Hume's 'Whatever *is* may *not
be*'. The exceptions pitched upon turn out to be either mathematical
entities which it is at least arguable that Hume never thought of as matters of
fact and existence, or tautologous existential statements, or cases where the

meaning given to the word 'necessary' breaks the entailment '*P* necessarily exists' entails '*P* exists'. (Just such an example is provided by Geach's suggestion that god should be spoken of as having an 'imperishable existence that has no liability to cease'.[5]) In short, Hume's general comment 'there is an evident absurdity in pretending to demonstrate a matter of fact' leading to his conclusion 'the words, *necessary existence,* have no meaning' is still a defensible position even if I have not here fully defended it.

Hume's objection to *demonstrating* the existence of a thing does however suffer from a disadvantage not yet discussed. This is the way in which he conflates (in the *Enquiry*) the psychological notion of inconceivability with the logical notion of (self) contradictory and, in like manner, the notion of 'perfectly conceivable' with the notion of 'implies no (self) contradiction'. This mixing of the logical and psychological shows itself in the premises of his objection to Clarke's *a priori* argument, particularly in the premise 'Nothing, that is distinctly conceivable, implies a contradiction'. After some preliminary prodding at this delicate area, Jonathan Barnes thrusts home an objection which he makes a cause for totally rejecting Hume's position:

> Although Hume gives no satisfactory account of what he means by 'conceive', what little he does say is enough for our purposes: his analysis of belief shows that '*P* is believed' entails '*P* is conceived' and hence '*P* is conceivable'. But it is certainly possible to *believe* propositions which are logically impossible (everyone who makes a genuine mistake in mathematics or logic does so); and so it is possible to *conceive* propositions which are logically impossible.[6]

Hence on this interpretation the premise in Hume's argument 'Nothing that is distinctly conceivable, implies a contradiction' is false. I disagree with Barnes here because I can find nothing in Hume's account of belief which nails him without possibility of escape to the position '*P* is believed' entails '*P* is *distinctly* conceived' and *distinct* conception is the term being used in Hume's argument. Certainly the converse is not Hume's position. As he says 'We conceive many things, which we do not believe' (*Treatise,* 94). But what happens when someone believes '37 + 58 = 85'? Is he not distinctly conceiving something which implies a contradiction? No. What I think Hume would say he is doing is entertaining a confused conception in such a way that the false arithmetical proposition is conceivable to the person just as long as the confused conception is retained. Thus when he spots that he added 7 and 8, made 15, put down the 5, and then in his excitement forgot to 'carry' 1, his distinct conception will be '37 + 58 = 95', i.e. as soon as the conception becomes distinct it will be realised that '37 + 58 = 85' was not a distinct conception. As a result of such indistinct conception it is possible to believe something which is a contradiction. The contradiction has not been recognised. But of course spoken of in this way, Hume's 'distinctly conceived' can practically be replaced by the phrase 'properly understood'. This, however, transfers the difficulty to matters of fact. While one may get away with saying that the negation of any matter of fact is 'conceivable' it is very doubtful if the negation of certain matters of fact can be 'properly understood', particularly some of those matters of fact which are concerned with existence. For example, although I can imagine my own non-existence after my death, I do not think I can properly understand what such non-existence would be since *my* understanding something always presumes a *me* who is doing the understanding and the case I am imagining presumes the non-existence of me. The point is that Hume's 'conceivable' seems to hang fire between 'understand' and 'imagine', tending to the one or the other according to the convenience of the context, and it is not unequivocally certain that in all contexts these two words can be replaced by 'possible' (i.e. non-contradictory). This, I think, is part of what Robert Adams is saying when he argues that the 'method of distinct conception' cannot establish 'that *everything* which can be conceived to exist can also (without logical impropriety) be conceived not to exist'[7] since this would involve conceiving one by one the non-existence of *every* thing and 'everything' is (presumably) an infinite class of objects. Adams goes on to say

> I think probably the only way in which the method of distinct conception could yield a general proof that non-existence is logically possible in *every* case would be by providing a proof that a state of affairs is logically possible in which nothing would exist at all. And it does not seem to me likely that such a state of affairs can be conceived in such a way as to exclude all rational doubt of its logical possibility.

The difficulty is a compounded version of my conceiving my own non-existence and I would reply again that the problem is not in *imagining* the non-existence of everything (every *thing* going out of existence leaving only empty space and Newton's absolute duration) but in *understanding* this situation. Likewise in the case of the Supreme Being I can conceive (imagine) a universe just like this one in which, or in relation to which, no such Being is ever to be found. But I cannot conceive (understand) what such failure to find would be like nor, for that matter, can I conceive (understand) what finding such a Being would be like. But if I can understand neither the existence nor the non-existence of such a Being this suggests a difficulty more general than merely 'The words *necessary existence* have no meaning'. The difficulty will now be the meaning of *any* talk about such a Being. I shall return to Hume's treatment of this problem at the end of Chapter 5.

But Hume's original 'decisive' objection to Clarke's *a priori* argument would certainly have stood on firmer ground could it have been expressed without reference to conceivability. Can it be so expressed while still retaining the main features of Hume's objection? If we bring together *Dialogues* 189 and *Enquiry*, 25: 40 and 163: 171, and read 'conceivable' as 'negation not contradictory' we get:

No assertion is demonstrable unless its negation is contradictory. No
negation of a matter of fact is contradictory. All assertions about the
existence of *things* are matters of fact. Therefore no negation of an
assertion that some *thing* exists is contradictory. Hence there is no thing
whose existence is demonstrable.

The emphasis given to the word *thing* is an attempt to indicate that the
scope of the argument does not extend to tautological existential statements
or the entities of mathematics. In this form Hume's argument makes an
appeal to the same epistemological distinctions as before but without some
of the bother inherent in relating the conceivable and the possible. It will
be questioned at the same points, to wit, whether it is true that 'No negation
of a matter of fact is contradictory' and whether the Supreme Being's
existence should be regarded as a matter of fact (how else it could be regarded
and the Supreme Being still be regarded as an adequate object of worship is
quite obscure to me).

Before leaving Hume's remarks about 'necessary existence' it is worth
noting the striking similarity between his contention 'The words, *necessary
existence,* have no meaning; or, which is the same thing, none that is consistent'
and Russell's very characteristic remark 'The word "necessary" I should maintain, can only be applied significantly to propositions. And, in fact, only
to such as are analytic — that is to say — such as it is self-contradictory to
deny'.[8] In short, Hume's objections to proving *a priori* the existence of
anything derive from his empiricist epistemology. Similar objections will be
raised by anyone, such as Russell, who adopts a similar epistemology. In our
own century these will include the logical atomists, the logical positivists,
and all those lesser empiricists who owe a significant part of their theory of
knowledge to the Hume/Russell tradition. For them, as for Hume, the
a priori arguments for god's existence are, and will remain, totally vacuous.

(ii)   THE INFINITE CHAIN OF INSUFFICIENT REASONS

Hume's second seminal objection to Clarke's hybrid *a priori* argument
focuses upon the argument's insistent demand for a sufficient explanation,
not merely of each item in any causal chain, but for the causal chain
considered *either* (1) as a whole, *or* (2) as having a terminus in that ultimate
cause which contains within itself the sufficient reason for its own existence.

(1) To the demand for explanation of any causal chain considered as a
whole Hume replies that the uniting of its parts into a whole is an 'act of
the mind', an artificial concept which 'has no influence on the nature of
things': 'Did I show you the particular causes of each individual in a collection
of twenty particles of matter, I should think it very unreasonable, should you
afterwards ask me, what was the cause of the whole twenty. This is

sufficiently explained in explaining the cause of the parts' (*Dialogues*, 190).
The fundamental assumption in this objection is one which almost totally
dominates all modern scientific and secular thinking. It is that there is no need
to go beyond the world and its contents in explaining either the world or any
of its contents. Is this a justifiable assumption?

If I explain that the flood in the lane outside my house is caused by a
collapsed conduit under the old railway, I have explained the cause of the
flood. If I am asked why the conduit collapsed, I can explain that it was
broken by the heavy lorries taking timber away from the wood. If I am
asked why this broke the conduit, I can talk about the crushing load on
salt-glazed six-inch pipes and *so on*. The 'so on' will indicate a series of
causal explanations which will terminate at a point where I run out of
information, or just have to say 'that's the way things are' (or lose my temper).
If my questioner then asks me the cause of the whole series of causes, and
if I do not know he is fishing for the answer 'god', I would be entirely at a
loss to know what manner of answer he could possibly expect since all
available causal explanations have already been given. But if I know he is
fishing for the answer 'god' I might in my turn ask him in what sense god
could be an explanation of the whole series? What new thing am I being told
or what old absurdity is being resolved? Since god is going to be in *every*
case the explanation why the causal series is what it is, I might well retort
that an 'explanation' which fitted *every* series was of no value in explaining
any of them: worthwhile explanations are of particular events or things and
there is no call for an explanation of everything considered as a whole. My
response is not unlike Russell's answer to Copleston's question 'Why shouldn't
one raise the question of the cause of the existence of all particular objects?' –
'Because I see no reason to think there is any. The whole concept of cause is
one we derive from our observation of particular things; I see no reason
whatsoever to suppose that the total has any cause whatsoever' (op. cit.
p. 179). But Hume's objection to asking for the cause of causal sequences is
not so much that there is none, but that the question is incoherent. It is a
request for an explanation of an illicit causal category. The request is akin
to finding that Benjamin is the parent of Harry, Harry is the parent of John,
and John is the parent of Rupert, then asking who is the parent of all four
people 'considered as a whole'.

But the assumption that there is no need to go beyond the world and its
contents in explaining the world or any of its contents need not be confronted
merely by questions (about causal sequences) which rely upon a category mistake.
My questioner about the broken conduit could have finished up asking me
why things are as they are (or why the world is as the most sophisticated
science finds it to be). Now clearly this question cannot be answered by
reference to the world and its contents. These are already bypassed in the
way the question has been formulated. The question is not looking for an
answer – an explanation – which is any longer of the same kind as answers
to all scientific and secular questions. This new cosmic question comes in

two ways. Why are things as they are? Why is there anything at all? Both are given an answer by reference to a self-sufficient reason.

(2) Hume's comment in the *Dialogues* on the demand that all causal sequences should have a beginning in that ultimate cause which contains within itself the cause of its own existence is brisk but incomplete: 'it seems absurd to enquire for a general cause or first Author' of an eternal succession of objects since a cause 'implies a priority in time and a beginning of existence'. Perhaps it does, but surely in the case of god, Clarke might say, what is being supposed is a being which has priority in time to all else but has no beginning of existence. The succession of objects is not eternal. If this account of god as first temporal cause or creator of things *ex nihilo* (as distinct from a sustaining cause) is to be rejected then one or other of two alternatives have to be viable. Either (a) at some time things just came into existence uncaused and out of nothing, or (b) the succession of causes is infinite, i.e. the universe of things in space had no beginning. If neither (a) nor (b) is viable, then we will be left with the conclusion that there is some being which exists independently and self-caused and in which all other causal sequences began. I shall call this being 'the first cause'.

In the *Treatise* (I, iii, 3) Hume argues a point which implies the possibility of (a). As in the *Dialogues,* Clarke is specifically mentioned, and in *A Letter,* 23, Hume admits that it is Clarke's *a priori* argument for the existence of god which is threatened. The point is this. If it can be shown that it is not necessarily true that *'whatever begins to exist must have a Cause of Existence'* *(A Letter,* 22; *Treatise,* 78), then the possibility that the totality of things exists without a cause becomes viable, and the logical pressure exerted by the demand for a self-sufficient first cause is relaxed.

Hume's argument in the *Treatise* is essentially an application of the epistemology already described in the first section of this chapter. The proposition is 'neither intuitively nor demonstrably certain'; an uncaused event is conceivable; it is no good objecting that an uncaused event would produce itself, i.e. exist before it existed, or would be produced by nothing:

> 'Tis sufficient only to observe, that when we exclude all causes we really do exclude them, and neither suppose nothing nor the object itself to be the causes of the existence; . . . If every thing must have a cause, it follows, that upon the exclusion of other causes we must accept of the object itself or of nothing as causes. But 'tis the very point in question, whether every thing must have a cause or not (*Treatise,* 81).

If an uncaused event — one that follows a preceding state of affairs but is in *no* other way related to preceding states of affairs — is possible, then there is at least a *possibility* that the things in the universe came into existence uncaused and out of nothing. Because Hume allows such a possibility, Anthony Kenny[9] couples Hume with 'big bang' cosmologies, and Aquinas with Hoyle and 'steady state' cosmologies. Hume admits the possibility of something coming 'into existence not only from nothing, but also by nothing; not only without matter, but also without a cause'. Aquinas and Hoyle on the other hand think 'that the origination of matter calls for a cause'. This may be so, but I would have thought that Hoyle's cause of matter — a sort of void into which other matter has decayed — comes much closer to a universe of things in space which has no beginning (that is, (b) above) than to a beginning in any Being 'quod omnes dicunt Deum', and alternative (b) is just as damaging to the *a priori* arguments (Aquinas' 'Third Way' included) as alternative (a).

Alternative (b) has in fact always seemed more plausible than (a), presumably because even the great 'atheistical' systems of antiquity accepted the maxim 'Nil posse creari de nilo'.[10] But if the first cause argument is to have logical force the possibility of an infinite regress of causes has also to be ruled out. Leibniz does just this: 'And so, however far you go back to earlier states, you will never find in those states a full reason why there should be any world rather than none, and why it should be such as it is'.[11] The words are echoed in Hume's paraphrase of Clarke's *a priori* argument: 'What was it, then, which determined something to exist rather then nothing, and bestowed being on a particular possibility exclusive of the rest?' *(Dialogues, 189).* The inference in each case is that a temporally infinite regress gives no answer to the cosmic questions: Why this? Why anything?

I myself can see no stronger commendation of the possibility of an infinite temporal regress than that provided by John Hick when he observes that the modern mind 'sees no *a priori* impossibility in the idea of a temporally as well as a spatially unbounded universe'.[12] In this sense Hume is a 'modern mind' (see, for example, *Dialogues,* 183) and any appeal to the need for a prime mover will fall on deaf ears with Hume as it will with us. But *should* Hume and a 'modern mind' see any impossibility, not in an infinite temporal regress of caused causes, but in an infinite regress of things whose existence is contingent upon other things?

In the last analysis the objections to such a regress seem to depend upon the sort of assumptions made by Aquinas in the 'Third Way': the argument which begins with caused contingent beings (i.e. ourselves and every observable thing in the universe) and concludes with an uncaused necessary Being (quod est per se necessarium non habens causam suae necessitatis aliunde). This Being is supposed to answer the cosmic questions: Why this? Why anything? But does this contingency of everything give any logical or rational force to the demand for such a necessary being?

A short answer (which might very well have been given by Hume) is once again provided by Russell: 'The difficulty of this argument is that I don't admit the idea of a necessary being and I don't admit that there is any particular meaning in calling other beings "contingent" . . . The word "necessary", it seems to me, is a useless word, except as applied to analytic propositions, not to things' (Russell and Copleston, op. cit., p. 170). But this, it may be said, is an appeal to an empiricist theory of knowledge which

Clarke and Leibniz certainly, and Aquinas possibly, would have rejected.
Very well. Let us try to put the point another way. Why should there be a
contradiction or even rational difficulty in holding that no being exists
which is necessary by contrast with the contingency of everything else? There
is no logical need for such a being precisely because it is possible that all
things exist contingently in an infinite temporal regress. The only rational
difficulty with such a regress comes from supposing that the regress is not
really infinite. This supposition then allows an insistent question about the
end and origin of the regress. But in an *infinite* temporal regress of events
the question of ends and origins could literally *never* arise. The contingent
existence of every thing would *always* be explainable in terms of other
contingent things. The pseudo-logical demand that contingency should
terminate in necessity is a demand which gathers its force from presuming
the impossibility of an infinite regress, not from demonstrating such an
impossibility, and *demonstration* of the impossibility that things could exist
from eternity is what the *a priori* argument requires in order to arrive at a
necessarily existent first cause. If we are left with competing possibilities —
possibly an infinite temporal regress (and this is the possibility Hume takes to
be obviously true — *Dialogues,* 190); possibly a finite temporal regress ter-
minating in a first cause — then this is no good. For the *a priori* argument
to be good the second possibility has to logically exclude the first. Then and
only then would the necessary existence of such a first cause entail the
existence of such a first cause.

But if there is no contradiction in supposing the universe to be spatially
and temporally limitless, what happens to the cosmic question 'why
anything?' It becomes simply unanswerable, not because of our lack of
information, but, in Hume's terms, because in general we lack any possibility
of understanding how we should settle questions about 'the origin of worlds'.
Thus the question 'why anything?', far from necessitating the answer 'god', is
not even comprehensible and what is more (Hume might have added), if
the universe had been empty, would the question 'why nothing?' have been
supposed to necessitate the same answer which the question 'why anything?'
is supposed to necessitate in the universe of things?

The second cosmic question 'why this?' will still be answerable in a
spatially and temporally limitless universe in the same ways in which such a
question is usually answered. If I ask what causes the stars to shine, old
port to give me evil dreams, and the ewes to go to the tups at the right
moment, I would normally expect three distinct answers. But if I got an
answer of the form: that which contains within itself the cause of its own
necessity — 'quod omnes dicunt Deum' — then I would have no answer at all
to my questions in the sense in which I had asked them. Even the psalmist
asking similar questions is not speering for a logically necessary answer about
some being which is the cause of its own necessity. He is commending men
to the mystery and majesty of the things done by his god. He is affirming
that a certain answer is appropriate to the cosmic question 'why these things?'

He is not using the question as a logical lever to force some remote semblance to that answer out of the intellectually unpersuaded.

There are thus three candidates for the ultimate origination of things. In the beginning things appeared from nothing and by nothing. In the *Treatise* Hume allows us to infer that this is at least a possibility. Secondly: In the beginning was the being which contains within itself the cause of its own necessity. This is the candidate which has to logically exclude the other two if it is to succeed in the cosmological argument or in Clarke's *a priori* argument. Thirdly: There never was a beginning. The universe is spatially and temporally limitless. In the *Dialogues* Hume does not argue but rather assumes this to be the case (as many of us now would). If it is the case, or even possibly could be the case, then the demand for 'some ultimate cause, that is necessarily existent' loses its compulsive force. There may be such a being. But the *possibility* is not enough for the *a priori* argument.

(iii)   EXISTENCE AND THE CONCEPTION OF A THING

Although Hume's few and brief remarks on the subject of *existence* were the catalyst which produced Kant's celebrated refutation of the ontological argument, it would now be a little ridiculous to use what Hume has to say as an excuse for entering full scale into the modern discussion of the subject. Even in the past ten years so much new material has appeared that there is now much to commend Hartshorne's remark 'we must do our own thinking, and not expect Kant or Hume to have done it for us'.[13] But let us at least get one thing straight. Hume did not say 'existence is not a predicate' nor does he so much as hint at such an expression. What he speaks about is 'ideas' and 'conceptions', and I think his main point can be discussed in these terms without indulging in the very questionable translation to talk about predicates. What he says is 'that the idea of existence is nothing different from the idea of any object, and that when after the simple conception of any thing we wou'd conceive it as existent, we in reality make no addition to or alteration on our first idea'. He continues with the particular case: 'Thus when we affirm, that God is existent, we simply form the idea of such a being, as he is represented to us; nor is the existence, which we attribute to him, conceived by a particular idea, which we join to the idea of his other qualities, and can again separate and distinguish from them' (*Treatise*, 94). Jerome Shaffer (op. cit., p. 235f) points out that in *Treatise*, 66, Hume appears to say something different from the above: 'To reflect on any thing simply, and to reflect on it as existent, are nothing different from each other. That idea, when conjoined with the idea of my object, makes no addition to it. *Whatever we conceive, we conceive to be existent*' (my italics). The final sentence is the trouble. This view, Shaffer remarks, 'is a most embarrassing one for Hume to hold' since it is entirely at variance with what else Hume has to say on existence. But when Shaffer has finished his chastisement he generously concedes 'Perhaps Hume was writing carelessly'. I can see no other credible interpretation of the sentence in italics. It concludes a passage in which Hume has said in a variety of ways that existence makes no difference to our idea of an object and the sentence has every appearance of intending to say this in yet another way rather than make a new, uncharacteristic and divergent point which is nowhere followed up.

Ignoring for the moment the old trouble that a conception wavers between an imagination and an understanding, what Hume seems to be saying is this. When I form a conception of a thing what I am doing is bringing together a number of simple ideas. These form a 'complex idea' (*Treatise*, 2f). But when I say 'the complex idea exists' I am not really saying anything more about the *idea*. I am not adding to or subtracting from my idea of the thing. Instead, I am saying that my idea has an instance in the real world, or that what I am forming an idea of can actually be found somewhere or in some way. For example: I have a very well-developed idea of a hobbit. But whether I say 'hobbits exist' or 'hobbits do not exist' makes no difference to my idea of a hobbit. Or again: I have an idea of a democracy but my idea is not altered by knowing whether there are or are not any democracies. Hume's own example on p. 94 of the *Treatise* (quoted above) is that the idea which we have of god does not alter in any way when we think of him as existent. In the footnote on p. 96 he underlines the point: 'in that proposition, *God is,* or indeed any other, which regards existence, the idea of existence is no distinct idea, which we unite with that of the object, and which is capable of forming a compound idea by the union'. But in the *Meditations*, when Descartes unearths his vision of the ontological argument, he finds that existence is implied by the idea which he has of a Perfect Being. Hence the existence of that Perfect Being, God, is as certain as a demonstration in geometry. But if Hume is right, no analysis of any compound idea could yield the idea of existence. Hence Descartes' ontological argument must be invalid or contain a false assumption.

To put it another way: what would be the result if existence were to be regarded as part of the idea of an object ('object' being used in the widest possible sense). The first result would be that existence would cease to be a relation between my idea and the object of which it is an idea, and would become instead merely part of my idea. But surely, Hume might have said, if I enquire whether hobbits exist, my enquiry does not concern the *idea* of a hobbit but the *exemplification* of that idea in the real world. If the notion of existence has been incorporated into the idea of a hobbit, and I know that it has, I still have no answer to the exemplification question, and the exemplification question is the fundamental existence question which survives after the notion of existence has supposedly been taken somewhere else, namely, into the idea of the object. So if Descartes insists that the idea of existence is contained in the compound idea we can form of the Perfect Being this is quite all right (Descartes, if not Hume, might comprehend how existence could be part of a compound idea). But it does not settle the question whether the idea of a Perfect (existent) Being is exemplified in the real world and *that* is the question which people are asking when they ask if god exists.

So at the very least, when followed out in their own terminology, Hume's observations suggest some sort of clarification of the verbal legerdemain which the ordinary man senses in Descartes' ontological argument. Even Samuel Clarke, although he could not quite bring himself to dismiss the Cartesian version out of hand, does complain of '*This* Obscurity and Defect' that 'it seems to extend only to the *Nominal Idea* or *mere Definition* of a Self-Existent Being' and does not clearly refer that definition 'to any *Real* particular Being *actually existing without us*' (op. cit., p. 20).

*   *   *

Clarke's *a priori* argument concludes with a being which 'cannot be supposed not to exist without an express contradiction'. Clarke derives this necessity from the cosmic demand for a first cause which contains within itself the sufficient reason for its own existence. Hume will have nothing to do with this notion or with *any* way of arriving *a priori* at a necessarily existent being: 'The existence, therefore, of any being can only be proved by arguments from its cause or its effect; and these arguments are founded entirely on experience' (*Enquiry*, 164 : 172).

In the *Dialogues* Hume's concluding comment on the *a priori* proof of god's existence is characteristic of his ability to lift his head from philosophical minutiae and put the issue in proportion:

> The argument *a priori* has seldom been found very convincing, except to people of a metaphysical head, who have accustomed themselves to abstract reasoning, and who finding from mathematics that the understanding frequently leads to truth, through obscurity, and contrary to first appearances, have transferred the same habit of thinking to subjects where it ought not to have place. Other people, even of good sense and the best inclined to religion, feel always some deficiency in such arguments, though they are not perhaps able to explain distinctly where it lies. A certain proof, that men ever did, and ever will, derive their religion from other sources than from this species of reasoning (*Dialogues*, 191f).

These judgements appear to me well-balanced and discerning. The *a priori* arguments contain insights of great consequence to religion, not proofs which could compel the belief of a rational man — albeit that philosophers will doubtless continue to sharpen their teeth on the dead bones of arguments which never did have much life.

5 Theology and Meaning

> I suppose it may be of use, to prevail with the busy mind of man to be
> more cautious in meddling with things exceeding its comprehension . . . and
> to sit down in a quiet ignorance of those things which, upon examination,
> are found to be beyond the reach of our capacities.
>
> Locke, *Essay*

One of Hume's conclusions in the *Enquiry* is that divinity and school
metaphysics are 'sophistry and illusion' unless they are found to contain
matters of fact or abstract demonstrations. Elsewhere he observes that
arguments about god's nature or the origin of worlds carry us 'quite beyond
the reach of our faculties', that we have 'no idea' of certain theological
positions and that if we predicate such a term as 'good' of the deity it can
only have the normal or anthropomorphic sense 'for we know no other'.
These and many other apparent strictures on the comprehensibility of
theology invite the questions whether, to what extent, and on what grounds
Hume regarded religious belief as incomprehensible and the language in
which it is expressed as meaningless. In this chapter I shall consider these
questions under three heads. First, the use Hume makes of his impression/
idea dichotomy as a criterion of meaning. Secondly, his requirement that
if ordinary language predicates are to be used meaningfully in theology
then they must be kept reasonably close to their normal meanings. Finally,
but most important of all, Hume's general thesis, which he shares with Locke,
that certain subjects lie beyond the limits of human understanding.

(i) WORDS AND IDEAS

In the manifesto at the beginning of the *Enquiry* Hume is very emphatic
about his purpose. It is 'to enquire seriously into the nature of human
understanding, and show, from an exact analysis of its powers and capacity,
that it is by no means fitted for such remote and abstruse subjects' (such
subjects as a considerable part of metaphysics and metaphysics used to give
'popular superstition' an air 'of science and wisdom'). One of the principal
mechanisms for executing this purpose is the impression/idea dichotomy
which Hume set out at the beginning of the *Treatise* and which he repeats,
with slightly different emphasis, in Section II of the *Enquiry*. In brief, his
position is as follows.

By 'impressions' are meant all our sensations, passions, emotions and
feelings 'as they make their first appearance in the soul' or as they are
actually experienced. By 'ideas' are meant *(Treatise,* 1) 'the faint images of

these in thinking and reasoning'. (Hume never uses the word 'image' again
in the first chapter of the *Treatise,* and in Section II of the *Enquiry* he
seems to go out of his way to avoid its use, speaking merely of 'ideas or
thoughts'. I shall try to indicate the importance of this later on.) Thus, for
example, the origin of our idea of a man or of our idea of the colour red is
in each case a previous experience – an 'impression' of a man or an 'impression' of red. The idea, together with the impression which is its origin, may
be 'simple' as in the case of red (i.e. not capable of being analysed into other
impressions or ideas) or 'complex' as in the case of man (i.e. capable of
being analysed into other complex and/or simple impressions or
ideas). Every *simple* idea takes its origin from a simple impression but some
complex ideas may be formed which are not derived from complex
impressions. Thus: 'I can imagine to myself such a city as the New
Jerusalem, whose pavement is gold and walls are rubies, tho' I never saw any
such' (*Treatise,* 3). I can do this because I have ideas (derived from
impressions) of walls, gold, rubies, streets and cities, and I can put these
together and form the complex idea of the New Jerusalem without ever
having had actual experience of it. An impression and an idea 'differ only
in degree, not in nature' (*Treatise,* 3) and the difference is the same as that
between an experience and an experience recalled in a thought: the former
is more lively, vivid and intense than the latter. But this would mean, if we
adopt the usual interpretation of Hume (namely, that by 'idea' he means
'mental image'), that the challenge which he throws down (*Treatise,* 4;
Enquiry, 19: 28) to 'show' or 'produce' a simple idea which is not derived
from an impression is not capable of being taken up. This is not for the
usually cited reason which Flew calls the Conventionalist Sulk (roughly, that
the proposition 'ideas are copies of impressions' is presented by Hume as a
contingent generalisation but becomes true by definition when needed to
rule out apparent counter-instances[1]). It is because in no ordinary sense of
the words is it possible to 'show' or 'produce' an idea when 'idea' is understood as a mental image which differs from an actual experience merely by
being less lively or vivid. Such a mental image of a lively experience is
unproducible as far as other people are concerned. What then could Hume
have intended by his apparently absurd challenge to 'produce' or 'show' an
idea?

The question admits no satisfactory answer if we stick to the conventional
misinterpretation of Hume that 'all ideas are for him (mental) images'. I say
*mis*interpretation because even if such an interpretation could be made to
stick to the *Treatise* on the evidence of its first page and of his occasional
talk about ideas 'copying' impressions, it will not stick in any consistent
way to his recharacterisation of the same doctrine in Section II of the
Enquiry. In that Section the contrast between ideas and impressions is never
presented as one between mental images and that which is imaged. Instead
it is regularly presented as the contrast between thoughts and experiences.
The word 'thought' or its cognates occurs nine times in the chapter. In six of

these it could apparently be replaced by the word 'idea' while in the remaining three (and again at the beginning of Section III) it is explicitly allowed as an alternative to the word 'idea' *as Hume intends the word 'idea' to be used.* Thus on p. 18:27 he remarks 'The less forcible and lively [perceptions] are commonly denominated *Thoughts* or *Ideas*' (Hume's italics). On p. 19:28 he speaks about what happens 'when we analyse our thoughts or ideas' and in the important footnote which appears at the end of the chapter in all the editions he firmly contrasts his use of the word 'idea' meaning 'thought' with Locke's different use of the term: 'Again, the word *idea* seems to be commonly taken in a very loose sense, by Locke and others; as standing for any of our perceptions, our sensations and passions, as well as thoughts'. The only evidence which Section II provides for the view that Hume thinks of an idea as a mental image is his occasional use of the phrase: ideas *copied* from a precedent feeling or sentiment. But there is also evidence to show — quite apart from his consistent choice of 'thought' rather than 'image' as an alternative to 'idea' — that he is not using the word 'copy' in anything like the sense 'mental photocopy' or 'preserved image', but rather as a philosophically familiar gloss of a notion which does not involve images at all: 'In short, all the materials of thinking are derived either from our outward or inward sentiment: the mixture and composition of these belongs alone to the mind and will. Or, to express myself in philosophical language, all our ideas or more feeble perceptions are copies of our impressions or more lively ones' (*Enquiry*, 19:28). In the context of a chapter where 'ideas' and 'thoughts' are used as freely interchangeable terms it is difficult not to conclude that the 'philosophical language' of 'ideas' and 'copies' should be interpreted by means of the layman's gloss of 'materials of thinking' and 'derived' rather than the other way round.

   A remarkable example of the staying power of the conventional generalisation that for Hume ideas are mental images is to be found in E. J. Furlong's *Imagination*[2] where the author absorbs both the generalisation and a part of the contrary evidence into the same expository paragraph

> First, to think is, for Hume, to have ideas. But all ideas are for him images. Hence to think is to have images, i.e. to imagine. A theory of thinking will be a theory of imagining. We therefore find Hume using 'imagination' where another man, uncommitted to the view that all ideas are images, would employ 'thought' or 'mind'. Sometimes, of course, Hume forgets, and we find him using 'mind' in a context where his theory would require 'imagination' . . . (p. 96f).

Of course Hume will 'forget' to live up to a generalisation if, as I have argued, he does not hold it. It is only fair to point out that in the context from which I have quoted, Furlong is mostly concerned with the *Treatise* and, if the tradition that for Hume all ideas are mental images can find support, it can be found there, not in the *Enquiry*. I am not arguing that Hume is

unequivocally consistent in what he says even in the *Enquiry*. But I am saying
that if his position can be summarised at all, the summary is that ideas are
thoughts, not that ideas are images.

Now if this is so, it makes a great deal of difference both to his challenge
to produce a simple idea which is not derived from an impression and to the
use which he makes of his impression/idea dichotomy as a criterion of
meaning. Let us take the challenge first. Although I cannot 'produce' or
'show' a mental image I *can* produce a thought or 'the materials of thinking'
because these are usually (perhaps always) words. That ideas are thoughts or
the materials of thinking, and that these are either identical with words or at
the very least become identical with words when the thought is articulated,
is something which Hume takes as understood when he speaks of 'words
expressive of ideas' (*Enquiry*, 21:32). But 'thoughts' and 'the materials of
thinking' are not interchangeable terms. So is an idea a thought or a material
used in thinking? From Hume's insistent use of 'thoughts' and 'ideas'
(always the plural) as synonyms, together with the words or phrases he
actually instances as 'expressive of ideas', it would appear that by 'ideas' he
means the phrases or single words which form the distinguishable parts of
whole thoughts (much as words form the distinguishable parts of sentences).
Thus ideas are thoughts in the sense that a thought is *composed* of ideas,
not in the sense that a thought is *identical* with an idea: ideas are the materials
of thinking. If this is so, then Hume's challenge to produce a simple idea
which is not derived from an impression is no longer an invitation to
perform an absurdity. It is an invitation to produce a word or phrase which
expresses an idea where the idea is not derived from experience. But how,
according to Hume, can we show that a word or phrase expresses an idea? Only
by pointing out the experiential situation — the impression — from which the
idea, and hence the word which expresses the idea, derives its origin or use:
'To give a child an idea of scarlet or orange, of sweet or bitter, I present the
objects, or in other words, convey to him these impressions' (*Treatise*, 5).
There is an obvious difficulty here. Ideas *not* derived from impressions appear
to be ruled out at source since Hume allows only one way in which an idea
can be acquired. I shall return to this point shortly.

But if words express ideas, what happens when the idea expressed is in
some way confused or altogether lacking? In the former case the words are
employed 'without a distinct meaning' (but the meaning could be made
distinct if a determinate idea could be formed); in the latter case the words
are employed 'without any meaning' at all (*Enquiry*, 22: 30). Thus with any
word or phrase ('term' in Hume's usage) there are three possibilities. First,
that the term expresses a determinate idea and has a distinct meaning.
Examples Hume gives are 'fear', 'sweet', 'orange' and 'golden mountain'
among others. Secondly, that the term expresses an idea which is in some
way confused or obscure and has no distinct meaning. Hume is not very
forthcoming with examples, but possibly 'freedom of the will' would do.
Finally, that the term expresses no idea at all and is employed without any

meaning. Examples to which Hume argues in the body of his work are 'power' and 'substance'. Thus in brief, ideas can be determinate, confused or lacking. Terms can have a distinct meaning, an unclear meaning or no meaning at all.

It is obvious that this trichotomy provides Hume with a very vigorous form of meaning empiricism with which to attack crucial philosophical and theological terms, and he uses it to good effect: we have no idea of a necessarily existent being; we have only a confused idea of a first cause; we have no idea of the general origin of worlds or of an immaterial substance; we have no idea of the best of possible worlds. But Hume does not say that we have no idea of god. We have no idea of 'power' or 'efficacy' in him any more than we have an idea of these in anyone else (*Treatise*, 160). Our 'idea of that supreme Being is derived from particular impressions' (*Treatise*, 248). More explicitly in the *Enquiry* we are told 'The idea of God, as meaning an infinitely intelligent, wise, and good Being, arises from reflecting on the operations of our own mind, and augmenting, without limit, those qualities of goodness and wisdom' (p. 19:28). This is to say that in Hume's view the meaning of the word 'god' at least *starts* its life in experience. But supposing Hume were to say that some cherished phrase or formulation in a religion lacked meaning. For example, it is said that God is 'three persons in one *substance*'. What reply can be made when Hume argues that we have no idea of substance? The reply could be, as Bennett[3] and others have pointed out, that 'substance' is one of the class of words to which Hume's meaning empiricism is inapplicable. The word does express an idea but the idea is not derived from experience. To this Hume has a number of possible counters. He can say there is no such class of immune words. It is true by definition that *every* idea is derived from impressions. But this invites the stalemate situation where his opponent simply refuses to allow the definitional truth. Hume can then say that the class of words for which immunity is claimed is so small and so peculiar (being almost entirely metaphysical or philosophical terms) that the authority which meaning empiricism gains elsewhere gives it authority as a normative generalisation to legislate for these few words as well. Again a determined rejection of the authoritarian claims would be hard to overrule. But Hume can also say that if immunity from meaning empiricism is claimed for 'substance' or 'necessary connection' or 'necessarily existent being' (all suspiciously out-of-the-ordinary terms) then the whole weight of showing that these terms do have meaning is thrown onto those who wish to use the terms. *They* have to provide a convincing account of what these terms mean since the presumption engendered by the wide applicability of the empiricist criterion of meaning is that the terms mean nothing. If our understanding of the idea of substance cannot be located in an experienced situation, where is it located? In general, if someone claims to employ a word with a distinct meaning but cannot locate the empirical situation in which its meaning could be displayed ('cashed' in Ian Ramsey's useful metaphor), it is at the very least a reasonable question to ask whether

and how he understands the word, or, in Hume's more usual terms, whether
he has in fact got any idea at all. It is a reasonable question because of the
very large number of terms for which empirical 'cashability' *does* count as
success in a quest for meaning. This 'prove yourself!' challenge to alleged
ideas which lack empirical 'cashability' is certainly weaker than Hume's
intended meaning empiricism, but it does keep a good part of his bite without
leaving the fierce but vulnerable dependence upon saying '*all* ideas derive
from impressions'.

It is in part from his meaning empiricism that Hume derives his *general*
presumption against claims to determinate understanding of matters which
lie beyond possible experience. But before I turn to this subject I wish to look
briefly at another important aspect of what Hume has to say about meaning.

(ii)   A MEANING WHICH CONFOUNDS EVERYTHING

Once stated, Hume's point is obvious. It is that if someone uses an ordinary
language word in contexts which do not satisfy the commonly accepted range
of application of the word then the result will be confusion or dishonesty.
In religious language, according to Hume, such confusion or dishonesty
results when the theologian insists upon applying such anthropomorphic
attributes as 'good' and 'intelligent' to a god whose apparent nature is
incompatible with the normal meanings of these words.

Suppose it is said that in the country of Ruritania the government allows
complete political freedom. But a visitor to Ruritania discovers that the law
only recognises one political party in the state; that political dissentients
are confined in corrective labour camps; that press, wireless and television
are controlled by the one Party; that public criticism of the government is
punishable by loss of job, pension and home and that private criticism is
suppressed by a secret police. Suppose all these things. Now what is the
visitor to say to Comrade Rassendyll when he insists that the Ruritanians
have political freedom? The visitor can either say that on the evidence
produced it is just false that they have freedom, or he can say that they do
not understand the word 'freedom' in the way in which he does. Perhaps they
are afraid to acknowledge the real position. Perhaps they have adopted a
political Newspeak in which freedom *is* slavery, war *is* peace, industrial
idleness *is* industrial action. . . .

Now it is Hume's contention in more than one of his writings on religion
that dishonesty through fear, or confusion through a religious version of
Newspeak, is characteristic of much of the language used to talk about god
or to address him. This is the case because we speak of God as good and
merciful and yet we (Christians and Mohammedans alike) say *both* that he
does not prevent the suffering in the world which he could prevent *and*
that he countenances and employs the everlasting torments of Hell. Concerning
the former I have already pointed out (Chapter 3) that in the *Dialogues*

Hume's (at least Philo's) suggestion for overcoming the dishonesty or double talk is that we should rescind the attribute good or benevolent and acknowledge that from the phenomena alone (and revelation apart) it appears that god has no moral attributes. Concerning the latter Hume says very explicitly in the essay 'Of the Immortality of the Soul' that god's sanction and use of eternal punishments for man's transient offences 'is inconsistent with *our* ideas of goodness and justice', and (*Dialogues*) 'we know no other' idea which the word 'good' can express than the idea it expresses in ordinary use. To say a man is good (ordinary sense) but god is 'good' (special sense) confounds everything because the second 'good' has the *appearance* of meaning the same as the first without the reality of doing so (just like the confusion in saying that in Scotland we are free while in Ruritania they are 'free'). The traditional Christian (although partly extricated by the doctrine of a Purgatory) is guilty of just this sort of un-witting dishonesty or double talk about his loving and merciful God who also[4] casts into the fires of Hell those who displease him. Likewise the Koran can threaten that 'Those whose scales are heavy shall triumph, but those whose scales are light shall forfeit their souls and abide in Hell for ever. Its flames will scorch their faces and they will writhe in pain' (ch. 'The Believers') and all this 'in the name of Allah, the Compassionate, the Merciful'. In each case the believer thanks God for 'mercies' which if performed by a man would constitute unimaginable vindictiveness (*N.H.R.*, 67) and the effect, according to Hume, is either to stand the meaning of words on their heads or to misrepresent the nature of the deity.

In the *Dialogues* Hume, through Demea and Philo, considers a way of escape from this misapplication of anthropomorphic language: 'How then does the divine benevolence display itself, in the sense of you anthropo-morphites? None but we mystics, as you were pleased to call us, can account for this strange mixture of phenomena, by deriving it from attributes, infinitely perfect, but incomprehensible' (*Dialogues*, 199). But as has already been pointed out by Cleanthes (*Dialogues*, 157-159) this will not do. Incomprehensible attributes are no more informative than sublime mysteries. They are both an excuse for saying nothing about god, and being able to say nothing about god is, as Cleanthes points out, not readily distinguishable from atheism. The silence (holy or sceptical) prevents the theist from saying that his god is intelligent, wise and good, and these things *must* be said if the god is to be anything of concern to mankind. But as soon as these things *are* said then the god has to satisfy the requirements of character and performance which would warrant use of these terms. Accord-ing to Hume the theistic god does not satisfy the requirements for moral attributes because he permits natural evil and, according to various revela-tions, sanctions and employs the torments of Hell. Since the god does not warrant use of these terms their continued use (like saying Ruritanians have freedom) is either false praise or misleading use of language. God, Hume might have said, is either good or not good or partly good or beyond good and evil. But he cannot be 'good' (outside a theological *Nineteen Eighty-Four*) without introducing a misuse of language which confounds everything.

At the end of Part III of the *Dialogues* Hume argues in similar vein about attributing to the deity intelligence as *we* understand the term:

> we may conclude, that none of the *materials* of thought [ideas] are in any respect similar in the human and in the divine intelligence [nor the *manner* of thinking] . . . it would, in such a case, be an abuse of terms to apply to it the name of thought or reason. At least, if it appear more pious and respectful (as it really is) still to retain these terms, when we mention the supreme Being, we ought to acknowledge, that their meaning, in that case, is totally incomprehensible; and that the infirmities of our nature do not permit us to reach any ideas, which in the least correspond to the ineffable sublimity of the divine attributes (*Dialogues*, 157: Demea speaking).

As before, Cleanthes insists this is no good. To attribute incomprehensible intelligence is to attribute 'intelligence' with no meaning in the word and such 'intelligence' is not worth insisting upon.

It will be noticed that none of this is an application of Hume's meaning empiricism. It is simply an appeal to the obvious fact about language that if you wish words to carry their common meanings (or even something like their common meanings) then you cannot insist that they be used regardless of their appropriateness. If you do insist that they be used regardless of appropriateness then you can take your pick between the unacceptable consequences: either the word means what it commonly means and what you say by means of it is false, or the word does not mean what it commonly means and either you convey nothing by its use or you convey something different from what you intended. In the case of the moral attributes of the deity this meaning-dilemma is acute. I shall investigate its implications in Chapter 9.

(iii) THE IMMENSE ABYSS

In the very last sentence of the *Treatise* Hume writes in a manner which recalls Locke's words quoted as motto to this chapter: 'Nothing is more suitable to that philosophy, than a modest scepticism to a certain degree, and a fair confession of ignorance in subjects, that exceed all human capacity'. In the Introduction to the *Treatise* he had already given a strong indication how subjects exceeding human capacity will be recognised: ''tis still certain we cannot go beyond experience; and any hypothesis, that pretends to discover the ultimate original qualities of human nature, ought at first to be rejected as presumptuous and chimerical'. In the *Enquiry* the most frequently repeated refrain in the book is that we must be content to limit our enquiries

to what is intelligible to us, and what is intelligible to us is marked out by
the limits of our experience. See *Enquiry*, 6:16, 72:73, 81:90, 103:111,
142:151, 162:170, *et al.* In the *Dialogues* the same sort of thinking pervades
Philo's remarks. A very characteristic passage occurs in Part I:

> But when we look beyond human affairs and the properties of the surround-
> ing bodies: When we carry our speculations into the two eternities before
> and after the present state of things; into the creation and formation of
> the universe; the existence and properties of spirits; the powers and
> operations of one universal spirit, existing without beginning and without
> end; omniscient, infinite, and incomprehensible: we must be far removed
> from the smallest tendency to scepticism not to be apprehensive, that
> we have here got quite beyond the reach of our faculties (*Dialogues,* 135;
> see also 177, 201 *et al.*).

Hume is particularly disparaging about arguments and disputes concerning
the ultimate origination of things: 'Our experience, so imperfect in itself,
and so limited both in extent and duration, can afford us no probable
conjecture concerning the whole of things' (*Dialogues,* 177; see also *Enquiry,*
162:170 for a very forceful repetition of this contention).

Hume's position is thus: (1) that our understanding is limited; (2) that
the limits are drawn in some way by our experience; (3) that we can and
should recognise and accept these limits; and (4) that conclusions about the
nature of the universal spirit and the ultimate origination of things are
characteristic of subjects which lie beyond our understanding. How does
Hume reach this position? How judicious is it? What are its consequences for
religious belief?

Of the four propositions by means of which I have characterised Hume's
position, (1) and (2) are fundamental. They are arrived at by several routes.
The first, most obvious and least interesting is via Locke. Hume shares with
Locke the basic assumption that in some form or other experience is the
source of all that can be known. I shall not dwell upon the Lockean origins
of Hume's position since these do not constitute any philosophically
arguable reason in favour of it or against it.

The second route to propositions (1) and (2), and to the link between
them, is Hume's theory of the meaning of terms: that for a word or phrase
to have meaning it must express an idea; that ideas are the materials of
thinking (*Enquiry,* 19:28; *Dialogues,* 156); that ideas can only be got from
experience. Hence thought — that which can be constructed from the materials
of thinking — is limited by experience. But wait a minute — proposition (1)
was that our *understanding* is limited, not that our *thought* is limited. So
how does thought relate to understanding in Hume's scheme of things? I am
inclined to answer that when we have clear and determinate thoughts (the
words which comprise the thoughts express determinate ideas; see p. 77
above), thought and understanding are the same. When we have confused

thoughts (the words which compose the thoughts express confused ideas or no
ideas at all), then we do not have understanding. In short, understanding is
clear and determinate thought. Thus in terms of (1) and (2), understanding or
determinate thought is limited by experience. Proposition (3) merely says
that we can recognise the truth of (1) and (2) — presumably when we note
the experiential source of determinate ideas. It then commends the attitude
of mind which accepts that our understanding has limits beyond which no
certain or dogmatic conclusions can be justified. Hume sometimes says that
conclusions are uncertain if they go beyond our experience (e.g. *Enquiry,*
142:151); sometimes that we sould confine our enquiries to our experience
(e.g. *Enquiry,* 160:170). There is no indication that he thinks these injunctions
are materially different from each other.

Hume's idea/impression dichotomy is thus one route to his typically
empiricist limitation upon what we can understand or clearly think. Another
route is his distinction between demonstrations and matters of fact (see
above, p. 61). Demonstrations are not only contrasted with matters of fact
in the degree of certainty which attaches to them (negation self-contradictory
v. negation false) but also in point of origin. The demonstration is 'discoverable by the mere operation of thought'. The matter of fact depends upon
'the present testimony of our senses' and 'the relation of *Cause and Effect'*
and this relation 'is not, in any instance, attained by reasonings *a priori*;
but arises entirely from experience, when we find that any particular objects
are constantly conjoined with each other' (*Enquiry,* 27:42f). Thus the source
of matters of fact is experience and no allowance is made for matters of fact
from any other source. But Hume is by no means eccentric or perverse in
what he calls a matter of fact. It would be quite hard to find an example of
what the layman would call a matter of fact whose source was *other* than
experience. The sort of positive pronouncements in 'school metaphysics and
divinity' to which Hume objects are rational attempts to prove 'the
existence of a Deity and the immortality of souls' in which the conclusions
are presented as having demonstrable or matter-of-fact certainty. They do not
have demonstrable certainty (their denial is not self-contradictory) nor do
they come within the scope of matter of fact certainly because these — Hume
would say we all agree and probably most of us do — are related to experience.

The conclusion so far is that propositions (1) and (2) are suggested to Hume
by his acceptance of Lockean presuppositions and recommended to us by his
theory of meaning and by his account of the different 'objects of enquiry'.
But it must not be thought that Hume's contrast between what we can
understand and what is beyond our understanding is the same as the positivist
contrast between verifiable propositions and all other propositions. What
Hume is saying is that when we can relate our thoughts to experience we
are thinking clearly and are able to give some sort of grounds for being sure
about our conclusions. When we cannot so relate our thoughts 'we are got
into a fairyland'. Hence, in Sections I and XII of the *Enquiry,* he contrasts
the conclusions of common life and experience with those of abstruse

philosophy and metaphysics which serve 'only as a shelter to superstition
and a cover to absurdity and error'. We are entitled to be confident about
the conclusions of common life because these relate to experience. But
nothing entitles us to be confident about the conclusions of abstruse
philosophy. Doubts about the former are impractical and foolish. Doubts
about the latter are nothing worse than the proper hesitations of a reasonable
man aware that he has no grounds for rational confidence about matters
altogether outside all possibility of experience. He cannot be confident in his
arguments and conclusions about the origination of worlds, the nature of god,
the ultimate destiny of things or the constitution of spirits. At least as a
rational man he cannot be confident and dogmatic about such things. He
can be and, as Hume observes, often is dogmatic about such subjects if he is
a man subject to the 'miracle' of religious faith. But this dogmatism is of
quite a different kind to the pseudo-rationalistic dogmatism in theology and
metaphysics which Hume is so anxious to condemn and which he constantly
contrasts with '*faith* and divine revelation': the true foundations of religion.

*   *   *

What Hume has to say about meaning and understanding has three applica-
tions to religious language and dogma. In the first place his impressions/ideas
dichotomy allows him to say that certain terms, for example, 'spiritual substance'
and 'necessary being' are meaningless. Secondly, he has the no-Newspeak-in-
theology argument to limit use of anthropomorphic language in stating god's
attributes. Thirdly, he has the general prescription that rational confidence
in matters which run wide of common life and experience is unjustified
because such matters are beyond the limits of our understanding. 'Our line
is too short to fathom such immense abysses'.

I shall shortly consider what Hume has to say about religion based upon
revelation or established as a natural instinct of mankind. But before doing
so I wish to look at one item in the philosophy of religion which stands
somewhat apart from the central issues of god's existence and attributes
which have so far occupied our attention. This item is the immortality of
the soul – a subject of controversy in the early eighteenth century (for
example, between Collins and Clarke) into which Hume impoliticly strayed
in one of the suppressed essays.

6 The Immortality of a Person

> The soul, secur'd in her existence, smiles
> At the drawn dagger, and defies its point.
> The stars shall fade away, the sun himself
> Grow dim with age, and nature sink in years;
> But thou shalt flourish in immortal youth,
> Unhurt amidst the war of elements,
> The wrecks of matter, and the crush of worlds.
>
> Addison, *Cato*, V i

At no time in his adult life did Hume ever believe in any form of personal immortality.[1] This biographical fact, so challengingly at variance with the beliefs of most of his contemporaries, is given little expression in his philosophical writings. There is the brief, aphoristic essay 'Of the Immortality of the Soul' which Hume perforce never published during his lifetime, and there are sections in the *Treatise,* in particular 'Of the Immateriality of the Soul' and 'Of Personal Identity', which can be construed as attacks upon certain versions of the immortality doctrine. There are a few wayward remarks elsewhere in his private papers and published works — mostly of biographical interest — and that is all. The excuse for devoting a chapter to the present topic is thus not its prominence in Hume's writing but its importance in the philosophy of religion together with the controversial significance of those relatively brief things which Hume has to say. These add up to a case against immortality which at least one recent writer has found 'almost irresistible'.[2]

(i) PERSONS AND IMMORTALITIES

'Whether we are to live in a future state, as it is the most important question which can possibly be asked, so it is the most intelligible question which can be expressed in language'. The confident opening sentence of Bishop Butler's dissertation 'Of Personal Identity' asserts one thing and asks another. It asserts, what subsequent philosophical discussion has taken to be highly debatable, that the immortality of a person is a coherent doctrine. It asks whether the doctrine is true. Now Hume's contribution to the subject is to argue that one very important version of the immortality doctrine is incoherent and that even if it were coherent it would, along with other versions of the doctrine, be false or pernicious or both. But first, what versions of the doctrine are there and what problems do they raise?

Leaving aside unproblematic palliatives such as speaking of a man's children or his works or his moral acts as 'his immortality', and leaving aside also those sophisticated and modernistic re-thinks of Christianity which would rob eternal life of any reference to life after death, the immortality doctrine exists in a number of forms of which the following are historically the most important.

(A)   *Bodily resurrection*

This is the orthodox Christian (and Moslem) doctrine. It is that at 'the general resurrection in the last day' the corruptible body which each person has in earthly life will be restored incorruptible: 'It is sown a natural body; it is raised a Spiritual body';[3] 'For this corruptible must put on incorruption, and this mortal must put on immortality'.[4] In case anyone should construe 'spiritual body' as a sort of ghost rather than flesh and blood there is St Augustine's authoritative and forthright gloss:

> Bodies which have a living soul, but not yet a life-giving spirit, are called *animal* (that is, bodies with *anima* — 'life' or 'soul'; and yet they are not souls but bodies). In the same way, those other bodies are called *spiritual*. Yet we must not allow ourselves to believe that they will be spirits: we must think of them as bodies having the substance of flesh, though never having to experience corruption or lethargy, being preserved from such a fate by the life-giving spirit. Then man will no longer be earthly, but heavenly, not because his body, made of earth, will not be the same, but because the heavenly gift will fit it for living in heaven itself, not by a loss of its natural substance, but by a change in its quality.[5]

About this doctrine as such Hume makes no *direct* critical comment although I shall argue that some of his remarks on the problem of personal identity could be developed into an objection to it as they could to almost any doctrine of personal immortality. But even in Christianity the doctrine of immortality by bodily resurrection in the last day or at death (which will be the same thing for those who are dead if there is to be no existence between death and the general resurrection) exists along with a second doctrine, one version of which is the main butt of Hume's attack.

(B)   *Immortal soul*

In this account of immortality man is thought of as the combination of a mortal and perishable body with an immortal and imperishable soul. The soul is identified with the essential person, with 'mind' or 'self' or the 'Hidden Thing within': that which is supposed to make me what I am, a thinking, conscious being apart from the accidents of the bodily encumbrance which I happen to carry in mortal life.[6] The body is subject to death. But the essential person survives death.

This account of immortality comes in at least two versions. In one the distinction is made between the material substance of the body and the immaterial or spiritual substance of the soul. The material body corrupts at death but the immaterial soul is released and remains incorruptible. In the other the distinction is again made between body and soul but the vehicle of the soul's immortality is not specified as a substance — immaterial or otherwise. It is mainly the former of these which Hume attacks: very sharply under the heading 'metaphysical topics' in 'Of the Immortality of the Soul'; less sharply, but with more sophistication, in the *Treatise* chapter 'Of the Immateriality of the Soul'.

The doctrine of an immortal soul has a venerable lineage from Plato's *Phaedo* and earlier to the present day. It still provides the commonest background assumption to popular talk about immortality. In Christianity, despite the more canonical bodily resurrection doctrine, talk about an immortal soul, whether or not the soul is identified with an immaterial or spiritual substance, is and always has been very common.[7] Because of this, Hume's attack upon the notion of an immaterial soul was commonly understood as an attack upon any belief in immortality. In *A Letter* (1745) he defends himself from this interpretation. But given his own disbelief in immortality the defence may well be disingenuous and adapted, like the *Letter* itself, for particular local purposes.

In some variations of the immortal soul doctrine (but not in the Christian assimilation of it) the soul is thought of as existing both before and after its sojourn in the mortal body. This is the version of the doctrine which Hume briskly rejects when he remarks 'The soul, therefore, if immortal, existed before our birth: And if the former state of existence no wise concerned us, neither will the latter'.

(C)   *Metempsychosis*

This is the doctrine that at death the soul of a human being or animal passes over into a new body of the same or a different species. As with the previous doctrine — with which it clearly shares certain basic metaphysical assumptions — the doctrine of metempsychosis is of immense antiquity. It was entertained by the Pythagoreans[8] among others and is still held in a somewhat different form by Buddhists. Hume mentions the doctrine disparagingly in a single sentence.

(D)   *Astral body*

The doctrine that a 'shadow' or 'astral' body breaks away from the physical body at death and in certain abnormal pre-mortem experiences has a certain vogue among modern devotees of psychical exotica. It has no place in eighteenth-century thinking nor in the great religions of the western world. Whether, as Geach remarks, the view is 'wholly devoid of philosophical

interest'[9] is debatable.[10] But the absence of empirical evidence in favour of
the view seems to render the philosophical interest (if any) of little practical
concern.

In this chapter I shall refer only to doctrines (A) and (B) since these alone
have real importance in the intellectual context in which Hume was writing.
Both pose question of the highest complexity. How is the resurrected body
or the immortal soul to be identified as the *same person* as some once living
man? What is meant by 'soul' or 'self'? (A problem spotted by Berkeley —
'the grand mistake is that we know not what we mean by we, selves, mind
etc.')[11] What is it to be the same person at different times? Is the phrase
'immaterial soul' intelligible? If these and other questions about coherence of
doctrines (A) and (B) can be given a satisfactory answer then the matter-of-
fact question can be asked: Is there any evidence that men have an immortality of the sort spoken of in either (A) or (B) or any combination of them?
In what follows, and in accordance with the design of this book, I confine
discussion of these and the like questions to points raised by Hume or
arising directly in connection with what he does say.

(ii)   HUME'S ARGUMENTS

In the short essay 'Of the Immortality of the Soul' (which I shall generally
refer to in this chapter simply as 'the essay') Hume divides the discussion
into metaphysical topics and physical and moral arguments. *Metaphysical
topics* are the difficulties with the immortal soul doctrine which result from
considerations of coherence or intelligibility. Taking the essay and the
Treatise chapters together these are (1) difficulties which arise from taking
the vehicle of the soul's immortality as an immaterial substance and
(2) identification difficulties which arise with the notion of an immortal
soul quite apart from whether the vehicle of its immortality is supposed to
be substantial. *Physical arguments* are those which would seek to show that
the doctrine of the immortality of the soul is false, even if we allow it to be
coherent. The most important of those touched upon in the essay are what
I shall call the Concomitant Variation Argument and the Secret Dread
Argument. *Moral arguments* are those objections which, according to Hume,
would be made on moral grounds to the Christian doctrine of immortality
supposing that doctrine to be both coherent and true.

Metaphysical topic (1)

At the beginning of the essay 'Of the Immortality of the Soul' Hume
remarks that 'metaphysical topics are founded on the supposition that the
soul is immaterial, and that it is impossible for thought to belong to a
material substance'. His reply is:

But just metaphysics teach us, that the notion of substance is wholly
confused and imperfect, and that we have no other idea of any substance
than as an aggregate of particular qualities, inhering in an unknown
something. Matter, therefore, and spirit are at bottom equally unknown;
and we cannot determine what qualities may inhere in the one or the other.

This reads very like a summary of part of Hume's argument in the chapter
'Of the Immateriality of the Soul' in the *Treatise*. His conclusion there is
that 'the question concerning the substance of the soul is absolutely
unintelligible' (*Treatise*, 250). This conclusion rests upon several arguments.

The first and most general of these arguments in the *Treatise* is that
since we have no idea of *any* substance ('matter and spirit are at bottom
equally unknown') we cannot dispute meaningfully whether something is
or is not a material or an immaterial substance. (This is the road which Locke
might have taken when he remarks 'Self is that conscious thinking thing,
whatever substance made up of (whether spiritual or material, simple or
compounded, it matters not) . . . .'[12] Locke's later preference for the soul
being an immaterial substance is the one which Hume attacks.) Hume's
reasons for concluding that the notion of a substance is meaningless form
a significant part of the critical epistemology of the *Treatise*. For example,
he says that we have no idea of any substance derived from our impressions
(our sensible and reflective experiences) therefore we can attach no meaning
to the term. And again, if we define a substance as 'something which may
exist by itself' then this is vacuous because it 'agrees to every thing, that can
possibly be conceiv'd; and never will serve to distinguish substance from
accident, or the soul from its perceptions' (*Treatise*, 233). Hume's objections
to the doctrine of substance — whether supposed to be material or spiritual —
are part of the history of philosophy known to every undergraduate and
discussed by every critic. I do not propose to rake over the ashes again here.
Suffice it to say that with certain additions and qualifications they are
widely held to be important objections to the notion of material substance
as Locke was supposed to have used it,[13] and may also be significant
objections to Berkeley's account of minds if his account can be shown to
depend upon us having a notion of a spiritual substance.

Hume's second argument to show that 'the question concerning the
substance of the soul is absolutely unintelligible' consists in an attack upon
one of the arguments which had been used to show that the soul must be an
immaterial substance. There is, he says, an argument for the soul's
immateriality which runs as follows. Thought or consciousness (the supposed
primary function of the soul) does not have extension or location. Everything
which is of material substance does have extension and location. Therefore
thought cannot inhere in a material substance. Therefore it inheres in an
immaterial substance (which is the indestructible stuff of the soul). In order
to discuss this argument Hume suspends his contention that all talk of substances is meaningless. His reply is then a prolonged advocacy of the thesis

that 'an object may exist, and yet be nowhere'. For example, 'A moral reflection cannot be plac'd on the right or on the left hand of a passion, nor can a smell or sound be either of a circular or a square figure' (*Treatise*, 236). The fact that it makes no sense to ask for the location of a thought or the extension of a consciousness does not, according to Hume, imply that these objects are non-existent or that they must exist in an immaterial substance which is incapable of location or extension. Instead it implies that thought and consciousness are not members of that category of objects to which the concepts 'location' and 'extension' can be meaningfully applied. The argument (that thought cannot inhere in a material substance therefore it inheres in an immaterial substance) is thus, according to Hume, a confusion derived from a category mistake. It leads to questions as absurd as 'Is the . . . immaterial substance . . . on the left or the right hand of the perception?' (*Treatise*, 240) and is, for example, as foolish as asking if the sportsmanship of the village cricket team is at deep mid-wicket or silly mid-on, failing to get an answer, and therefore concluding that the sportsmanship inheres in a locationless spiritual ether. Hume does not use the modern expression 'category mistake'. But he does in effect characterise the mistake and use it to ridicule the contention that thought must inhere in an immaterial substance.

His third argument is an attack upon yet another argument for the soul's immateriality. Motion and matter, it is sometime said, however subdivided or compounded, are still motion and matter and never become pleasures or moral reflections or thoughts. 'Now as these different shocks, and variations, and mixtures are the only changes, of which matter is susceptible, and as these never afford us any idea of thought or perception, 'tis concluded to be impossible, that thought can ever be caus'd by matter' (*Treatise*, 247). This argument is the fusion of two arguments. One concludes that the movements and combinations of physical things are in a different category from thoughts, hopes, pleasures and intentions. The other concludes that the movements of matter can never produce (cause) thoughts etc. The former conclusion is true but, as Hume has already indicated, does not imply that thoughts must exist in a non-material substance. The latter conclusion asserts a matter of fact which on the best information available seems to be just false. As Philo remarks 'we every day see [reason] arise from [generation] and never [generation] from [reason]' (*Dialogues*, 197). The line Hume takes in the *Treatise* is a more general rejection of the matter of fact argument: 'as the constant conjunction of objects constitutes the very essence of cause and effect, matter and motion may often be regarded as the causes of thought, as far as we have any notion of that relation' (*Treatise*, 250).

It may well be true that thought is commonly observed to be an effect of some modification of matter and hence that it is not *necessary* for thought to inhere in some immaterial substance. But it is a pity Hume's own preconceptions prevent him using the most obvious argument against thought belonging to an immaterial substance. If he had been able to accept that he was acquainted with material things and that these, not their qualities (the Cheshire cat but not its grin), are substances, that is, can significantly be said to exist separately or in their own right, then he could have attributed thought to the corporeal person and left the immaterial soul-substance as a pseudo-notion.[14] As it is, he will have nothing to do with any talk of substances: an unwillingness which both deprives him of a good argument against immaterial substance and puts some of his own metaphysic in question. In particular, for Hume, the essential person or soul is left as *neither* material *nor* immaterial substance and this means that he is officially unable to say that the person is corporeal: an official prohibition which he comes close to waiving on at least one occasion (see below p. 98).

There is a fourth and somewhat curious reason given by Hume for reaching the conclusion that 'the question concerning the substance of the soul is absolutely unintelligible'. It is this. If Spinoza's doctrine of the unity of the substance of the universe (each individual object being merely a modification of it) is held to be absurd and atheistical then 'this hideous hypothesis is almost the same with that of the immateriality of the soul, which has become so popular' (*Treatise,* 241). It is almost the same because the whole of our experience can be considered in two ways. 'I observe first the universe of objects or of body', the sun, moon, mountains etc. and these, for Spinoza, are all modifications of one substance. 'I then observe a universe of thought, or my impressions and ideas' and there I discover another sun, moon, mountains etc. These, for 'certain theologians' (Berkeley?), are all modifications of one single immaterial substance which is my soul. Both hypotheses are equally absurd according to Hume. I say this in a 'somewhat curious' argument because its force depends on the one hand upon a carelessly developed paraphrase of a profoundly complicated philosophical position while on the other hand it depends upon Hume's readers being prejudiced against Spinoza on the grounds of his supposed atheism. Neither of these characteristics is likely to commend Hume's argument in the present matter to the modern reader and his thesis that 'immaterial substance' is meaningless is sufficiently argued without the Spinoza outburst. (Whenever Hume mentions Spinoza he does so in order to condemn him (see, for example, *A Letter,* 13). I have never been able to decide if this is because Hume genuinely disliked Spinoza's 'absurd' metaphysics or because he thought it prudent to identify himself on occasions with those who condemn Spinoza's 'atheism'.)

Hume has thus argued 'concerning *the Immateriality of the Soul* (from which the Argument is taken for its natural Immortality, or that it cannot perish by Dissolution as the Body)' (*A Letter,* 13) that the notion of an immaterial substance is unintelligible and that nothing shows that thought must 'inhere' in such a substance. Hence if immortality depends upon the soul being an immaterial substance no coherent account of immortality is possible.

Hume's parting shot on the subject is in 'Of the Immortality of the Soul'. If we suppose 'spiritual substance' (Hume uses 'immaterial' and 'spiritual' interchangeably, as I have done) to be a coherent concept and to be instantiated, then nature appears to employ such a substance much as she does ordinary matter:

> [Nature] modifies it into a variety of forms and existences; dissolves after a time each modification; and from its substance erects a new form. As the same material substance may successively compose the bodies of all animals, the same spiritual substance may compose their minds: Their consciousness, or that system of thought, which they formed during life, may be continually dissolved by death; and nothing interests them in the new modification . . . And that an immaterial substance, as well as a material, may lose its memory or consciousness, appears, in part, from experience, if the soul be immaterial.

The suggestion is strikingly destructive. What Hume is saying is that even if we allow that the soul is immaterial the immortality of its stuff may be of no more significance to our immortality as persons than is the immortality of the stuff of our bodies. In this sense the doctrine of metempsychosis could be true but totally banal. The soul may transmigrate but the transmigration would be of no more interest to the person whose soul it was, and no more identical with him as a person, than the maggots which devoured the dead body of the king would be of interest to or identical with the king. Hume's piquant conclusion to the passage quoted — if experience shows anything it shows that immaterial substance can lose its memory — refers, presumably, to both geriatric and post-mortem amnesia!

It will be observed that in all this Hume has said and implied nothing about the doctrine of immortality through bodily resurrection. The final shot apart, all he has said is that the soul cannot be immortal if the vehicle of its immortality is the incoherent doctrine of immaterial substance. As he remarks in his own defence: 'The Author has not anywhere that I remember denied the Immateriality of the Soul in the common Sense of the Word. He only says, That the Question did not admit of any distinct Meaning; because we had no distinct Idea of Substance. This Opinion may be found everywhere in Mr *Lock*, as well as Bishop *Berkley*' (*A Letter*, 30). But this is slightly disingenuous. What is 'the common sense of the word' (presumably the word 'soul') which differs from the sense Hume gives it? If the soul is the essential person, and the soul cannot be said to be an immaterial substance and thus both immune from the body's corruption and able to provide some sort of vehicle for continuing personal identity, how is anyone going to be able to characterise immortality except through the *intrinsically* improbable credo of bodily resurrection or through some unexplained non-substantial person for which the word 'soul' is supposed to stand? The suspicion that Hume means more destruction than he finds it prudent to admit is, I think, confirmed by the remainder of his discussion which is capable of application to doctrines of immortality which do not depend upon speaking of an immaterial soul-substance.

Metaphysical topic (2)

It is widely agreed among modern writers on the subject that the major
'metaphysical' (i.e. coherence) difficulties with doctrines of immortality[15]
are those which centre around the criteria for personal identity. How is an
observer to know that X at time t_1 is the same person as Y at time t_2?
How do I know that I am the same person at different times? Now apart
from one undeveloped suggestion, Hume does not explicitly apply his
discussion of these questions to the problem of immortality. But his discussion
is applicable.

Very briefly his account of personal identity is that no person can ever
find within himself any unchanging entity which is always present and
which constitutes soul, myself or me. All he ever finds is a sequence of
changing perceptions. Self must therefore consist only in the sequence of
perceptions. 'It is the successive perceptions only, that constitute the mind'
(*Treatise*, 253). The scenes are ever-changing but there is no abiding theatre
in which the scenes take place. The demand for such a theatre results in
fictions like 'the notion of a *soul*, and *self*, and substance, to disguise the
variations'. The same is true with material objects, with shoes and ships
and sealing wax, with cabbages and the physical bodies which are kings.
According to Hume we disguise the actual variable and interrupted character
of these things by supposing a mysterious and inward substance which is the
thing's real identity. But no such real identity is to be found. The thing
consists only in 'a succession of related objects', just as the identity of a mind
consists only in a succession of related perceptions. Memory 'acquaints us
with the continuance and extent of this succession of perceptions' (*Treatise*,
261), but the nature of the relation eludes Hume: nothing simple and individual can be found in which the perceptions inhere, nor can the mind 'perceive some real connexion among its perceptions' (*Treatise*, 636). In all this,
'perception' is being used in the exceptionally wide sense of sensation,
passion, emotion, thought or observation by sight, touch, taste, smell or
hearing which is explained at the beginning of the *Treatise*. It should also
be noted that Hume uses 'soul', 'mind', 'self' and 'myself' indifferently for
what might also be called 'the essential person' and that in this usage
reference to 'soul or myself' carries no implication of a substantial object
(material or immaterial). What Hume is seeking to do is to characterise the
essential person as a sequence of perceptions. The enterprise, but not the
conclusion, is similar to Locke's quest for the essential person which led him
to the wider and somewhat more useful suggestion that consciousness is the
essential characteristic.

Hume's account of personal identity, stimulating as it has proved to be
in the history of philosophy (despite his own hasty retreat from it in the
Appendix to the *Treatise*), clearly contains serious mistakes. In particular
Hume fails to observe the importance of his own distinction between
'numerical and specific identity' (*Treatise*, 257). If a man hears the identical

note struck several times successively on a piano, the identity of the note is
its specific identity not its numerical identity. There are several notes all
specifically the same. The saying 'as like as two peas' refers to the *specific,*
not the numerical identity of the peas. If it referred to the numerical identity
there would be one, not two peas. Now Hume, in seeking the identity of a
person, sets out to look for something which would be specifically identical
throughout time (i.e. continuous and unchanging). He fails to find this
something and quite correctly finds instead only changing perceptions —
man, alas, being totally subject to change and decay. He then prematurely
abandons the search for the criteria of *numerical* identity which would be an
indispensible part of the sort of identity actually contained in the notion
'same person'.[16]

Leaving aside for the moment Hume's real or supposed mistakes, there are
at least two points at which his account of personal identity touches upon
doctrines of immortality. One is an application of his account which Hume
himself suggests but does not follow up. The other is in his remarks on
memory as a criterion of personal identity.

The application is this. Having accurately observed that in myself I never
stumble upon anything other than a perception, Hume remarks:

> When my perceptions are remov'd for any time, as by sound sleep;
> so long am I insensible of *myself*, and may truly be said not to exist. And
> were all my perceptions remov'd by death, and cou'd I neither think, nor
> feel, nor see, nor love, nor hate after the dissolution of my body, I
> shou'd be entirely annihilated, nor do I conceive what is farther requisite
> to make me a perfect non-entity (*Treatise,* 252).

And again, somewhat similarly, in the 'appendix' to the *Treatise* (p. 636)
'The annihilation, which some people suppose to follow upon death, and
which entirely destroys the self, is nothing but an extinction of all particular perceptions; love and hatred, pain and pleasure, thought and sensation.
These therefore must be the same with self; since the one cannot survive the
other'. Both these observations take the form: *if* we lost all our perceptions at
death, *then* we are annihilated as persons. The antecedent is never positively
affirmed by Hume. Of course in the final analysis it cannot be affirmed. Men
do not live through death to tell us what it is to die. (The two possible
exceptions were not forthcoming — 'He told it not; or something seal'd the
lips of that Evangelist'). But does the antecedent need to be positively
affirmed? If the essential person consists in having perceptions, isn't there
already an enormous and unbroken weight of inductive evidence to show that
having perceptions and having the body of a living man are inseparable? Do
we not observe and experience a concomitant variation in the state of the
body and the state of the sequence of perceptions which is, according to
Hume, the person? Certainly we do not know from experience that having
a body is necessary to having perceptions, but we do know that all the

experience we have is of a body with its perceptions. This suggests both a matter-of-fact argument to which I shall return later and the identity problem carried a stage further. If to be a person is to have perceptions, how are persons to be distinguished from one another or identified once they lose the physical identifying features provided by their bodies? The point is that I know X and Y are the same person because of their connection with a numerically identical body, and that X and Z are different persons because of their connection with numerically distinct bodies. But in the case of disembodied perceptions knowledge of this connection is *ex hypothesi* unavailable. For the observer this difficulty seems to be insoluble. For the disembodied person himself, for me, all that can be said is that having died, I seem to be still having perceptions. But wait a minute – this very formulation is at error. What is this 'I' which is 'having' perceptions? Should I (now living) say 'there will be perceptions when I am dead?' But how are *those* perceptions going to be identified with *these* perceptions which are the essential me now? This is a puzzle which applies equally to the immortality of the soul and the resurrection of the body. Locke's answer is that memory relates the pre-mortem and post-mortem perceptions. But this, as Hume points out, is not good enough.

In the *Essay* (II, xxvii, 9) and in the controversy with the Bishop of Worcester, Locke had argued that by a person is meant 'a thinking intelligent being, that has reason and reflection and can consider itself as itself, the same thinking thing in different times and places; which it does only by that consciousness which is inseparable from thinking . . .'. Hence personal identity consisted in 'the sameness of a rational being: and as far as this consciousness can be extended backwards by any past action or thought, so far reaches the identity of that person'. Commentators have generally abbreviated this by saying that for Locke, consciousness is essential to being a person, and memory is essential to personal identity: if the memory is preserved forever, the person is preserved in immortality.

One difficulty in Locke's thesis which Hume pinpoints is that we are always prepared to extend our identity as person beyond the limit of our present memories. I do not remember *any* of the events at school recorded in a diary written by me when I was sixteen, nor do I remember writing the diary though I have it before me now. But the diary is mine; I wrote it at the time and I have no doubt that I did and experienced the things recorded in it. Thus Hume, echoing the words of Bishop Butler, remarks 'memory does not so much *produce* as *discover* personal identity' (*Treatise*, 262). But the difficulty goes much deeper. Just as my lack of memory of doing X does not entail that I did not do X, so the presence of my memory of doing X does not entail that X was done by me. Memory beliefs, and therefore honest memory claims, are generally true, but that is as far as we can go. The very common situation of amnesia and the only slightly less common situation of paramnesia prevent memory *per se* from being a criterion of identity which could function even for me independently of physical remains (such as my diary) or the memories which other people have of what I did. In short, a distinction has to be made (and can be made) between seeming memories and actual or veridical memories. The same holds for my knowledge of the identity of other persons. The seeming memories of other persons are not veridical in the absence of physical checks, nor am I able to identify the other person whose memories we are talking about except through his or her physical continuity in one body. 'Did the person who remembers doing X actually do X?' is a question which is perfectly senseless unless we can refer to the bodily identity of the person quite apart from what he claims to remember. But now consider what problems this poses for the memories of disembodied persons. A certain disembodied person has memories which, we shall suppose, bear a one-to-one correspondence with the memories Ron Frab had at the completion of his life. Is the disembodied person the same person as Ron Frab? Suppose we are presented with two living men having specifically the same memories. Do we have one person or two? If we have only one what will be left if I kill one of the two men? So presumably we give due weight to the numerical non-identity of the two men and say what we have is two persons with the same memories. Now what happens at death's door which makes me less inclined to say that Ron Frab, the living man, and the disembodied person are two persons with specifically the same memories? Nothing, except that one of the two memory sets has gone out of existence in the form in which we always recognise persons, that is, *via* their bodily continuity, while another memory set has supposedly come into existence in a form in which we never recognise or identify persons. So why not two persons with the same memories one of whom has gone out of existence? A similar but less acute puzzle of recognition and identification occurs with immortality through bodily resurrection. The discontinuous bodily identity makes us uncertain whether we should side with Locke in saying that what has 'a different beginning in time and place' is different, or whether we should say the specific identity is sufficient for us to ignore the numerical non-identity. As Penelhum remarks 'The crucial difference between a person's looking forward to his own resurrected future and his predicting the future existence of a being like himself seems to depend on a decision which can, in default of bodily continuance, be taken equally well one way or the other'.[17]

My object in following this subject as far as I have[18] is to indicate the direction in which Hume's remarks on personal identity could develop in relation to problems of identity in immortality. If Hume is right and perceptions are even a *part* of the essential person then there are two possibilities. If perceptions cease at death, there would be no personal immortality of any sort and there would be an end of it. If perceptions do not cease at death then intricate and perhaps insoluble difficulties present themselves in attempting to identify whatever is left after death with the 'whole man' person known in life.

Physical arguments

These are Hume's several (brief) arguments in the essay which maintain that even if it were coherent the doctrine of the immortality of the soul would very probably be false. There are four.

(1) The first is what I shall call the Concomitant Variation Argument. It is an application of what J. S. Mill was to call the 'Method of Concomitant Variations' in his list of sound experimental procedures. Hume's statement of the method in the essay is this:

> Where any two objects are so closely connected, that all alterations, which we have ever seen in the one, are attended with proportionable alterations in the other; we ought to conclude, by all the rules of analogy, that, when there are still greater alterations produced in the former, and it is totally dissolved, there follows a total dissolution of the latter.

Now, argues Hume, there is a very striking concomitant variation in the state of our body and the state of our soul (where 'soul' or 'mind', as before, is understood to mean the sequence of perceptions which is the essential person). For example:

> Sleep, a very small effect on the body, is attended with a temporary extinction; at least, a great confusion [dreams? — *J.G.*] in the soul.
> The weakness of the body and that of the mind in infancy are exactly proportioned; their vigour in manhood; their sympathetic disorder in sickness; their common gradual decay in old age. The step further seems unavoidable; their common dissolution in death.

These reflections are by no means original. They have a history going at least as far back as the Epicureans, and Bertrand Russell is unlikely to be the last distinguished thinker who will appeal to them.[19] But what *is* unusual in Hume's use of them is that he makes the argument an application of a respectable general procedure for securing true results in empirical investigations. If we are to think of a living man as a conjunction of two parts, a soul (or essential person) and a body, then to all appearances the two parts have a common rise and fall. The argument to their mutual dissolution is of exactly the same character as the observation that the health of the red corpuscles in the blood varies with the health of the marrow and if the latter is destroyed by disease so is the former. If this argument is sound, why should the body-soul argument not be sound? It will be observed that this argument is primarily applicable to forms of the immortality doctrine in which the soul, substantial or otherwise, operates as the bearer of the person's immortality.

(2) The second argument to show that the soul is mortal looks like an

extension of the first but on closer inspection it proves to be something more: 'Every thing is in common betwixt soul and body. The organs of the one are all of them the organs of the other. The existence therefore of the one must be dependent on that of the other'. Now this certainly could be read as a reassertion of the Concomitant Variation Argument. But it could also be read as Hume's nearest approach to saying that soul and body are not separable, independent objects, but interrelated features of one unified thing — the whole corporeal man. In 'Of Personal Identity' Hume set out with a preconception which he shared with Locke: that he should look for and that it would be possible to find a single non-corporeal criterion of personal identity which would be decisive in all cases however peculiar. Having failed to find anything which would do the job he admitted failure in his quest and never returned to it. What he should have done, we may say, was to pay more attention to this hint in the essay and say that the quest was futile. It is futile for the reason quoted: the quest depends upon being able to isolate parts of the whole man and treat one of the parts as the essential person. But there are no separable parts in the sense supposed. There are only different aspects of the whole man: body and soul make one, not two. As Bernard Williams has remarked, 'when we are asked to distinguish a man's personality from his body, we do not really know what to distinguish from what'.[20] There is thus no single criterion of personal identity but a cluster of criteria — bodily continuity, memory, etc. — no one of which can be used in isolation. Now if 'every thing is common betwixt soul [essential person] and body' and the identity of the whole man consists in body and soul, then if the body is destroyed the soul is destroyed. Once again it will be noted that there is much less difficulty here for immortality by bodily resurrection complete with soul.

(3) The third 'matter of fact' argument which Hume produces is an appeal to the universality of Heraclitean flux.

> Nothing in this world is perpetual. Every being, however seemingly firm, is in continual flux and change: The world itself gives symptoms of frailty and dissolution: How contrary to analogy, therefore, to imagine, that one single form, seemingly the frailest of any, and, from the slightest causes subject to the greatest disorders, is immortal and indissoluble? What a daring theory is that!

The reference of the word 'form' (it appears from a few sentences earlier) is 'the soul'. Why, asks Hume, and with good reason, should this one part or aspect of the whole man be excepted from the universal rule of change, decay, corruption.

(4) The final 'physical argument' is a reversal of the old argument that since men look for immortality there must be something there to look for. The old argument can be found, for example, in several of Berkeley's sermons and elsewhere in his work.[21] It is also given splendid rhetorical statement by Addison in the lines which precede the motto to this chapter:

It must be so — Plato, thou reason'st well! —
Else whence this pleasing hope, this fond desire
This longing after immortality?
Or whence this secret dread, and inward horror,
Of falling into nought? why shrinks the soul
Back on herself, and startles at destruction?

If we call this the Pleasing Hope Argument then Hume's counter to it (apart from his point that it is highly suspect because it is interested pleading) could be called the Secret Dread Argument: if the pleasing hope requires an object so does the secret dread. If, according to Hume in the essay, the horror of annihilation were an 'original passion' it would prove the mortality of the soul since nature, which does nothing superfluously 'would never give us a horror against an impossible event' — 'She may give us a horror against an unavoidable event, provided our endeavours, as in the present case, may often remove it to some distance. Death is in the end unavoidable; yet the human species could not be preserved, had not nature inspired us with an aversion towards it'. It is not entirely clear that Hume intends to say the Pleasing Hope and the Secret Dread Arguments are both nonsense because if one is valid, the other is valid and they cannot both be valid because they establish contradictory conclusions. He could be saying this, or he could be saying that the Pleasing Hope Argument is unsound because the Secret Dread Argument shows not that annihilation is objectively real, but that aversion to death is useful as a means of preserving the species in a way in which the hope for immortality is not. Either way the Pleasing Hope shrivels (like Lamia) under the cold touch of Hume's philosophy.

I have listed these four 'matter-of-fact' objections to the immortality of the soul more or less as Hume gives them. The last two are also objections to a rational belief in bodily resurrection though not to the coherence of such a doctrine if it could be otherwise established, say by divine revelation. Hume does not develop these arguments elsewhere either in private or published writings although he does affirm his disbelief in any form of immortality — a disbelief which we can only assume to be influenced by arguments of this sort.

There is one other matter-of-fact (or perhaps it should be called matter-of-taste) argument against immortality which Hume produces in the essay and which he returned to in his deathbed interview with Boswell. In the essay he puts it thus: 'How to dispose of the infinite number of posthumous existences ought also to embarrass the religious theory . . . For these, then, a new universe must, every generation, be created, beyond the bounds of the present universe.' In Boswell's report the same objection — 'That immortality, if it were at all, must be general' — reduces to Hume saying that if he is immortal, then Wilkes must be immortal: a consideration which perhaps makes the thought of personal immortality unseemly without diminishing its probability. But as Hume says in the essay (concerning a universe crowded with the dead)

'The want of arguments, without revelation, sufficiently establishes the negative'. No need then to fear Wilkes in the future state, or the tedious company of 'every stupid clown that ever existed'!

Moral arguments

It will be noticed that nothing which Hume has so far said is specifically directed at immortality by bodily resurrection. But he does confront the Christian doctrine with just about the most damaging objection which could be devised. He says, not that it is incoherent or false, but that it is immoral. It is immoral in three ways according to Hume in the essay.

First, given the fine balance between our needs and our ability to satisfy our needs, all our energy and attention have to be directed to this world (the point is in the essay but is repeated in *Dialogues,* 208) and in practical life we cannot regulate our conduct by reference to an hereafter. Secondly, the benefits of the after-life are unreasonably reversed for one species of virtue but:

> According to human sentiments, sense, courage, good manners, industry, prudence, genius, are essential parts of personal merit [a point argued at length in the *Enquiry concerning the Principles of Morals* — J.G.]. Shall we therefore erect an elysium for poets and heroes, like that of the ancient mythology? Why confine all rewards to one species of virtue?

Thirdly, the use of heaven and hell as an ultimate, everlasting reward and punishment is a moral scandal. This is because
(a) 'Punishment, without any proper end or purpose, is inconsistent with *our* ideas of goodness and justice; and no end can be served by it after the whole scene is closed'.
(b) 'Punishment, according to *our* conceptions, should bear some proportion to the offence. Why then eternal punishment for the temporary offences of so frail a creature as man?'
(c) 'Heaven and hell suppose two distinct species of men, the good and the bad. But the greatest part of mankind float betwixt vice and virtue'.
(d) The very concepts of reward and punishment are inappropriate to non-rational creatures and very many men come into this category, for example 'Nature has rendered human infancy peculiarly frail and mortal; as it were on purpose to refute the notion of a probationary state. The half of mankind die before they are rational creatures'.

Hume's emphasis on the word *'our'* ideas of goodness and justice should be noted. It is a point which has already been considered (see Chapter 5). Hume's return to it under the topic of immortality emphasises its importance: 'To suppose measures of approbation and blame, different from the human, confounds every thing'.

The contention that the Christian view of immortality is immoral is in striking contrast to the often heard view that the 'weights' of heaven and

hell are at least a significant motive to do good and may even be the ultimate
pivot upon which the justice or injustice of things is balanced. As D. Z.
Phillips remarks 'In this world, there may be moments when one wonders
whether justice and goodness are worth pursuing. One's immediate reading
of the scale of probabilities makes the matter look doubtful. At such times,
Geach would say, what we need to do is to extend the scale so that it
includes an assessment of life after death'.[22] I would not care to conjecture
from the source given[23] whether Geach would or would not say exactly this,
but there is no doubt that very many people would say it. To such people
Hume's reasoned contention, that immortality of the type popularly and
traditionally supposed in Christianity is flagrantly contrary to all human
moral decencies, may even now come as a startling affront to their religion.
But I suspect Hume's intention is not to say that the Christian scheme of
immortality is in fact morally offensive, but that because it would be morally
offensive there can be no such scheme.

$$*\qquad\qquad*\qquad\qquad*$$

Hume did not believe in any form of personal immortality. His reasons
for this negative belief are as complete as the nature of the case will permit.
The belief in its vulgar (and not so vulgar[24]) form as the immortality of an
immaterial soul (thought of as the essential person and characterised by
consciousness or perceptions or thoughts) is incoherent. The question
concerning the materiality or immateriality of the soul is wholly unintelligible. There is nothing to show that thought does inhere in an immaterial
substance nor even that it would be meaningful to say that it did so inhere.
Even if it did there is nothing to show that the immaterial stuff preserves its
form any more than the material stuff does. Such observations as we can make
show that whenever thought occurs it occurs in conjunction with a body. The
notion of a person is such that if we make memory the criterion for personal
identity then for personal immortality there must be memory independent
of bodily identity. Such independence is difficult, perhaps impossible, for an
immaterial soul. For a resurrected body complete with memories there is at
least an ambiguity in whether it should or should not be said that this is the
same person as some once living man. The concomitant variation of bodily
vitality and the vitality of the soul or supposed essential person, the
inextricable fusion of body and soul which makes the identity of the living
man, the precariousness of human life and our consequent *interest* in securing
immortality — all this argues against that aspect of the living man which
we call 'soul' being immortal. But, finally, even if the immortality promised in
the Christian religion were coherent and true it would be morally offensive.

Hume's final flourish in the essay is to concede that only divine revelation
could give us information about immortality: 'Nothing could set in a fuller
light the infinite obligations which mankind have to Divine revelation; since
we find, that no other medium could ascertain this great and important

truth'. Since not even divine revelation could substantiate an incoherence, Hume is presumably not referring here to immortality via an immaterial soul but to some other characterisation of immortality such as the survival of disembodied experiences or the resurrection of the body complete with soul. That the Christian belief should be whole-person immortality — preserving body and soul into everlasting life — and therefore least *metaphysically* objectionable is not a consideration which gives the belief any rational probability. Hume's prudential device of foisting improbable beliefs onto divine revelation — the subject of my next chapter — is not a covert way of saying that he accepts these beliefs. It is more like saying that the beliefs are probably false and certainly independent of evidence, though they are of too much public importance to be freely dismissed.

I said at the start of Section (ii) of the present chapter that a sentence in the essay 'Of the Immortality of the Soul' reads very like a summary of part of the chapter in the *Treatise* called 'Of the Immateriality of the Soul'. But there is more to it than that. At the end of the chapter 'Of the Immateriality of the Soul' Hume remarks: 'In both cases the metaphysical arguments for the immortality of the soul are equally inconclusive; and in both cases the moral arguments and those deriv'd from the analogy of nature are equally strong and convincing' (*Treatise*, 250). In the light of what I have been saying, to describe the metaphysical arguments as 'inconclusive' is erring on the side of modesty; but to describe the moral and physical arguments as 'strong and convincing' is downright deception *unless one had already read* 'Of the Immortality of the Soul'. If one had read that essay it would not require much intellectual detective work to notice the *irony* (no longer the deception), and one would easily appreciate what is now completely hidden: that Hume means 'strongly and convincingly *against* the immortality of the soul'. This cross-reference between the essay and 'Of the Immateriality of the Soul', together with the appearance which the metaphysical topics in the essay have of being a *summary* of the *Treatise* section, leads me to the following conjecture. We know that Hume produced 'Of the Immortality of the Soul' and 'Of Suicide' in 1755 in a hurry to fill up a gap in a volume at the printers (*Letters*, II, 253). I would suggest that the immortality essay came so easily to hand because it was one of the parts of the *Treatise* which twenty years earlier he had been advised not to publish for fear of public outcry (see *New Letters*, pp 2-3). It could have been a separate section coming immediately after the section 'Of the Immateriality of the Soul' or, much more likely, it could have formed the concluding pages to that section itself. When the two were pulled apart the essay required a summary (which it has) of the metaphysical topics which had originally preceded it in detail, while the *Treatise* section required a new and truncated ending — possibly the paragraph on the middle of p. 250 beginning ' 'Tis certainly a kind of indignity . . .' This would then leave the irony of the 'strong and convincing' physical and moral arguments high and dry (as it now is) and without any reference to what precedes it in the *Treatise* as actually published.

Part 11 Revealed Religion and Natural Belief

7 Miracles and Revelation

We know that thou art a teacher come
from God: for no man can do these miracles
that thou doest, except God be with him.
John, III ii

It often happens, such is our natural love for
the marvellous, that we willingly contribute our
own efforts to beguile our better judgements.
Scott, *Guy Mannering,* Chapter IV

The stimulating and confusing thing about Hume's chapter on miracles in
the *Enquiry* is that it brings together, interrelates and applies to the biblical
miracles two items which for the sake of clarity should perhaps be kept apart,
namely, the credibility of witnesses and the intrinsic probability or improbability of the event allegedly witnessed. The result is a piece of argument
which has provoked more comment, criticism and abuse than anything else
in Hume's philosophical writing. To the philosopher 'Of Miracles' offers, at
the very least, an almost irresistible opportunity to try to distinguish between
a miracle, a very unusual event, and an event which provides a falsifying
instance of a natural law; to the historian or jurist it offers a fascinating
discussion of the credibility of witnesses; to the believing Christian it
threatens to demonstrate that no wise man would give any credit to the New
Testament miracles; and, which is not now so readily perceived, to an
eighteenth-century reader (or to a twentieth-century reader asking questions
of the 'Who moved the stone?' type) it offered a direct confutation of the
crucial argument upon which the rational credibility of the Christian
Revelation had been and is still sometimes made to depend, namely, the
historical truth of the Resurrection. I begin with the eighteenth-century
background in order to bring out the significance of Hume's conclusion
'that a miracle can never be proved, so as to be the foundation of a system
of religion'. I then proceed to a discussion of Hume's argument about
evidence before adding a few footnotes to the already vast literature
relating to the philosophical and interpretive problems raised by Hume's
outburst in Part II of the chapter about the 'absolute impossibility' of an
event.

(i) THE EIGHTEENTH-CENTURY CONTROVERSY

'Whatever God hath revealed is certainly true; no doubt can be made of it.
This is the proper object of faith: but whether it be a divine revelation or

no, reason must judge' (Locke, *Essay*, IV, xviii, 10). But how was reason
to judge? The eighteenth-century answer was found in two arguments, one
referring to the fulfilment of prophecy, the other to the performance of
miracles. Both arguments were set out with great vigour by Samuel Clarke
in the Boyle Lecture of 1705: 'The Proof of the Divine Authority of the
Christian Revelation, is *confirmed and ascertained,* by the *Exact Completion
both of all those Prophecies that went before concerning our Lord,* and *of
those that He Himself delivered concerning things that were to happen after'.*[1]
And, concerning miracles, 'The Christian Revelation is positively and directly
proved, to be actually and immediately sent to us from God, by the many
infallible *Signs and Miracles,* which the Author of it worked publickly as the
Evidence of his Divine Commission'.[2]

The argument from miracles to the authenticity of the Christian revelation
is exceedingly ancient. But in the Restoration period it had been formulated
by Stillingfleet[3] and was repeated by Locke in his *Discourse of Miracles.*[4]
Indeed it was an argument whose strength was conceded by most writers in
the period, the deists included.[5] Together with the argument from prophecy
it made up the orthodox early eighteenth-century case for maintaining that
the Christian revelation ought to be accepted by every rational man.

The structure and assumptions of the argument from miracles were as
follows: Granted both that the power of performing miracles could only be
conferred upon a man by God, and that God would not confer such a power
upon those misrepresenting him, then any man who performed miracles
gave evidence in so doing that he had authority from God to deliver a
revelation, and hence that the revelation was true. The argument from prophecy took the same general form, but with the important and distinctive
addition that in the New Testament accounts Jesus both delivered prophecies,
and more significantly, fulfilled in his own person the prophecies concerning
a messiah which had earlier been delivered by others. These arguments were
both challenged in the 1720s, and in the course of the controversy which
followed the reasonableness of accepting the Christian revelation came to
rely mainly upon one particular version of the argument from miracles — the
version which Hume attacks.

The controversy concerning prophecy began in 1724 with a tract from
the scholar and mathematician William Whiston which naively and inadver-
tently provided Antony Collins with an opportunity to attack the argument
from prophecy.[6] The argument thus begun continued at a high level of
polemic[7] until diverted in 1727 by a new subject even more alarming to
orthodox apologists. In that year there appeared the first of six *Discourses
on the Miracles of our Saviour* by Thomas Woolston. In the first five discourses Woolston examined fourteen of the miracles with an eye to establishing:
'That the literal History of many of the Miracles of *Jesus,* as recorded by
the *Evangelists,* does imply Absurdities, Improbabilities, and Incredibilities;
consequently they, either in whole or in part, were never wrought [but
must be understood in an allegorical or mystical sense] '.[8] In the final

discourse (1729) he dealt with the story of the Resurrection — 'that Sandy Foundation of the Church' — which he set out to show 'to consist of Absurditys, Improbabilitys and Incredibilitys', and to be a fabrication by the Apostles.

Woolston's argument was vigorous rather than profound, but vigorous upon a most sensitive topic. It was directed at the heart of the argument from miracles, and hence at what was considered to be the essential rational foundation of the Christian revelation. It called forth a storm of refutations[9] of which only those from Sherlock and Pearce (another bishop) need be mentioned. Pearce tacitly admitted that the argument from miracles needed defending. He suggested that if the miracle of the Resurrection could be established as an undoubted historical fact, then this would be sufficient to prove to a rational man that God had invested Jesus with special authority to deliver a revelation. He states the logic of the situation as follows:

> Here then a Rational man will take his Stand, and being once convinced that *Jesus* did truly rise from the Dead . . . he will easily admit all the Miracles wrought by *Jesus*, when Alive, to have been True and Real ones: For the Divine Power (we may be sure) would [not have raised up a charlatan]: And if he wrought Undoubted Miracles, will not this Conclusion necessarily follow, That he came from God, teaching the Divine Will, because he made use of his Miracles as so many Proofs of his having a Commission from Heaven?[10]

It was, however, Thomas Sherlock in the *Tryal of the Witnesses of the Resurrection*[11] who argued carefully and persuasively that the testimony of the Apostles established the Resurrection as an historical fact.

The *Tryal* was immensely successful if we may measure success by the number of editions which a book makes in the first twenty years of its life. It was widely acclaimed as a decisive move in the controversy with the deists. Even Annet, one of Sherlock's critics, conceded ten years after its publication that 'The conquest he has gain'd has spread itself far and wide, and reach'd even the remotest corners of infidelity'.[12]

In 1733 Woolston died in prison on a charge of criminal blasphemy, and Chubb and Annet who survived to challenge Sherlock drew abuse and ridicule upon themselves. In these circumstances it is not surprising to find that Hume hesitated to enter the controversy. In a letter of 1737, addressed to Henry Home (of a branch of the Home or Hume family which had not adopted the reformed spelling of its name), Hume explained why he had decided to omit his remarks on miracles from the *Treatise*: 'Having a frankt Letter I was resolv'd to make Use of it, & accordingly enclose some Reasonings concerning Miracles, which I once thought of publishing with the rest, but which I am afraid will give too much Offence even as the World is dispos'd at present' (*New Letters*, 2). But in 1748 Hume did publish his reasonings — or some later revision of them — in the *Enquiry*. 'I won't justify the prudence of this step', he wrote to the same correspondent, 'any other way than by expressing my indifference about all the consequences that may follow' (*Letters*, I, 111). Hume's new recklessness may have been encouraged by his increasing fame and maturity and by the cooling of tempers and the decline of controversy between 1737 and 1748. Be that as it may, 'Of Miracles' has strong appearances of being intended, at least in part, as an answer to Sherlock's highly successful *Tryal of the Witnesses*.

We know that as a general policy Hume deliberately avoided personal exchanges which could lead to pamphlet war between himself and others. It is therefore not surprising to find no reference to Sherlock either in the *Enquiry* or in the rather meagre collection of Hume's letters surviving from the years 1737 to 1748. The evidence that Hume is answering the *Tryal* is textual and circumstantial. It consists of five items:

(1) Sherlock's sole concern in the *Tryal* is with weighing and assessing evidence, where the evidence consists exclusively in the reports of witnesses. As Flew observes, this is also Hume's fundamental concern throughout 'Of Miracles'.[13]

(2) This similarity of subject-matter becomes more significant when it is noticed that Hume's final conclusion 'a miracle can never be proved, so as to be the foundation of a system of religion' directly contradicts the conclusion which Sherlock tries to establish, namely, that one particular miracle, the Resurrection, *has* been so conclusively evidenced that it could be used as the rational ground for accepting a system of religion.

(3) Sherlock confines his discussion to the particular question whether the evidence for the Resurrection is good enough to establish that the event in question took place. Hume's argument is sufficiently general to cover the evidence for any miracle but his interest in the particular case of rising from the dead is obviously stressed at several points in his argument. On p. 115: 122 in the middle of his 'proof . . . against the existence of any miracle' he remarks: 'But it is a miracle, that a dead man should come to life; because that has never been observed in any age or country' and on the immediately following page he drives home his reference in another way: 'When anyone tells me, that he saw a dead man restored to life, I immediately consider with myself, whether it be more probable, that this person should either deceive or be deceived, or that the fact, which he relates, should really have happened'. Again, on p. 128:138, immediately following his conclusion that 'a miracle can never be proved, so as to be the foundation of a system of religion', he discusses what the reaction would be to reports attributing a resurrection to Queen Elizabeth.[14] He would not have 'the least inclination to believe so miraculous an event'. 'But should this miracle be ascribed to any new system of religion; men, in all ages, have been so much imposed on by ridiculous stories of that kind, that this very circumstance would be a full proof of a cheat. . . .' The reference to the Resurrection, and, *via* the conclusion that a miracle can never be proved so as to be the foundation of a

system of religion, to the Resurrection used to 'ground' the Christian revelation, is thinly disguised.

(4) Hume could well be alluding to Sherlock on p. 130:140 of the *Enquiry*. At the end of his discussion of miracles he invites his readers to examine the miracles related in scripture 'according to the principles of these pretended Christians, not as the word or testimony of God himself, but as the production of a mere human writer and historian'. Who are 'these pretended Christians'? At the beginning of the *Tryal* it is agreed that the 'Argument should be confined merely to the Nature of the Evidence' and the whole work treats the scriptures expressly and exclusively as the production of human writers and historians. Hume might have had other names in mind, but none would fill the place more easily than Sherlock's, given the character of the *Tryal* and its fame at the time Hume was writing.

(5) From a comparison of the arguments deployed by Hume and Sherlock it would appear that Hume is answering certain vital points in Sherlock's case. This fifth item requires further discussion.

In the *Tryal* the *dramatis personae* include Judge, Jury, Counsel for Woolston (whose business it is to press the charges against the Apostles) and Counsel for the Apostles. The Judge puts three charges: *First,* that there is fraud and deceit in the transaction, i.e. that Jesus himself is a 'trickster' (this is the word being used at the time); *secondly,* that the evidence is forged by the Apostles; *thirdly,* that no evidence would be sufficient to support the credit of so extraordinary an event.

Sherlock dismisses the first charge after a careful cross-examination of the four narratives. Hume does not re-open this question although he does insinuate the suggestion that there may be 'a cheat' in the business (*Enquiry,* 118:126 and 121:129) and his remarks throughout Part II are reminiscent of the violent language in which the controversy had been carried on. The terms 'lies', 'forged miracles', 'imposture', 'holy fraud' and 'cheat' occur in the chapter.

The second charge — that the evidence is forged by the Apostles — is countered by Sherlock with the following superficially powerful argument:

> The Counsel for *Woolston* tells you, that 'tis common for Men to die for false Opinions; and he tells you nothing but the Truth. But even in those Cases their suffering is an Evidence of their Sincerity; and it would be very hard to charge Men who die for the Doctrine they profess, with Insincerity in the Profession. Mistaken they may be; but every mistaken Man is not a Cheat. Now if you will allow the Suffering of the Apostles to prove their Sincerity, which you cannot well disallow; and consider that they died for the Truth of a Matter of Fact which they had seen themselves, you will perceive how strong the Evidence is in this Case (*Tryal,* p. 77).

This argument can be weakened by establishing a non-identity between

the witnesses of the events and the narrators of the Gospels, or by establishing
a possibility that the witnesses may have genuinely deceived themselves
about the nature of the events they describe. Clearly, although Hume may
have entertained doubts about the authorship of the Gospels, he did not have
the critical equipment required to urge the first alternative very convincingly.
He does however adopt the second line of attack. If a report asserts very odd
and unlikely events, it must, among other things, be attested 'by a sufficient
number of men, of such unquestioned good-sense, education, and learning, as
to secure us against all delusion in themselves'. (The passage could be Hume's
amplification of Sherlock's concession (p.46) that miracles 'require more
Evidence to give them Credit than ordinary Cases do'). The hint is given, and
Hume goes on:

> But if the spirit of religion join itself to the love of wonder, there is an
> end of common sense; and human testimony, in these circumstances, loses
> all pretensions to authority. A religionist may be an enthusiast, and
> imagine he sees what has no reality: He may know his narrative to be
> false, and yet persevere in it, with the best intentions in the world, for the
> sake of promoting so holy a cause (*Enquiry,* 117:125; see also 126:136:
> 'Even a court of judicature' may have difficulty in settling what is true).

The *possibility* that the Apostles reported an illusion, or persisted in a
falsehood for the sake of 'so holy a cause' is sufficient to upset Sherlock's
argument that it is altogether beyond belief that the Apostles could have
suffered in a false cause. A good example of the sort of way in which the
enthusiastic distortion described by Hume could work in an actual example
is given by Conyers Middleton. Speaking of Irenaeus he says:

> . . . but I have shewn also, that this single witness was of a character, on
> which we cannot reasonably depend for the truth of a report so extra-
> ordinary. I have shewn him to be of so credulous, superstitious and
> enthusiastical a turn of mind, as would dispose him to embrace and assert
> any fabulous tale, which tended, as he thought, in any manner, to advance
> the credit of the Gospel, or to confute an Heretic.[15]

There can be little doubt that Hume would have liked to say this sort of
thing about the Apostles had the evidence been available or contemporary
opinion permitted.

It is, however, with the third and final charge against the witnesses of the
Resurrection — that no evidence would be sufficient to support the credit
of so extraordinary an event (see *Tryal,* pp. 43-48 and 73-74) — that Hume
is primarily concerned. As Sherlock observes, if this charge can be sustained
it 'excludes all evidence out of the case'. In developing the charge the Counsel
for Woolston is made to raise two issues[16] which Sherlock in the person of
the Counsel for the Apostles then answers.

The first is that the Resurrection is not an event of the kind which is capable of being established by sense-perception (*Tryal*, p.43). To this Sherlock replies:

> A Man rising from the Grave is an Object of Sense, and can give the same Evidence of his being alive, as any other Man in the World can give. So that a Resurrection consider'd only as a Fact to be proved by Evidence, is a plain Case; it requires no greater Ability in the Witnesses, than that they be able to distinguish between a Man dead, and a Man alive: A Point, in which I believe every Man living thinks himself a Judge (*Tryal*, p. 46).

Hume does not discuss this matter, although, as already pointed out, he draws attention to the difficulty which a court of law might experience in distinguishing a true from a false report — even when the report concerns the most recent and public events (*Enquiry*, 126:136).

The second issue is that the Resurrection cannot be proved to the satisfaction of a rational man (*Tryal* pp. 43-44). It is a tribute to Sherlock's intellectual honesty that the case he makes for this position is a great deal stronger than anything actually to be found in Woolston's *Discourses*. He argues thus on Woolston's behalf in more than one place:

> In common Affairs, where nothing is asserted but what is probable, and possible, and according to the usual Course of Nature, a reasonable Degree of Evidence ought to determine every Man. For the very Probability, or Possibility of the thing, is a Support to the Evidence. . . . But when the thing testified is contrary to the Order of Nature, and, at first sight at least impossible, what Evidence can be sufficient to overturn the constant Evidence of Nature, which she gives us in the uniform and regular Method of her Operations? (*Tryal*, p. 43)
> The Testimony of Nature, held forth to us in her constant Method of working, [is] a stronger Evidence against the Possibility of a Resurrection, than any human Evidence can be for the Reality of one *(Tryal*, p. 73).

This is substantially the same sceptical argument[17] as that developed at greater length by Hume in the first part of the chapter on miracles. Sherlock's reply is as follows: 'Our Senses then inform us rightly what the usual Course of Things is; but when we conclude that things cannot be otherwise, we outrun the Information of our Senses' (*Tryal*, p.47).

Thus although experience indicates that resurrections are uncommon, it does not entitle us to infer that they can never take place. This is a good point. But it is only effective against the version of the sceptical argument which concludes that a miracle is impossible. Sherlock does not state this version. The version he has set himself to answer (the one which Hume officially reiterates although he later gets carried away by his own argument) concludes that 'the wise man' — the man who learns from the regularities in his experience and proportions his belief to the evidence — will only believe in a miracle if it is supported by overwhelming evidence: evidence stronger than is ever likely to be produced. Against this position Sherlock produces only one reply of consequence. If the sceptic cannot believe reports of a resurrection then: 'A Man who lives in a warm Climate [Hume calls him 'the Indian prince'], and never saw Ice, ought upon no Evidence to believe that Rivers freeze and grow hard in cold Countries; for this is improbable, contrary to the usual Course of Nature; and impossible according to his Notion of Things' (*Tryal,* p.45).

Let us call this the Indian Prince Argument. The reasoning of the Indian Prince is clearly mistaken. Ice may be impossible according to his experience: but his experience is limited. If the cases are parallel, then the experience of the sceptic is also limited, and his decision to reject resurrection reports is unjustified.

The Indian Prince Argument is given an important place in the *Tryal.* Hume answers it (*Enquiry,* 113:121) both in the text and in a lengthy footnote.[18] The gist of his answer is that the cases differ; the experience of the Indian Prince is limited in a way in which the sceptic's is not. The Indian prince has an obvious gap in his experience, namely, cold and its effects. But the sceptic's experience that men die and do not rise from the dead has no obvious gap in it. There is no reply to the sceptic which could take the form 'in *these* conditions, which you have not experienced, resurrections occur'.

It is possible that Sherlock might defend the Indian Prince Argument as follows: Hume is begging the question. If the Gospels are true then a resurrection *has* occurred, and the sceptic's experience is therefore limited in contrast with the experience of the Apostles even if the sceptic's experience has no 'obvious' gap in it. But for the sceptic the fundamental question *is* whether the Gospels are true. Hume does not discuss this question in a direct manner. He does, however, give an account of the way in which a wise man would react to *reports* of a resurrection (and the Gospels considered as historical evidence are merely ancient reports). The wise man would disbelieve the reports unless and until overwhelming evidence was produced that the reports were genuine. The Indian Prince 'reasoned justly' when he required 'very strong testimony' before he would believe reports of events outside the range of his experience. But once very strong testimony was produced, the Indian Prince, as a rational man, was bound to believe in the freezing of water. Likewise very strong testimony would oblige the sceptic to believe reports of a resurrection. But has sufficiently strong testimony ever in fact been produced? Hume's official answer in 'Of Miracles' is that it *has not.* But at points in what he has to say a second and more problematic answer appears: that sufficiently strong testimony *could not* be produced. I will first consider his official answer. The problematic answer will be considered in the last section of this chapter.

(ii) THE RELIABILITY OF WITNESSES

Hume attributes to Archbishop Tillotson the apologetic corrective which he turns against 'all kinds of superstitous delusion'. But the argument which he actually sets out in the first part of the chapter on miracles bears a remarkably close resemblance to the one devised by Sherlock on behalf of Woolston: 'The Testimony of Nature, held forth to us in her constant Method of working, [is] a stronger Evidence against the Possibility of a Resurrection, than any human Evidence can be for the Reality of one' (*Tryal,* p.73). Hume's official, full-dress version of this argument, rather than the argument as some of his critics have interpreted it and as Hume himself in off-duty moments seems to want us to use it, is as follows:

(1) A weaker evidence can never destroy a stronger.

(2) A wise man proportions his belief to the evidence.

(3) Some things happen invariably in our experience, e.g. that all men die. In matters of fact these invariable experiences constitute certainties and are called laws of nature — 'a firm and unalterable experience has established these laws'.

(4) Other things happen less than always in our experience, e.g., that a day in June is warmer than a day in December. In matters of fact these constitute probabilities which admit of degrees ranging from strong (almost always happens) to weak (very seldom happens).

(5) The veracity of human testimony is, from experience, normally a strong probability and as such amounts to a proof that what is reported took place.

(6) But sometimes the veracity of testimony is a weak probability as when 'the witnesses contradict each other; when they are but few, or of a doubtful character; when they have an interest in what they affirm; when they deliver their testimony with hesitation, or on the contrary, with too violent asseverations' etc. (*Enquiry,* 112:120). *Therefore* (from 3 and 4) when testimony is given which is contrary to our invariable experience, a probability, whether strong or weak, is opposing a certainty and (from 1 and 2) the wise man will believe the certainty.

Now by 'miracle' is meant 'a transgression of a law of nature by a particular volition of the Deity' (*Enquiry,* 115n:123n) and 'a firm and unalterable experience has established these laws':

There must, therefore, be a uniform experience against every miraculous event, otherwise the event would not merit that appellation. And as an uniform experience amounts to a proof, there is here a direct and full *proof,* from the nature of the fact, against the existence of any miracle; nor can such a proof be destroyed, or the miracle rendered credible, but by an opposite proof, which is superior.

The plain consequence is, .\ . 'That no testimony is sufficient to establish a miracle, unless the testimony be of such a kind, that its falsehood would be more miraculous, than the fact, which it endeavours to establish . . .' (*Enquiry,* 116: 123; quotation marks in original)

It is in large measure due to Professor Flew (op. cit., Chapter VIII) that there can now be no excuse for ignoring Hume's all too easily ignored official restrictions and reservations on this argument. In the first place it does not set out to demonstrate that certain conceivable events, whether called miracles or not, are logically impossible. Thus Hume is not abandoning, out of prejudice against miracles or for any other reason, his fundamental thesis that 'The contrary of every matter of fact is still possible; because it can never imply a contradiction, and is conceived by the mind with the same facility and distinctness, as if ever so conformable to reality' (*Enquiry,* 25:40). Even if a miracle is at variance with all known facts, if it is conceivable, like the sun not rising tomorrow, then it is logically possible. The second restriction upon Hume's argument is that it is intended as a check upon superstition[19] not as a demonstration that a miracle could never occur in a religion. Thirdly, the argument is addressed to the wise, to the man who does in fact proportion his belief to the evidence, not to him for whom belief is conditioned by real or imagined factors other than evidence (factors such as election by divine grace). Finally, Hume's argument is concerned with the testimony of witnesses and historians, not with what a man might observe for himself, experimentally reconstruct, or infer from the physical relics of past events.

This last restriction is of great importance and is still being ignored by commentators. Hume's argument tells me that if *I* have seen a miracle I should not expect any reasonable or wise man to believe my report. But my outrage at such scepticism is no objection to Hume (as Newman[20] and Ninian Smart would have it be). Hume is simply warning that incredulity is what I should expect. His argument refers explicitly and totally to the credibility of reports of miracles not to the possibility of actually experiencing one take place. Thus my own experience of seeing water turn into wine is not within the range of his argument. But the report of my experience given to someone else is within its range. From the other person's point of view my experience is simply someone's testimony, and Hume's argument warns me, very realistically I would have thought, that if my experience were very far-fetched I should expect to be pooh-poohed when I tell other people about it. In his otherwise valuable discussion Ninian Smart misconstrues Hume's argument at just this point: 'Hume's general argument, then, fails. We cannot rule out *a priori,* i.e. without recourse to observing the way the world is, the possibility of miracles; and therefore we cannot frame a rule about believing in them which would rule out the legitimacy of believing what we see, if we were to see a miracle'[21] But in Hume's official argument there is no attempt to rule out *a priori* the possibility of miracles or anything else taking place and at no point, not even during incautious over-statements of his position, does he ever rule out the legitimacy of believing what we see. His argument is not about what *we* see but about what *others* tell us that they saw. As such, is it a good argument? I shall argue that it is decisive when applied to weak evidence but indecisive when applied to evidence which would be regarded as conclusive apart from the improbability of what is reported.

When Hume lists the factors which put the veracity of an historical report in question, the effect of his argument is to include among them the probability of the event reported. There is nothing particularly odd about this but it has significant consequences when the report concerns events improbable enough to be called miracles. In such reports the improbability of the event, when measured by our normal experience, is so great that it vitally affects the credibility of the evidence. If, on other grounds, the evidence has already been judged weak then the improbability of the event augments this weakness. In Hume's phraseology, a weak probability (the truth of the report) is confronted with a certainty (our experience that events of the kind reported do not happen) and the wise, or even the mildly stupid man, will not believe the report. In just this sort of way the fabulous or miraculous episodes in a legend, which might in other respects contain elements of historical truth, are readily dismissed: no wise man is going to start looking for the skull of a tall one-eyed man from the evidence contained in Book IX of the *Odyssey*. Likewise no wise father is going to look for the old woman on hands and knees his young son says is crawling round the house, although the father may go out and chase the sheep away. Disbelief, when the report is suspect and what is reported is grossly improbable, is both normal and rational, and Hume's argument does little more than codify this response.

But what happens when the evidence is strong when considered in isolation from the probability of what is evidenced? In such a case, as Hume says (*Enquiry,* 116: 123) the evidential proof is diminished by the strength of my certainty that some things just do not happen. Now it is in this situation, when it is 'supposed that the testimony upon which a miracle is founded may possibly amount to an entire proof' that Hume's argument engenders a little unease. There is an uncomfortable sense that by means of it one may well justify disbelieving reports of things which did in fact happen — like your disbelief in my report of seeing water turned into wine if my report had also been vouched by numerous other good and impartial witnesses. While it is certainly true that when something altogether extraordinary is reported, the wise man will require more evidence than ususal and will check and re-check the evidence very carefully, nevertheless at some stage in his accumulation of respectable evidence the wise man would be in danger of becoming dogmatic and obscurantist if he did *not* believe the evidence. Such dogmatic obscurantism looks capable of some sort of justification according to Hume's argument, and in a few off-duty moments Hume is himself guilty of it. But, as if sensing that his argument could be unconvincing when brought to bear upon evidence which in itself

amounted to a full proof, he begins Part II with what is clearly a premeditated
retraction. As far as miracles are concerned his argument has never been
confronted with evidence which amounted to a full proof: 'it were easy to
shew, that we have been a great deal too liberal in our concession, and that
there never was a miraculous event established on so full an evidence'.
'Never was' is stronger and more difficult to establish than is required in
order to confute the apologetic position adopted by Sherlock, Pearce, Sykes
and the rest, but it has the advantage of comprehending the dangerous
particular case — the Resurrection — without naming it.

The Hume offers four considerations which would justify saying that no
miracle has ever been satisfactorily evidenced. He does not quite say in as
many words that the biblical narratives in general and the Resurrection
story in particular are unsatisfactory and weak as evidence when judged by
these, but he does come as close to saying this as a prudent regard to the
contemporary state of law and opinion would allow. Thus, as I have already
pointed out, at several points in the chapter he adverts to the case of a man
rising from the dead and, lest any doubt should remain about the application
of his argument, he finally invites his readers to consider the Pentateuch
'according to the measures of probability above established'.

The first consideration which leads Hume to say that a miracle never
has been supported by conclusively strong evidence is just a list of tough-
minded requirements for such evidence. Hume bluntly says these have never
been satisfied. They include guarantees against delusion, deception and
falsehood concerning events 'performed in such a public manner, and in so
celebrated a part of the world, as to render the detection unavoidable'. In
the light of modern scholarship it might seem absurd to expect the biblical
narratives to satisfy such requirements and it should come as no surprise to
us when Hume implies that the biblical narratives do not satisfy the
requirements. But Hume's background was a theology which took the
Gospels as straightforward factual reports. Against *that* background it would
be quite in order (as Sherlock shows) to expect the Gospels to satisfy tough
evidence criteria and to be shocked if it is said or implied that they do not.

The second develops an old observation about human credulity. Although
belief in a wise man is fixed by evidence, there is in human nature an
irrational interest in and love of the marvellous. As Scott was to observe a
little later — 'such is our natural love for the marvellous, that we willingly
contribute our own efforts to beguile our better judgements'. In just such a
way could we account for the spread of stories about the odd, strange,
interesting or marvellous.

But if the spirit of religion join itself to the love of wonder,
there is an end of common sense . . . A religionist may be an enthusiast,
and imagine he şees what has no reality: He may know his narrative to be
false, and yet persevere in it, with the best intentions in the world, for the
sake of promoting so holy a cause (*Enquiry,* 47:25).

The remark about enthusiastic self-deception is of particular importance in relation to what C. D. Broad calls the indirect evidence for the Resurrection:

> The direct testimony for this event appears to me to be very feeble . . . But the indirect evidence is much stronger. We have testimony to the effect that the disciples were exceedingly depressed at the time of the Crucifixion; that they had extremely little faith in the future; and that, after a certain time, this depression disappeared, and they believed that they had evidence that their Master had risen from the dead.[22]

As already indicated, a good part of Sherlock's case rests on indirect evidence of this sort and the possibility of enthusiastic self-deception is one of Hume's few available counters to it apart from questioning the *entire* record of events (which, it seems to me, he does in fact wish to do).

The third consideration which leads Hume to say there never was a miracle established on full evidence is the way in which miraculous narratives are devalued by abounding among primitive and barbarous peoples and in 'the first histories of all nations'. So common are miracles in such histories (and so easily dismissed by the wise) that in the essay 'Of the Authenticity of Ossian's Poems' Hume is able to make the *lack* of miracles in the narrations an objection to their authenticity: 'Why is this characteristic wanting, so essential to rude and ignorant ages? . . . the incidents, if you will pardon the antithesis, are the most unnatural, merely because they are natural'.

The fourth consideration is what I shall call the Contrary Miracles Argument. It is this:

> that, in matters of religion, whatever is different is contrary; and that it is impossible the religions of ancient Rome, of Turkey, of Siam and of China should, all of them, be established on any solid foundation. Every miracle, therefore, pretended to have been wrought in any of these religions (and all of them abound in miracles), as its direct scope is to establish the particular system to which it is attributed; so it has the same force, though more indirectly, to overthrow every other system. In destroying a rival system, it likewise destroys the credit of those miracles, on which that system was established; so that all the prodigies of different religions are to be regarded as contrary facts, and the evidences of these prodigies, whether weak or strong, as opposite to each other (*Enquiry*, 121:129).

Hume's paraphrase of this argument is perhaps clearer than the original: 'If a miracle proves a doctrine to be revealed from God, and consequently true, a miracle can never be wrought for a contrary doctrine. The facts are therefore as incompatible as the doctrines' (*Letters*, I, 350).

A formal version of the argument would, I think, be as follows: A set of miracles m_1 is claimed to establish the truth of the religion (or doctrine)

R_1. Another set of miracles m_2 is claimed — presumably by different people — to establish the truth of another religion (or doctrine) R_2. R_1 and R_2 are contraries, that is, such that they cannot both be true but could both be false. Hence m_1 and m_2 cannot both have occurred. Hence whatever evidence substantiates m_1 detracts from — is contrary to — the evidence which substantiates m_2 and vice versa. As Broad (op. cit.) observes, there is in this a suppressed premise — 'that miracles *only* occur in connexion with *true* religion' — but this is of course not an illicit assumption of Hume's. It is also a suppressed premise in the argument from miracles which forms the mainstay of the position Hume is attacking. Thus by means of the Contrary Miracles Argument Hume contrives to show that when miracles are used to confirm some religion, the evidence for such miracles is not only diminished by the force of our everyday experience, but also by whatever evidence can be produced in favour of the miracles which might confirm some contrary religion.

The Contrary Miracles Argument is particularly applicable to Christianity. This is because the miracles associated with early Christianity appear to have been regarded from the very beginning (and not merely in eighteenth-century misunderstandings of Christianity) as signs of the truth of what was being preached. Thus at the conclusion of Mark's Gospel it is said: 'And they went forth, and preached every where, the Lord working with them, and confirming the word with signs following'. Even Jesus is reported to have warned against misleading miracles: 'For false Christs and false prophets shall rise, and shall shew signs and wonders, to seduce, if it were possible, even the elect' (Mark, XIII, 22). Samuel Clarke is thus in no way unorthodox or historically unusual when he specified the purpose of miracles as '. . . for the Proof or Evidence of some particular Doctrine, or in attestation to the Authority of some particular Person'.[23] But it might be argued that the biblical miracles do not confirm *particular* doctrines, such as transubstantiation or the doctrine of the Trinity, but the general system of Christianity. This is precisely the point. They confirm, and were always taken to confirm, the general system of one religion as opposed to another: Christianity as opposed to the religion of Zoroaster or Mithras for example. Now while it might be possible to allow at the same time the general claims of, say, the religion of Olympus and the religion of Valhalla, this is not possible in the case of monotheistic religions of the Christian type. The Christian religion contains within itself a claim to uniqueness — 'there is but *one* true and living God. . . .' The crux of the matter is that the claims of the early church about its God made him existentially incompatible with all other gods. The miracles associated with different religions do not all merely show, as Richard Swinburne suggests, 'that there is a god concerned with the needs of those who worship'.[24] At least for the Christian, evidence of the activity of his God is evidence of the non-existence of the gods of Olympus. These gods *cannot* exist if the Christian God exists and miracles which might appear to confirm their activity cannot have taken place if the Christian

miracles took place. In this way the evidence for the occurrence of a
Christian miracle and the evidence for the occurrence of a pagan miracle
form contrary pieces of evidence which, from the point of view of the
uncommitted, detract from each other.[25]

But there are at least two replies to the Contrary Miracles Argument
which need to be taken into account.[26] The first is that R_1 and R_2 being
contraries does not show that m_1 and m_2 (the occurrences which are
evidence for R_1 and R_2) are contraries. Two theories may be such that they
cannot both be true. But the overthrow of one does not show that the
phenomena explained by it — the evidence for it — are not genuine phenomena.
I would agree, provided 'evidence' and 'theory' in religion were related to
each other as they are normally related in the sciences. But in the Christian
use of the argument from miracles, miracles and the existence of God are
not related as evidence and theory in science. The claim is that the miracle
can occur if and only if it is brought about by the one true God (cf. *John*,
III, 2). It is God and God alone who can bring about a miracle and if the
claim is made that a miracle has taken place in a religion incompatible with
Christianity, then whatever evidence substantiates that claim diminishes the
evidence that a Christian miracle has taken place and vice versa. The second
reply to the Contrary Miracles Argument is that the old-fashioned Christian
could allow that, as demons, the Olympians could perform (rather scruffy)
miracles. But of course *this* upsets not only the Contrary Miracles Argument
but also the whole rationale of using miracles to validate a revelation.

Now if the New Testament — and not just the Pentateuch as Hume tact-
fully suggests — is examined, not as the testimony 'of God himself, who
conducted the pen of the inspired writers', but 'as the production of a mere
human writer and historian', what happens? Manifestly the narratives cannot
satisfy the tough-minded criteria for evidence which Hume first produces.
The early spread of Christianity in Roman society *could* be accounted for
by enthusiastic self-deception together with the interest always excited by
the marvellous or odd. Christianity *did* start among uncultured and uncritical
people in a remote part of the Roman world, and, because of the exclusivist
'one true God' claims of the early Church, Christianity *is* subject to the
Contrary Miracles Argument. But of course none of this would be very new
or shocking, at least to modern German New Testament scholars. With the
exception of contrary miracles it is exactly the sort of thing which they have
been saying in vast detail throughout the present century. As C. S. Peirce
remarks 'The whole of modern "higher criticism" of ancient history in
general, and of Biblical history in particular, is based upon the same logic
that is used by Hume'.[27]

Thus Hume's contention at the beginning of Part II, that the evidence for
a miracle has never amounted to a full proof, if not capable of justification for
all cases, is at least justified when applied to the miracles which really
matter: the biblical miracles in general and the Resurrection miracle in
particular. This being so, the full force of Hume's original argument, as it

applied to weak evidence, can be turned upon the Resurrection narrative, that is, upon the keystone of eighteenth-century attempts to show that the Christian Revelation was so well-authenticated that it could not be rejected by any rational and unbiased man:

> It is experience only, which gives authority to human testimony; and it is the same experience, which assures us of the laws of nature. When, therefore, these two kinds of experience are contrary, we have nothing to do but subtract the one from the other, and embrace an opinion, either on one side or the other with that assurance which arises from the remainder. But according to the principle here explained, this subtraction, with regard to all popular religions,[28] amounts to an entire annihiliation; and therefore we may establish it as a maxim, that no human testimony can have such force as to prove a miracle, and make it a just foundation for any such system of religion (*Enquiry*, 127:137).

What Hume does not do in this argument, what he does not need to do, and what it may not be possible to do, is to show that miracles could never happen and that the evidence for a miracle could never be credible to a rational man. But giving his argument the limited application which it requires in order to upset the position of eighteenth-century rational apologists (and modern fundamentalists) it does all that Hume could have required of it. This success is however achieved by playing down the occasional extravagances in Hume's statements, by giving more weight than he himself always gives to the restrictions on his argument, and by ignoring the contentious points which have always proved an irresistible fly-paper to the passing philosopher.

(iii)   LAWS OF NATURE

Among the incautious, possibly incorrect, and certainly debatable items which appear in 'Of Miracles' the following stand out: Hume's inference that if an event happened more than once it would not be a miracle; the conflict between his own account of laws of nature and the definition of a miracle which he quotes; his apparent gaffe in talking about the 'absolute impossibility' of an event and his over-hasty dismissal of the evidence for unusual events which may indeed have happened whether or not they warrant the title 'miracle'.

The most detailed definition of a miracle which Hume offers is in the footnote on p.115:123: '*a transgression of a law of nature by a particular volition of the Deity, or by the interposition of some invisible agent*'. In the main text, just preceding this note, he remarks: 'Nothing is esteemed a miracle, if it ever happen in the common course of nature' and 'There must, therefore, be a uniform experience against every miraculous event, otherwise

the event would not merit that appellation'. These observations contain both
a mistake and an insight. The mistake is in thinking that an event would not be
a miracle if it happened more than once. But if due weight is given to a
miracle being a particular volition of the Deity it is manifestly possible that
the Deity, like all lesser agents, is able to will the same thing more than once,
and, if resurrections are miracles and took place as reported, he *has* willed
the same thing more than once (Jesus, Lazarus and Jairus' daughter). The
insight, on the other hand, is in noticing that no happening 'in the common
course of nature' could be called a miracle even if, in some way, it could be
known to be a regular volition of the Deity. To be recognised a miracle has
to be a *particular* volition. To mortal man a *regular* volition would be
indistinguishable from a law of nature. If occasionalism were true, no
miracle could be recognised, which is as good as to say, no miracle could
happen.

But for anyone already believing in a god who works miracles, the
possible repetition of a miracle and our inability to recognise a miracle
occurring in the common course of nature, are not in any real, practical,
conflict. Providing the Deity does not will resurrections for a significant
proportion of men within three days of their deaths it seems perfectly
possible to preserve the universal generalisation that death is forever except
for the three or four occasions when the Deity has particularly willed it
otherwise. These particular occasions, the believer may say, no more
invalidate the universal generalisation than a man picking up a stone
invalidates the law of gravity. But the case is different for a man who does not
already believe in a god who works miracles. A unique event which his devout
friend calls a miracle may ultimately have to be just accepted by the sceptic
as an unpalatable aberration in the nature of things. But an odd event repeated
several times would almost certainly be taken as a challenge to explanations
of the way the world works: revise your old explanations or devise new ones
to account for the repeating oddity. Thus faith healings appear to constitute
a sufficiently numerous and well-attested class of events for the sceptic to
look seriously for the conditions which produce them quite apart from
reference to repeated volitions of the deity. The difficulty for the believer
occurs when the sceptic comes up with a sufficient explanation for the odd
events he is investigating. The believer then has to face the alternatives of
retracting his judgement that the odd events were miracles or revising his
definition of what constitutes a miracle so that an explainable event can still
'be seen to have religious significance' or something of that sort. The believer
in miracles is always vulnerable to this sort of attack but he is much less
liable to be attacked if his miracle constitutes a unique event rather than one
of a class of oddities.

The second debatable topic in 'Of Miracles' is the tension between Hume's
own account of what constitutes a law of nature and the definition of a
miracle. For Hume, a law of nature is, very roughly, the way in which we
describe what always happens in our experience together with an expectation

that our experience will be the same in the future as it has been in the past. In 'Of Miracles' this appears simply as 'a firm and unalterable experience has established these laws'. (Even here there is an incipient mistake. The word 'unalterable', although possibly justifiable on some account of the laws of nature, is not justifiable on Hume's. What he should have written is something like 'unvaried'.) Now if a miracle is 'a transgression of a law of nature' this simply means it is at variance with all our past experience and consequently with our expectations. But an event of this sort could equally well be either a transgression of a law of nature or an indication that our experience has not been sufficiently extensive for us to be able to formulate the laws of nature correctly; what we have could be either a miracle or a very uncommon natural event. Flew puts his finger right on the crucial point when he writes: 'Hume can provide no conception of a law of nature sufficiently strong to allow for any real distinction between the miraculous and the extremely unusual' (op. cit., p. 204). But of course (a point Flew does not miss) the converse of what is a weakness in Hume's account of laws of nature is a weakness in the religious man's definition of a miracle as 'a transgression of a law of nature' etc. It is incumbent upon *him* to be able to identify a transgression of a law of nature which results from a particular volition of the deity and to differentiate it from the odd event which can safely be left to the scientist to absorb into an amended statement of the laws. Hume on the other hand does not really *need* to make this highly complex and problematic distinction (albeit that he could not), but to the believer in miracles it is of the utmost importance. Nevertheless Hume does pitch headlong into a somewhat similar distinction which he is just as unentitled to make. It is the distinction between what could happen and what is 'absolutely impossible'.

It is as clear as anything could be that in his own person Hume strenuously and totally disbelieved in miracles. This disbelief breaks through his official argument both in an over-hasty rejection of his own examples and in two appeals to the impossibility of something happening. The first of these occurs when he is considering the miracles performed at the tomb of the Abbé Paris. He concludes 'And what have we to oppose such a cloud of witnesses, but the absolute impossibility or miraculous nature of the events, which they relate? And this surely, in the eyes of all reasonable people, will alone be regarded as a sufficient refutation'. The second occurs in his invented resurrection of Elizabeth I — 'I should only assert [her death] to have been pretended, and that it neither was, nor possibly could be real'. How should these outbursts be interpreted?

The interpretation which has provoked most discussion is that Hume is appealing to a distinction between the very unusual and the totally impossible which, like the distinction between the marvellous and the miraculous, he is simply not in a position to make. The distinction is doubly unfortunate from Hume's point of view. On the one hand he almost seems to say, as R. C. Wallace puts it, 'that occurrences are to be ruled out as impossible, solely on the grounds that they would conflict with the scientists' nomologicals',[29]

and Hume can give no sufficient account of such nomologicals. (It is an open
question whether anyone has or could, but that is not to the point.) On
the other hand if he is in fact using 'law of nature' as 'firm and *unalterable*
experience' (that is, with a different meaning to that employed in the rest
of his philosophy), then, again in Wallace's words, he is 'using a line of
argument which would exclude not only miracles, but also events which at
present appear to be anomalous and inexplicable, but which may in time be
incorporated into our pattern of explanation' (op. cit., p. 236). In short,
Hume's account of the laws of nature is either too weak to facilitate the
distinction which he seems to use between the impossible and the unusual or
too strong to admit the unusual when the unusual is a genuine indication
that the laws of nature should be re-formulated.

   In an exceedingly interesting attempt to find a way out of this difficulty,
Flew (op. cit., p. 186f) suggests that when Hume talks about the impossibility
of an event he is talking about physical impossibility and 'the criterion of
physical as opposed to logical impossibility simply is logical incompatibility
with a law of nature, in the broadest sense'.

> The qualification *in the broadest sense* is necessary. The expression *law of
> nature* is sometimes taken as a prerogative of science. Whereas the notion
> of physical or empirical impossibility is quite untechnical, and surely
> antedates the emergence of science proper. . . . It is only and precisely our
> knowledge, or presumed knowledge, of such nomological propositions
> which enables us to make the ordinary lay distinction between the immense-
> ly improbable and the sheerly impossible.

Now in speaking of 'absolute impossibility' it is unreasonable to presume that
Hume is suddenly and inconsistently abandoning his distinction between
matters of fact whose negation is conceivable and relations of ideas whose
negation is not, in other words, he is not attempting to say that certain
events are *logically* impossible. The impossibility he is talking about almost
certainly is something like what Flew calls physical impossibility. But the
questions are, is Hume entitled to talk about such impossibility and in what
sense does such impossibility entail that certain conceivable events could not
happen? In answer to the first question it would seem that Hume is just as
entitled as anyone else to use the lay distinction between the highly
improbable and the absolutely impossible. It is just impossible for me to be
beheaded and then for the headless body to get up an hour later and walk
away. It is just impossible for the sun to stand still in the sky in response to
the fiat of a man. These things are equally impossible in my understanding of
the world and in Hume's. They simply do not happen in the nature of things
and there is nothing in Hume's account of the laws of nature (as invariable
experience plus strong expectation) which prevents him from saying they are
impossible in the sense of *do not happen*. But does impossibility of this sort
mean that these things *could not happen*? Since logical impossibility is ruled

out, the force of 'could not' can only be either an emphatic and deceptive repetition of 'do not' or shorthand for a statement of the sort 'is logically incompatible with a universal statement to which we attribute a law-like· character'. The second of these alternatives does not however get us very close to the notion of 'could not happen'. The difficulty is in the word 'attribute' and it is one which has already shown up in Flew's phrase 'knowledge, or presumed knowledge'. Our attribution could be incorrect, and if our knowledge could be presumed knowledge, it could also be false belief. The point is that, once formulated, our nomologicals certainly imply the physical impossibility of events incompatible with them, but their real authority to say certain events could not happen is no better than the evidence which has been used to establish the nomologicals in the first place. But there is no means of knowing that such evidence is of the sort (whatever that sort would be) which could give the nomological the pseudo-logical strength which it would require in order to rule out certain events as physically impossible in the sense of *could not happen*. Consider an example. Hume could have said (with complete justification) that it was physically impossible, according to the best nomologicals at his disposal, for a man in England to be able to talk to and see a man who is at the same time in America. Now if he had taken this to mean 'it could not happen that . . .' then we would simply retort it *has* happened. In short, if we are to employ the notion of physical impossibility, the most this can mean is that: within 'our' experience of the world the event has not happened, nor are we able to conceive how it could happen, nor could it possibly happen *if* the laws of nature have in fact the form and content which we attribute to them. What force then has such impossibility got as used by a 'just reasoner' against a report of a miracle? No more force than Hume's original argument that the event is against all our past and what we presume to be our invariable experience. That is, there is a strong and rational presumption against the event but not a demonstration of its 'absolute impossibility' in any sense of that phrase in which it can be taken to imply *'could not happen'*. When Hume is on his guard he shows himself perfectly well aware of this:

> I beg the limitations here made may be remarked, when I say, that a miracle can never be proved, so as to be the foundation of a system of religion. For I own, that otherwise, there may possibly be miracles, or violations of the usual course of nature, of such a kind as to admit of proof from human testimony; though, perhaps, it will be impossible to find any such in all the records of history (*Enquiry*, 127:137)

Hume's 'absolute impossibility' is thus merely a robust appeal to the familiar and useful notion of 'physical impossibility' where that is construed in such a way that it does *not* entail that the impossible event *could not* happen — however confident we may be that in fact it will not happen.

If all this seems over-subtle and refined a much simpler interpretation is available: In Hume's observation about laws of nature the word 'unalterable' should have been 'unvaried'. The 'impossibility' gaffes are nothing but overstatements of his official argument brought on by his enthusiastic disbelief in miracles. They are at variance with his official argument and its appendage that *in fact* 'there never was' a miracle founded on good evidence. They are at variance with what he needs to establish in confronting the apologetic position of Sherlock and the rest. They are, in their simplest and most obvious meaning, at variance with his own philosophical position about matters of fact and they are minute points in a much longer argument.

However the most objectionable aspect of the chapter consists not in Hume's proper or improper appeals to physical impossibility, but in his precipitate readiness to play the Indian Prince and dismiss events which could very well have happened (and not even be miracles) solely on the grounds that they do not conform to his rather imperfect grasp of what constitute laws of nature. It is not that *we* have a perfect grasp of such laws but that, in general, a certain humility about our knowledge seems appropriate. Thus Hume's impatient dismissal of the Abbé Paris cures and of the Vespasian cure of the blind man seems both obscurantist and unnecessary and quite a lot else in the tone of the chapter conveys a sense of undue and slightly arrogant confidence about what is or is not physically possible.

*   *   *

'Of Miracles' has received more critical attention than anything else Hume wrote on religion. Its particular merits may not justify this but its importance in his whole critique of religion within the limits of reason alone can scarcely be over-estimated. It is the only piece in which he systematically attacks the reasonableness of belief in revealed religion. He does so by means of an argued rejection of the thesis that miracles in general and the Resurrection in particular authenticate the Christian revelation in a manner which should satisfy any reasonable man. But despite this and his highly critical survey of the arguments of natural religion he does not say that no reasonable man can believe in any religion. A reasonable man can have a belief which goes beyond the evidence, but his belief will subvert 'all the principles of his understanding' and be brought home to him 'by the immediate operation of the Holy Spirit'. This operation Hume graciously — or sarcastically — leaves undiscussed as, simply, 'a miracle'.

8 Scepticism and Natural Belief

Quod enim omnium·gentium generumque
hominibus ita videretur, id satis magnum
argumentum esse dixisti cur esse deos
confiteremur. Quod cum leve per se
tum etiam falsum est.
                          Cicero, *De Nat. Deo.* I, xxiii

Hume's well argued scepticism with regard to miracles and immortality, his
total rejection of the *a priori* arguments for god's existence, his damaging
critique of the *a posteriori* argument, his use of the problem of evil to question
god's moral attributes, the doubt which he sheds on the meaning of the
language of 'divinity and school metaphysics'; all these lead to the question:
If there are no good and sufficient reasons for belief in god, why is the
belief in him so very widely held? One possible answer, to which I shall
return in Chapter 9, is that there are causes in human nature (psychological,
anthropological, or sociological) which tend to produce belief in god quite
apart from the evidence which might substantiate the belief. Another, and
quite different answer, which I shall now investigate, is that belief in god is
what Hume calls an 'original instinct'. The expressions 'original instinct',
'natural instinct', and 'natural belief' are all used. The first two are Hume's. The
third is his commentators'. The sense is the same in each case. I shall generally
use the expression 'natural belief'. Any occasional preference for either of
the alternatives will be merely a stylistic device to avoid deceptive contrast
or ugly repetition. The doctrine of natural belief is a response by Hume to
some of the unacceptably sceptical positions which he finds himself driven
to by philosophical considerations taken in isolation. I shall first show how
Hume's various subdivisions of scepticism lead to talk about natural belief
as a check on excessive scepticism, and then how his theory of belief leads
to a category of non-rational beliefs which include both irrational and natural
beliefs. I shall then use the results of these investigations to ask what the
defining characteristics of a natural belief are. Finally I shall argue
that belief in god is not a natural belief and hence, for Hume, since it is not
an irrational belief either, it must be a reasonable belief with minimum content.

(i)   VARIETIES OF SCEPTICISM

Most of what Hume has to say about scepticism and quite a lot of what he
has to say about natural belief is to be found in Section XII of the *Enquiry*
and in the Sections on 'Scepticism with Regard to Reason' and 'Scepticism with

Regard to the Senses' in the *Treatise*. There is a mild difference of emphasis on these subjects in the two works but no conflict. Hume returns to the subject of scepticism in Part 1 of the *Dialogues* in order to apply to religion his distinction between excessive and mitigated scepticism.

In the *Enquiry* he rejects extreme Cartesian doubt as a desirable or even possible antecedent to doing philosophy. Such doubt cannot be achieved, and if it were, no one could ever rid himself of it. But there is a more modest version of antecedent scepticism which is of value:

> It must, however, be confessed, that this species of scepticism, when more moderate, may be understood in a very reasonable sense, and is a necessary preparative to the study of philosophy, by preserving a proper impartiality in our judgements, and weaning our mind from all those prejudices, which we may have imbibed from education or rash opinion (*Enquiry,* 150:159).

This account of *antecedent* scepticism presents no philosophical problems and Hume has little more to say about it. But there is, according to Hume, another species of scepticism which is *consequent* upon the pursuit of philosophy (*Enquiry,* 150:159). This has both an acceptable and an unacceptable form. The acceptable form is *mitigated* scepticism. The unacceptable form is *excessive* scepticism.

Mitigated scepticism is the due recognition that certain conclusions are altogether beyond our grasp: 'Our line is too short to fathom such immense abysses'. In the very last sentence of the Appendix to the *Treatise* Hume indicates his approval of this sort of scepticism: 'Nothing is more suitable to that philosophy than a modest scepticism to a certain degree and a fair confession of ignorance in subjects, that exceed all human capacity'.[1] Similarly in the *Enquiry,* 162:170, having just contrasted mitigated scepticism with violent and obstinate dogmatism, Hume remarks: 'Another species of *mitigated* scepticism, which may be of advantage to mankind, and which may be the natural result of Pyrrhonian doubts and scruples [i.e. excessive scepticism], is the limitation of our enquiries to such subjects as are best adapted to the narrow capacity of human understanding'. I have already indicated in Chapter 5 by what means Hume hoped to mark out those areas which are beyond the capacity of human understanding. Certainly dogmatic theology (but not necessarily belief in god) is one of them: 'The whole is a riddle, an enigma, an inexplicable mystery. Doubt, uncertainly, suspense of judgement appear the only result of our most accurate scrutiny, concerning this subject' (*N.H.R.,* 76). The reference of 'this subject' is not absolutely clear but must be something like the theological disputes he has just been talking about.

Mitigated scepticism is thus the wise and apt recognition that in certain metaphysical and theological disputes no conclusion is possible because the whole subject matter lies outside the range of possible knowledge. For

example: 'It seems to me, that this theory of the universal energy and operation of the Supreme Being, is too bold ever to carry conviction with it to a
man, sufficiently apprized of the weakness of human reason, and the narrow
limits, to which it is confined in all its operations' *(Enquiry,* 72:83). But
these areas of futile dispute in metaphysics and theology are perfectly remote
from all common life and experience *(Enquiry,* 72:83). We may be sceptical
with regard to *them* without undermining any of our knowledge of 'matters
of fact' or 'relations of ideas'.

Excessive or *Pyrrhonian scepticism* on the other hand is the extravagant
and inappropriate despair which not only acknowledges the limitations of
human understanding but also abandons all confidence in even the most
commonsense beliefs about the world:

> There is another species of scepticism, *consequent* to science and enquiry,
> when men are supposed to have discovered, either the absolute fallacious-
> ness of their mental faculties, or their unfitness to reach any fixed
> determination in all those curious subjects of speculation, about which
> they are commonly employed. Even our very senses are brought into
> dispute, by a certain species of philosophers; and the maxims of common
> life are subjected to the same doubt as the most profound principles or
> conclusions of metaphysics and theology *(Enquiry,* 150:159).

At one stage Hume had been a victim of such excessive scepticism:

> The *intense* view of these manifold contradictions and imperfections in
> human reason has so wrought upon me, and heated my brain, that I am
> ready to reject all belief and reasoning, and can look upon no opinion
> even as more probable or likely than another . . . I begin to fancy myself
> in the most deplorable condition imaginable, inviron'd with the deepest
> darkness, and utterly depriv'd of the use of every member and faculty
> *(Treatise,* 268-69).

The psychological antidote to this anguish and confusion is simple. Since
philosophy cannot dispel the doubts, practical life must. Hume recommends
the treatment thus: 'I dine, I play a game of back-gammon, I converse, and
am merry with my friends; and when after three or four hours' amusement,
I wou'd return to these speculations, they appear so cold, and strain'd and
ridiculous, that I cannot find in my heart to enter into them farther
(Treatise, 269). In the *Enquiry* the same antidote is recommended more
succinctly: 'The great subverter of *Pyrrhonism* or the excessive principles of
scepticism, is action, and employment, and the occupations of common
life' (p. 158: 167).

The philosophical antidote on the other hand involves a robust practical
check to the pretensions of metaphysical and sceptical argument. It is the
doctrine of natural belief. A natural belief is one which in practical life

cannot be abandoned and which we *all* hold and are absolutely justified in holding (*Dialogues,* 134) irrespective of philosophical objections. An example of such a belief would be belief in the continuous existence of an external world independent of my perceptions. If, on analysis, it appears that neither reason nor sense experience can confirm this belief, then this does not mean that the belief should or even could be abandoned since without it practical life in the ordinary world would be impossible. Though the belief be false, "tis the most natural of any, and has alone any primary recommendation to the fancy'. It must be emphasised that a natural belief can only be a check to *excessive* scepticism — which is just that sort of scepticism which threatens to destroy our most fundamental, practical, commonsense beliefs about the world, (i.e. our natural beliefs). These specially sacrosanct beliefs cannot check, would indeed have nothing to say about, *mitigated* scepticism — scepticism which says in effect that some subjects are too abstruse and remote from common life and experience for us to form any view of them. Thus excessive scepticism *is* doubting natural belief. Natural belief cannot be doubted in practice. Hence excessive scepticism is untenable.

(ii) REASONABLE BELIEF

Hume's remarks on belief are scattered throughout his philosophical writings but major clusters of them occur in *Treatise,* 94-106, *Treatise,* 628-629 (the Appendix) and *Enquiry,* 47-55:61-68. A passage from the *Treatise* (which he repeats verbatim in the *Enquiry*) contains the main outline of his final[2] theory:

> . . . 'tis evident, that belief consists not in the nature and order of our ideas, but in the manner of their conception, and in their feeling to the mind. I confess, that 'tis impossible to explain perfectly this feeling or manner of conception. We may make use of words, that express something near it. But its true and proper name is *belief,* which is a term that every one sufficiently understands in common life.[3] And in philosophy we can go no farther, than assert, that it is some thing *felt* by the mind, which distinguishes the ideas of the judgement from the fictions of the imagination. It gives them more force and influence; makes them appear of greater importance; infixes them in the mind; and renders them the governing principles of all our actions (*Treatise,* 629; *Enquiry,* 49: 63).

And again: 'It follows, therefore, that the difference between *fiction* and *belief* lies in some sentiment or feeling, which is annexed to the latter, not to the former, and which depends not on the will, nor can be commanded[4] at pleasure'. It is axiomatic for Hume that while I may *imagine* what I please, I cannot *believe* something at will: 'We can, in our conception, join the head of a man to the body of a horse; but it is not in our power to believe that such an animal has ever really existed' (*Enquiry,* 48:61).

In his account of belief Hume thus adopts a position characterised by the following points: (a) The word 'belief' signifies an attitude to or feeling about what is believed. This attitude or feeling can be recognised (introspectively) but is difficult to characterise further. (b) The belief-feeling or attitude influences action. (c) The belief-feeling or attitude cannot be commanded at will.

Leaving aside most of the usual criticisms of this position, it remains clear that there are problems in it for anyone wishing to distinguish between *reasonable* beliefs on the one hand and *irrational* or *unreasonable* beliefs on the other: a distinction of great importance in any account of natural beliefs since such beliefs are in a certain sense non-rational. (I shall use the term 'non-rational' whenever it is unnecessary to draw attention to sub-distinctions of the non-rational implied by the words 'irrational', 'unreasonable' etc.).

Problem A. If believing *P* consists in having a belief-feeling for *P*, this belief-feeling will presumably be the same whether the belief is reasonable or non-rational. How then should reasonable and non-rational beliefs be distinguished?

Problem B. If belief is some attitude which cannot be given or withheld at will, 'Hume seems to be leaving no room for the possibilities either of legitimately criticising people for holding irrational beliefs, or of altering our own beliefs or those of others with the help of argument'.[5]

Some of the teeth of problem A can be drawn by admitting that for the believer there is *no* difference between the belief-feeling for a reasonable belief and the belief-feeling for a non-rational one. Both are his beliefs and their rationality depends upon something other than the manner in which they are entertained. Upon what does it depend? Hume does not say, but he does not *prevent* us from saying (unoriginally) that the rationality of a belief depends (a) upon the person's ability to justify his belief that *P* (the justification involving the production of reasons or evidence that *P* is the case, or the pleading of successful action undertaken on the presumption that *P* is the case) and (b) upon the person's ability to *modify* the belief-feeling for *P* in the face of fresh evidence. But according to problem B this modification is just what the believer cannot undertake at will. Now there is no doubt that Hume, like everyone else, does wish to distinguish between reasonable and non-rational beliefs, 'weaning our mind from all those pre-judices, which we may have imbibed from education or rash opinion' (*Enquiry*, 150:159). What account then can be given, within Hume's theory of belief, of a reasonable man altering his beliefs in the light of fresh evidence?

Consider an example: if I truly announce 'I believe I shall be killed if I enter an aeroplane', then Hume is *right* in saying I cannot at will abandon my belief-feeling about this proposition. The belief stole in on me over a longish period, unnoticed and unreasoned, and I cannot shake it off when it suits me to do so. Nor can I decide to adopt a belief (say, belief in god) in the way in which I could, presumably, decide to *think* about the existence of god. But what can happen (and this is the part of the story which Hume does not specifically mention although what he says allows for it) is that various considerations such as accident statistics can be put before me which might be expected to result in a modification of my belief about the danger of flying. I do not at this stage *decide* to change my belief-feeling, but I attend to the evidence which tells against what I believe and if my belief satisfies the conditions for what is called 'reasonable' belief, my belief-feeling will be found to alter. This situation is exactly paralleled in Hume's account of ethical disputes. If I say 'X is wrong' and you say 'X is right' this means that I approve of X and you disapprove. I cannot decide to change my approval, but on hearing and agreeing with your account of the misery produced by X, my feeling of approval may wear off and become one of disapproval *provided* that my ethical view is reasonably based. (See, for example, *Moral Enquiry*, 180:13.)

Likewise my belief-feeling cannot be changed at will but if it has as its object a reasonable belief it can change as a result of my attention to and assessment of the evidence, and such attention is voluntary. There are of course numerous well-tried methods of preventing modification of the belief-feeling — for example, giving attention to a partial selection of evidence or by 'forgetting' that one's reasons for the belief are insufficient — but these do not alter the general case that with reasonable belief the belief-feeling occurs or fails to occur or is modified as the involuntary accompaniment of an honest assessment of the evidence. If we wish to call this assessment 'deciding to believe' (or 'deciding not to believe') this would probably be in conformity with ordinary usage, but it would also, according to Hume, muddle an important distinction between the evidence which I can review at will and the belief-feeling which I cannot.

There are however a number of beliefs, according to Hume, which are *not* the resultant of a conscious rational assessment of evidence and which are *not* upset by such an assessment except in brief moments of 'philosophical melancholy and delirium' (*Treatise*, 260).

> It seems evident, that men are carried, by a natural instinct or prepossession, to repose faith in their senses; and that, without any reasoning, or even almost before the use of reason, we always suppose an external universe, which depends not on our perception, but would exist, though we and every sensible creature were absent or annihilated (*Enquiry*, 151:160).

They are, as he says, 'a species of natural instincts, which no reasoning or process of the thought and understanding is able either to produce or prevent' (*Enquiry*, 47:60). Nevertheless one does not wish to call these beliefs either irrational or unreasonable although they may be non-rational. They belong to the class of beliefs which Hume sometimes speaks of as 'original instincts' — that is, the class of natural beliefs which have already been encountered as Hume's philosophical check to excessive scepticism.

In summary: there are, according to Hume, two types of belief:
(1) Those in which thinking and assessing influence the belief-feeling. These
are reasonable beliefs. (2) Those in which thinking and assessing do not
influence the belief-feeling. These are non-rational beliefs. Among non-
rational beliefs, some, called natural beliefs, are in some way justifiable.
The rest are in a straightforward way irrational or unreasonable. Three
questions now occur: which beliefs are to count as natural beliefs? What
characteristics do they have which make them natural beliefs rather than
irrational or unreasonable beliefs? What is this 'justification' which is strong
enough to check excessive scepticism and yet manages to side-step the
normal demand for reasons and evidence?

(iii)   NATURAL BELIEF

Hume distinguishes at least three[6] 'species of natural instincts' or 'natural
beliefs':

(1) Belief in the continuous existence of an external world independent
of our perception of that world (*Enquiry,* 151: 160, etc.)
(2) Belief that the regularities which have occurred in our experience form
a reliable guide to those which will occur.
(3) Belief in the reliability of our senses qualified to take account of
acknowledged and isolatable areas of deception and confusion (many
locations). Professor R. J. Butler[7] would add a fourth belief: Belief in an
orderly universe stemming from an agent designer commonly called god. I do
not think this belief is a natural belief nor that Hume regarded it as one, but
these points will be discussed later. Now what is it that makes these beliefs
natural beliefs in Hume's sense?

According to Butler (p. 78) 'Hume indicates that natural beliefs are
non-rational, that they have a certain degree of force, and that they are
unavoidable'. In the subsequent discussion he points out that the first of these
considerations does not separate natural beliefs from irrational beliefs while
the second is not a distinguishing mark because according to Hume it is a
characteristic of all beliefs. The third on the other hand is one which Hume
never abandons although he might be forced into the position of admitting
that not all natural beliefs are true. Unfortunately Butler does not explain
in what sense natural beliefs are unavoidable, nor, it appears to me, does he
state all their characteristics. This I shall now try to do.

If we examine Hume's list of natural beliefs and what he has to say about
them we find that they have four distinctive characteristics, namely:

First, they are beliefs of naive commonsense. Hume would argue that
philosophical conclusions must therefore keep close to them: 'philosophical
decisions are nothing but the reflections of common life, methodized and
corrected' (*Enquiry,* 162: 170, see also *Dialogues,* 134).

Secondly, if their rational basis is probed very closely — as Hume probes it — then, according to Hume, if one takes a certain strong sense of the word 'rational' there is no rational justification for holding them: they are non-rational but not irrational or unreasonable beliefs (*Enquiry*, 153:162, etc.).

Thirdly, neither the excessively sceptical philosopher, nor anyone else, can *act* in the world unless he has these beliefs of naive common sense. This is the vital point which makes these beliefs 'unavoidable' and it is their absolute justification. Hume is very emphatic about it in more than one of his works: 'Here I find myself absolutely and necessarily determined to live, and talk, and act like other people in the common affairs of life' (*Treatise*, 269; see also *Treatise* 183, 184, 187, 193, 197, 213, 216, 273, etc.). The same point is made in the *Enquiry* with the conciseness usually displayed in the later work:

> Nature is always too strong for principle . . . [And Pyrrhonian scepticism] can have no other tendency than to show the whimsical condition of mankind, who must *act and reason and believe*; though they are not able, by their most diligent enquiry, to satisfy themselves concerning the foundation of these operations, or to remove the objections, which may be raised against them (*Enquiry*, 160:168-9 (my italics); see also *A Letter*, 19).

Significantly this same point is brought out very forcibly by Philo at the beginning of the *Dialogues* and is never controverted by any other speaker: 'To whatever length any one may push his speculative principles of scepticism, he must act, I own, and live, and converse like other men; and for this conduct he is not obliged to give any other reason than the absolute necessity he lies under of so doing' (*Dialogues*, 134). If, in a moment of 'philosophical melancholy and delirium', one loses these beliefs then one can only remain in a state of paralysed non-communication with the world, 'utterly depriv'd of the use of every member and faculty' (*Treatise*, 269).

Fourthly, and this is a consequence of the third, these beliefs are universally, if inarticulately, held. For example, *everyone* acts as if there were an independent, continuous physical world.

In short, natural beliefs are beliefs of naive common sense. They are non-rational but necessary as a precondition of action, and they are universally held. Which of these criteria distinguish natural beliefs from irrational or unreasonable beliefs?

(a) As with irrational beliefs there is inability to produce good evidence that the belief is true. *But,* unlike irrational beliefs, there is no evidence which makes it more reasonable to adopt any alternative set of beliefs. The sceptical criticism of natural beliefs establishes no others in their place (*Enquiry*, Section XII).

(b) Unlike irrational beliefs there *is* justification for acting as if they are true. The justification is the discovery that there is no other course open to us. If we do not act as if these beliefs are true, we do not act at all. As Hume remarks in the *Abstract*[8] ' . . . upon the whole [our Author] concludes, that we assent to our faculties, and employ our reason only because we cannot help it'. This is why excessive scepticism — scepticism with regard to natural belief — cannot be maintained: 'the first and most trivial Accident of Life must immediately disconcert and destroy [it]' (*A Letter*, 19). Excessive scepticism does not just subvert some *special* system of life such as Christianity or Idealism or Anarchism. It subverts the practical ways of encountering and understanding the world and ourselves which form the bases for *all* systems of life; a special system of life may be subverted, but not all systems. Thus one may opt to disregard the thoughts of Chairman Mao. But surely disregard of the thoughts of Chairman Mao could upset life rather badly for some people? Precisely! For *some* people in *certain* societies it may. But consistently believing that the future will not be like the past and trying to act on this belief would totally disrupt anyone's life in any society. To disregard Chairman Mao might be political heroism (or obscurantism); to disregard a natural belief would more likely be regarded as madness than philosophical acumen. I labour this point because when we consider the case of belief in god it will be vital that the universality and practical inevitability of natural beliefs should have been noted.

In summary: a natural belief is in a certain sense 'non-rational' but it is *not* irrational or unreasonable and it *does* have the very important practical justification that things 'work out well' if I have the belief and *cannot work out* if I do not have the belief.

(iv) BELIEF IN GOD

Professor Butler's thesis (see note 7) is that since Hume speaks in several of his works as if the existence of god could never be doubted, since the question in the *Dialogues* concerns god's attributes and not his existence, and since each of the participants in the *Dialogues* appears to assent to belief in god as something natural and unavoidable, then this belief *is* a natural belief in Hume's sense. Philo's criticism of the argument from design 'should be viewed as an attempt, not to deny that God exists, but to break down Cleanthes' initial opinion that theological beliefs may find rational support in the recognition of evidence' (Butler, p. 87). Up to and including *Dialogues* XI Hume's argument takes the form: no evidence either *a priori* or *a posteriori* justifies belief in god, 'but we commonly act in accordance with belief in design. Therefore belief in design must be a natural rather than a rational belief' (p. 88). In the final section of *Dialogues* XII Philo explains just how little this natural belief involves. It amounts only to acknowledging 'the fact of design' which is unavoidably impressed upon us by 'our belief in an ultimate principle of order in the universe, and this belief, like our belief in causation, is unavoidable: nobody behaves as if the universe were ultimately a chaos!' (p. 98). Belief in design is equivalent to belief in a designer, and this belief 'would make no sense if God lacked intelligence; . . . But nothing can be said *about* God's intelligence as contrasted with man's' (p. 90).

Professor Butler's thesis, to which my précis does scant justice, has striking merits. It makes Hume's theory of belief and his account of religious belief into a connected whole. It makes Philo's apparent confession of belief in god in Section XII of the *Dialogues* into a comprehensible development of his own argument instead of something apparently at variance with his earlier utterances. It makes Hume's repeated assertions[9] that there is a god into honest reports of his belief rather than asides calculated to allay criticism of his atheism. But these and other advantages of interpretation also attach to a quite different understanding of Hume's thought, namely that:

(1) Belief in god does not satisfy all the criteria for a natural belief in Hume's technical sense of that term.

(2) Hume knows that it does not satisfy the criteria and Philo admits by implication that it does not: yet both assent to the existence of god in the highly attenuated sense explained by Philo at the end of the *Dialogues*. This assent is therefore to a reasonable belief and not to a natural belief.

(3) This rational assent is given to a proposition so limited that it is of no significance to religion.

Examined under the criteria for a natural belief, belief in god fails at least two of the four tests. In the *first* place, is belief in god a belief of naive common sense? This criterion is the most difficult to apply because of vagueness about what counts as common sense, but belief in god would seem to be inculcated by education or cultural background, that is, by factors which could be absent, rather than by factors present in the experience of all men as such. It is in this respect not like belief in an external world which is the untaught assumption of every sane man. *Secondly,* is it the case that belief in god lacks rational foundation? Without begging the question of a very large area of philosophy no general answer can be given and even Hume's answer is, at first sight, equivocal. He seems to say in different places that theological reasoning is 'too sublime for our understanding' or 'sophistry', *and* that the Christian religion is founded on faith not on reason *and* that every reasonable man will believe in god. These positions are, I think, compatible, but for the moment their complexity forestalls an answer to the question 'does Hume think that belief in god is reasonable?' *Thirdly,* is belief in god unavoidable in the crucial sense (which Butler does not point out) that no one can *act* in the world if he lacks this belief? Surely not. Only too clearly men can and do live in a coherent and successful manner without belief in god. In some rather deep sense they may not live as satisfactorily as those who have the belief but they *can* function in the world and in society without it or any form of it. Thus scepticism with regard to belief in god would be mitigated scepticism: more like disregarding the thoughts of Chairman Mao than the excessive scepticism of refusing to believe that the past is a guide to the future. One very important system of life would not be possible if one were sceptical about god's existence; but other systems of life would still be practical, even if psychologically difficult. In the *Dialogues* Philo brings out this point very clearly right at the beginning. If the philosophical sceptic discovers no rational justification for believing, say in an external world, he still 'must act, and live, and converse like other men' (*Dialogues*, 134). The sceptic is under an 'absolute necessity' to do so, and his excessive philosophical scepticism must give way whenever he attends to the ordinary world of his experience. But the religious sceptic is not in this situation. His mitigated scepticism is not rendered academic and unrealistic when he attends to the ordinary world of his experience. Quite the reverse. Such is the remoteness of theological speculation by contrast with our normal experience that 'We must be far removed from the smallest tendency to scepticism not to be apprehensive, that we have here got quite beyond the reach of our faculties' (*Dialogues*, 135; Philo speaking).

The *fourth* criterion of a natural belief is that it is universally held. Hume sometimes speaks as though a shadowy form of belief in god were almost universal but he is careful not to commit himself: 'The belief of invisible, intelligent power has been very generally diffused over the human race, in all places and in all ages; but it has neither perhaps been so universal as to admit of no exception, nor has it been, in any degree, uniform in the ideas, which it has suggested' (*N.H.R.*, 21). Hume's caution is amply justified by the atheistical philosophies of the modern world: whatever might once have been the case it is now false to say that all men believe in a god.

Thus the first criterion is indecisive, the second cannot be applied as yet, but the third and fourth tests rule out belief in god as a natural belief. What is more, Hume himself knows that belief in god does not satisfy all the criteria for a natural belief and Philo admits by implication that it does not. Philo's implied admission is important because what Philo says is also very likely to be Hume's own opinion.[10]

In the *Dialogues*, Cleanthes, Philo's opponent, does indeed express himself in a manner which suggests that belief in god, via the argument from design, could be a natural belief: 'Consider, anatomize the eye, survey its structure and contrivance, and tell me, from your own feeling, if the idea of a contriver does not immediately flow in upon you with a force like that of sensation' (*Dialogues*, 134). But this part of Cleanthes' case is not endorsed by Philo, and in a letter, unequivocally in his own person, Hume admits that he cannot establish via the design argument that belief in god is unavoidably forced upon us like belief in our senses:

The Propensity of the Mind towards it [the design argument], unless that Propensity were as strong & universal as that to believe in our Senses &

Experience, will still, I am afraid, be esteem'd a suspicious Foundation. Tis here I wish for your Assistance. We must endeavour to prove that this Propensity is somewhat different from our Inclination to find our own Figures in the Clouds, our Face in the Moon, our Passions & Sentiments even in inanimate Matter. Such an Inclination may, & ought to be control'd, & can never be a legitimate Ground of Assent (*Letters*, I, 155).

The most straightforward reading of the conditional 'unless that Propensity were as strong and universal as that to believe in our Senses and Experience' would suggest that Hume thinks the condition is not satisfied. This reading is confirmed elsewhere. In the *N.H.R.* he comes close to speaking of belief in god as a natural belief but shies off it: 'The universal propensity to believe in invisible, intelligent power, if not an original instinct, is at least a general attendant of human nature' (*N.H.R.*, 75). In the 'Author's Introduction' to the same work he had already admitted that belief in god is not universal and is not an original instinct: 'Some nations have been discovered, who entertained no sentiments of Religion, if travellers and historians may be credited; . . . It would appear, therefore, that this preconception springs not from an original instinct or primary impression of nature' *(N.H.R., 21)*.

Elsewhere (but notably in the *Enquiry*) Hume maintains that it is a mistake to try to establish religion (but he does not say belief in god) upon good reasons and arguments (see, for example, *Enquiry*, 130:140 and 135:145). Thus he appears to conclude that belief in god is not an original instinct; that it is not universal; that it does not 'flow in upon you with a force like that of sensation' and that religion *in general* cannot be established by reason.

The difficulty with the last item in this summary of his views is that in several of his writings he affirms belief in a deity by way of the design argument: 'The whole frame of nature bespeaks an intelligent author' (*N.H.R.*, 21). At the end of the *Dialogues* Philo also affirms his reasoned belief in a divine Being: 'No one has a deeper sense of religion impressed on his mind, or pays more profound adoration to the divine Being, as he discovers himself to reason, in the inexplicable contrivance and artifice of nature. A purpose, an intention or design strikes everywhere the most careless, the most stupid thinker' (*Dialogues*, 214; see also 202). This is puzzling, particularly the phrase 'as he discovers himself to reason', since the whole burden of Philo's argument appears to have been that he does not discover himself to reason. But this crucial phrase is repeated by Philo three pages later: 'Here then the existence of a Deity is plainly ascertained by *reason*' (my italics). If we adopt Kemp Smith's argument (see note 10) that Philo very largely speaks for Hume in the *Dialogues*, it might appear that Hume is here admitting that belief in god, like belief in an external world, survives the destruction of its supporting arguments, his continued use of the word 'reason' being merely perverse and confusing. He should have used the phrase 'natural instinct'. But this appearance is misleading. In the first place, Philo has

already asserted in his discussion with Cleanthes concerning scepticism that
'If we distrust human reason, we have now no other principle to lead us into
religion' (*Dialogues*, 193). This assertion is never disputed by Cleanthes
despite his attempt to argue the fact of design as something unavoidably
obvious. It is surely as clear a warning as could be given by Philo that it is
not part of his programme to allow that belief in god is a natural belief or
'original instinct', in other words one which must survive after the supporting
philosophical arguments collapse because it is a universal requirement for
living in the world.[11] In the second place, as Kemp Smith and Butler both
point out, Philo's profession of belief, qualified as it is by the phrase 'as he
discovers himself to reason', amounts to exceedingly little. Just how little
is emphasised by Hume in an addition to the text dating from 1776 (the
year of his death). The paragraph is given to Philo and is the last in the book:

> If the whole of natural theology, as some people seem to maintain, resolves
> itself into one simple, though somewhat ambiguous, at least undefined
> proposition, *that the cause or causes of order in the universe probably bear
> some remote analogy to human intelligence*: If this proposition be not
> capable of extension, variation, or more particular explication: If it
> affords no inference that affects human life, or can be the source of any
> action or forbearance: And if the analogy, imperfect as it is, can be carried
> no farther than to the human intelligence; . . . what can [a man] do more
> than give a plain, philosophical assent to the proposition, as often as it
> occurs (*Dialogues*, 227; Hume's italics).

I would thus argue that Philo does not concede that belief in design (as
Butler maintains) 'must be a natural rather than a rational belief'. Instead he
concedes that belief in a designer is after all a *rational* belief: one to which the
mind has a strong propensity but which is 'somewhat ambiguous', probable
rather than certain, incapable of rational development or extension,
dependent upon an imperfect and very limited analogy, and which commits
the believer neither to action nor forbearance from action. This is the substance of the existential assent to belief in god which is found so frequently
in Hume's writings and which Philo reserves for himself despite his arguments.
As Hume says in an early letter: He has an objection 'to every thing we
commonly call Religion, except the Practice of Morality & the Assent of the
Understanding to the Proposition *that God exists' (New Letters*, 13).

It is this assent of the understanding to the very limited proposition 'there
is a god' together with the 'propensity' of the mind to give the assent when it
contemplates the orderliness of nature, which might suggest that Hume
considers belief in god a natural belief. But it is not. The assent is not
universal and, unlike a normal religious belief in god, it does not even
influence action, let alone form a prerequisite of action. In this respect
Butler is mistaken when he argues that our belief in an ultimate principle of
order in the universe is unavoidable: 'nobody behaves as if the universe were

ultimately a chaos'. I do not behave as if *ultimately* the universe were one way or the other. My behaviour is not regulated by whether I infer an ultimate principle of order or of chaos. But my intellectual assent might be given to the probability of the former and I might name this principle of order 'god'. But use of this word is religiously neutral. Assent to the existence of god in this sense carries no duties, invites no action, allows no inferences, and involves no devotion. It is, as Hume argues through Philo in *Dialogue* XII, and as Lysicles the sceptic in Berkeley's *Alciphron* had argued in strikingly similar terms,[12] a proposition so hedged by doubts, restrictions and ambiguities that by suitable prompting both the religious man and the speculative atheist can be brought to give their assent to it. But the assent is *not* to a natural belief.

*   *   *

Hume's conclusion that belief in god is not a natural belief has two immediate consequences. One is that to doubt the belief (even if Hume himself did not doubt one very attenuated form of it) would not be excessive scepticism. The other is that the belief is subject to the normal reasonable/ unreasonable dichotomy. From Hume's repeated affirmations of a deity, together with Philo's assent to a very restricted sense of the proposition 'there is a god', I conclude that Hume regards belief in a god as reasonable rather than unreasonable and he thinks the reasonableness is recognised by most men when they survey the order in nature (*something* of the design argument remains). But this reasonable belief amounts to so very little that the theist and the atheist can agree about it. The belief is without religious significance and leaves Hume free (a) to adopt an attitude of mitigated scepticism to all theological arguments because they are beyond our understanding; (b) to attribute belief in a particular revelation to an irrational faith which he sarcastically refers to as a miracle, and (c) to criticise and condemn religion 'as it has commonly been found in the world'. It is failure to notice the genuineness of Hume's rational assent to the existence of some sort of a god which has made it appear as if his assent is insincere, or inconsistent with his critique of religion, or the expression of a natural belief. It is none of these; but neither is it of any advantage to the religious apologist.

My contention that, for Hume, a certain minimal belief in god is reasonable may, however, still be questioned at two points. One is whether Hume's talk about a 'propensity' of the mind to such a belief should suggest that he thinks belief in god is, in some sense, quasi-natural. The other is whether the conclusion of Philo's vestigial design argument — that there is an ultimate *principle* of order (*Dialogues,* 174) — is sufficient to justify Hume's assent of the understanding to the existence of a *god.* My answer to the first question is that no evidence can be found to show that Hume wants to make any allowance for a category of quasi-natural beliefs. What is more were he to make such allowance, it would be unclear which of the full-blown criteria for natural beliefs would have to be modified (and with what justification) and whether quasi-natural beliefs would still be entitled to the all-important examption from rational justification which is allowed to natural beliefs. The second question — whether assent to a principle of order justifies assent to the existence of a god — misses the point of what I have been saying about the sort of god to which Hume gives his assent. His god is somewhat more than a principle of order. As already pointed out (p. 36) Hume, through Philo, finds a vestigial design argument convincing: probably there is an ultimate principle of order. But to call such a principle 'god' would indeed merely confound everything by putting a religious name onto atheism; atheist and theist could agree that there is a principle of order, but the agreement would get them nowhere. Something more is required to justify Hume's retention of the word 'god', even when employed in his attenuated sense. The something more is given by the conclusion which Philo draws from his exacting scrutiny of the design argument, namely, that the principle of order may possibly be remotely analogous to human intelligence. It is this modest addition which allows Hume to retain the word 'god', to differentiate his position from that of atheism, and to regard belief in such a god as reasonable rather than natural or irrational. But as already emphasised: although the position is different from complete atheism it has in it nothing of recognisably religious value.[13]

But if belief in god is not a natural belief how is it that so very many people at all times and in all places have believed in a god or gods and have believed in a way which is much more significant and influential than Hume's minimal 'assent of the understanding'? Hume's answer, which I shall now examine, is that 'popular religion' has a causal origin in human nature. It also has evil effects in human society.

Part III Historical and Personal Religion

9 The Causes and Corruptions of Religion

> The theologian may indulge the pleasing task of
> describing Religion as she descended from Heaven,
> arrayed in her native purity. A more melancholy
> duty is imposed on the historian. He must discover
> the inevitable mixture of error and corruption, which
> she contracted in a long residence upon earth, among
> a weak and degenerate race of beings.
>
> Gibbon, *Roman Empire,* Chapter XV

Hume's critique of religion includes not only the traditional arguments for
rational theism and the supposed authenticating marks of revelation but also
the causes of religion in human nature and its effects in society. The
effects of religion upon society are the concern of Hume the historian and
moralist rather than Hume the philosopher. But an adequate account of the
causes of religious belief, though not itself philosophy, is an essential
complement to his philosophical thinking about religion. If, as Hume seems
to conclude, the arguments of natural religion are bad or establish only a
hesitant and highly attenuated conclusion, and if the authenticity of revelation
is suspect, then an appeal will almost inevitably be made by the believer to
the argument from general consent: why is it that religious belief is and always
has been so very prevalent? The argument, as J. S. Mill observes, 'admonishes
us to look out for and weigh the reasons on which this conviction of mankind
or of wise men was founded'. The short and conciliatory answer — that belief
in god is a natural belief — is, as I have shown, not adopted by Hume and not
adopted for the very good reason that belief in god does not satisfy the
conditions for a natural belief. Thus the only answer which remains for
Hume, in the absence of new and valid reasons, is that there must be causes
for religious belief which operate sufficiently widely for them to influence
most men. 'What those principles are, which give rise to the original belief,
and what those accidents and causes are, which direct its operation, is the
subject of our present enquiry' (*N.H.R.*, 21; 'Introduction').

In this chapter I shall give some account of what Hume has to say in the
Natural History of Religion[1] and some account of his insufficiently noticed
distinction between 'true' and 'corrupt' religion. I shall then explore some of
the lesser known areas of his writing which make clear his passionate hostility
to what he regarded as the evil effects of religion.

(i)　AN ORIGIN IN HUMAN NATURE

The main points which Hume makes in the *Natural History of Religion* are these:

(1) 'It is a matter of fact incontestable that about 1,700 years ago all mankind were polytheists' (*N.H.R.*, 23). This assertion would now be subject to many qualifications and footnotes. There is, for example, a dim possibility that some primeval religion might be more aptly described as monotheistic. Nevertheless, what Hume says here (as in the rest of the *N.H.R.*) could be re-dressed in modern terms as acceptable generalisations. Something very like it is affirmed, for example, by Ninian Smart: 'whether or not primeval religion was monotheistic, early religion was polytheistic but shows a tendency to evolve towards monotheism or monism'.[2]

(2) Polytheism does not owe its origin to contemplation of the order of nature by rational men:

> But farther, if men were at first led into the belief of one Supreme Being, by reasoning from the frame of nature, they could never possibly leave that belief, in order to embrace polytheism; but the same principles of reason, which at first produced and diffused over mankind, so magnificent an opinion, must be able, with greater facility, to preserve it (*N.H.R.*, 25; see also 26).

(3) The origin of polytheism is fear of the unknown causes of the apparently capricious events which govern human life:

> On the other hand, if, leaving the works of nature, we trace the footsteps of invisible power in the various and contrary events of human life, we are necessarily led into polytheism and to the acknowledgement of several limited and imperfect deities . . . the first ideas of religion arose not from a contemplation of the works of nature, but from a concern with regard to the events of life, and from the incessant hopes and fears ['especially the latter' – p.28] which actuate the human mind (*N.H.R.*, 27).

Thus in (1) to (3) Hume is saying that because polytheism is the primary religion of mankind; because 'the primary religion of mankind arises chiefly from an anxious fear of future events' (*N.H.R.*, 65); *therefore* the origin of religion as a whole lies in fear of the unknown, not in a rational contemplation of the order of nature. To the twentieth-century reader this may seem so obvious as to be scarcely worth insisting upon. But in the eighteenth century it was strikingly at variance with the sort of thinking (not all of it heterodox) which gave rise to deism and an excessive reliance on the arguments of natural religion. An assumption of deism, quite often shared by orthodox divines, was that monotheism was both the rational and natural religion of mankind.

'Natural' in the sense that, quite apart from the influence of priests and revelations, all men could and should arrive at it. 'Natural Religion is the Belief we have of an eternal intellectual Being, and of the Duty which we owe him, manifested to us by our Reason, without Revelation or positive law'[3] In such a context 'reason' is thought of as a timeless and classless capacity by which man will always be able to reach the conclusions of rational theism. No, says Hume; fear, not reason, is the source of religion. Polytheism, not theism, is the original religion of mankind.

(4) 'The only point of theology, in which we shall find a consent of mankind almost universal, is, that there is invisible, intelligent power in the world; (*N.H.R.,* 32), but whether this power be one or many, supreme or subordinate is in perpetual dispute. In other words there is no significant common notion of god which influences all belief or which looks in the direction of theism. The contrast between this and the tone of an earlier enquiry into the most general features of religions — Herbert of Cherbury's *De Veritate* (1624) — could hardly be more striking:

> No general agreement exists concerning the gods, but there is universal recognition of God. Every religion in the past, every religion in the future, did and will acknowledge some sovereign deity among the gods. . . .
> Accordingly that which is everywhere accepted as the supreme manifestation of deity, by whatever name it may be called, I term God.[4]

Lord Herbert's quest for monotheism in the diversity of actual world religions leads him to call by the name 'God' what Hume finds to be merely the tendency of polytheism to promote one deity above the rest: 'They may either suppose, that, in the distribution of power and territory among the gods, their nation was subjected to the jurisdiction of that particular deity; or, reducing heavenly objects to the model of things below, they may represent one god as the prince or supreme magistrate of the rest . . .' (*N.H.R.,* 43).

(5) From fear of this dominant god, his praises are ever extended and magnified, 'till at last they arrive at infinity itself' and thus theism is reached not by reason, 'but by the adulation and fears of the most vulgar superstition' (*N.H.R.,* 43).

(6) Although attributes are ascribed to the single, theistic deity which are quite inappropriate to a man or anything like a man, nevertheless the common people still try to propitiate him in a way appropriate to the old, local, anthropomorphic deity.

(7)   So remote and incomprehensible are the attributes of the theistic god — infinity, perfection, etc. — that 'they require to be supported by the notion of inferior mediators or subordinate agents' (*N.H.R.,* 47), which in turn become objects of devotion (such as the Virgin Mary), until a reaction towards pure theism intervenes. Thus there is a flux and reflux of polytheism and theism.

(8) The effects of polytheism are in many ways preferable to those of

monotheism. Polytheism is more tolerant (by its very nature). It does not appeal to reason and therefore avoids the entanglement of philosophy with religion which is characteristic of monotheism. This entanglement starts with the recognition by philosophy of the reasonableness of the basic tenet of monotheism. It finishes with philosophy 'perverted to serve the purposes of superstition' (*N.H.R.*, 54; see also *Enquiry*, 15:25). But worst of all, monotheism as it occurs in the popular religions of the world, has a pernicious and distorting effect upon morality. The main reason for this mentioned in the *N.H.R.* is that 'as men farther exalt their idea of their divinity; it is the notion of his power and knowledge, not of his goodness, which is improved' (*N.H.R.*, 6?

Although the authorities and evidence which Hume produces for his conclusions in the *N.H.R.* are almost all drawn from the observations of ancient authors, the problem which he discusses – the psychological and anthropological causes and origins of religious belief and its effects – is, as Mossner observes, essentially modern, 'and to Hume should go the credit for being the first great modern to treat of it systematically. From it arises much modern thinking on the subject' (*Life,* 333). But quite apart from the *N.H.R.* being the first move in what might now be called the sociology of religion, some of what Hume has to say has a bearing upon the philosophical acceptability of religion to a reasonable man. For one thing Hume does not distinguish between the historical conditions in which religious belief originated and the conditions which continue to operate to produce religious belief in subsequent periods. For example, if the origins of religion are fear and ignorance, he takes it for granted that fear and ignorance will at other times be the factors which foster religion, and with which religion will tend to be associated. If this is so, then a reasonable man, not a prey to the conditions Hume describes, may well conclude that he should have nothing to do with religion, its miserable effects or its degrading causes. But Hume appears to have a way out for the reasonable man. He is always careful to speak of 'vulgar religion', 'popular superstition', 'the opinion of the vulgar', 'barbarous and ignorant nations' etc. and to contrast this with a not very conspicuous alternative – 'the notion of a perfect being, the creator of the world' – which is conformable to 'the principles of reason and true philosophy' (*N.H.R.*, 43). Thus it is implied that the religion of the reasonable man, if he has any religion, will be something very different from the causally conditioned religion of the vulgar. His religion will be philosophical, rarified, 'true' by contrast with religion as it has commonly been found in the world. By opening up this distinction we shall see both what Hume thinks religion should be and why he condemns what it is.

(ii)   TRUE AND CORRUPT RELIGION

Hume's account of the 'true religion', hinted at in the *N.H.R.*, is given in the

Dialogues and in an unpublished preface to volume II of the *History*. The preface has been printed in full in Mossner's *Life*, pp. 306-7. A truncated and amended version of it also appears as a footnote on p. 449 of volume II of the first edition of the *History* (London 1757). It disappears altogether in later editions. In a sentence which appears identically in the preface and in the footnote true religion is described in terms which have a mildly masonic flavour: 'The proper office of religion is to reform men's lives, to purify their hearts, to enforce all moral duties, and to secure obedience to the laws and civil magistrate'.

In the *Dialogues* similar words are given to Cleanthes and Philo does not demur at the description: 'The proper office of religion is to regulate the heart of men, humanize their conduct, infuse the spirit of temperance, order and obedience' (*Dialogues,* 220). Now this characterisation of religion by means of its non-distinctive features, morality etc., without reference to any of its distinctive features, devotion, prayer etc., is entirely consistent with what one would expect from a man who could admit in his deathbed interview with Boswell 'that he had *some* belief' but who also kept to his earlier 'Objection both to Devotion & Prayer & indeed to every thing we commonly call Religion, except the Practice of Morality, and the Assent of the Understanding to the Proposition *that God exists' (New Letters,* 12). On this ground alone, apart from the evidence of the repetition of the account, there can be little doubt that Hume speaks sincerely. He does think true religion would have the functions he suggests. But later in the footnote, and also in Cleanthes' next sentence, it is made abundantly clear that Hume does not think this sort of religion would be at all conspicuous in the world, or active as an influence in history: 'and as its operation is silent and only enforces the motives of morality and justice, it is in danger of being overlooked, and confused with these other motives' (*Dialogues,* 220). But Philo takes the matter further. Although true religion thus described has no pernicious consequences, 'we must treat of religion, as it has commonly been found in the world'.

It has commonly been found, according to Hume, in the corrupt forms of superstition and enthusiasm. He characterises and condemns these (in the essay 'Of Superstition and Enthusiasm') in a conventional eighteenth-century manner: enthusiasm is a species of emotional fanaticism or religious mania; superstition is a state in which 'unknown evils are dreaded from unknown agents'. Its source is 'weakness, fear, melancholy . . . and ignorance' and it manifests itself in 'ceremonies, observances, mortifications, sacrifices, presents' directed towards the unknown agent. However, what is not conventional eighteenth-century thinking is Hume's analysis of the prevalence of these corruptions, particularly of superstition. Again in the unpublished preface to the *History* (but this time not surviving in the footnote) he writes:

The Idea of an Infinite Mind, the Author of the Universe seems at first Sight a Worship absolutely pure, simple, unadorned; without Rites,

Institutions, Ceremonies; even without Temples, Priests, or verbal Prayer
& Supplication; Yet has this Species of Devotion been often found to
degenerate into the most dangerous Fanaticism. When we have recourse
to the aid of the Senses & Imagination, in order to adapt our Religion, in
some degree to human Infirmity; it is very difficult, & almost impossible,
to prevent altogether the Intrusion of Superstition, or keep Men from
laying too great Stress on the ceremonial & ornamental Parts of their
Worship.

As we have seen, in the *N.H.R.*, a reason for the prevalence of superstition is
suggested: namely, that religion in general and superstition in particular have
the same causes, to wit, fear and ignorance.

Each element is subjected to its invisible power or agent. . . . Nor are the
operations of the same god always certain and invariable. Today he protects:
Tomorrow he abandons us. Prayers and sacrifices, rites and ceremonies,
well or ill performed, are the sources of his favour or enmity, and produce
all the good or ill fortune, which are to be found amongst mankind
(*N.H.R.*, 27).

The similarity between this account of the origin of religion in general and
the account of the origin of superstition in which 'unknown evils are dreaded
from unknown agents' is too obvious to need further elaboration.
    The point is that, for Hume, religion as it has commonly been found in the
world, the vulgar religion whose causes and effects are considered in the
N.H.R. and whose working in human history and society is so baleful, *is*
superstition. Thus in the *N.H.R.* 'popular religion' and 'superstition' are
treated as interchangeable terms. It is recognition of Hume's identification
of popular religion with superstition which provoked much of the uproar over
the *N.H.R.* and the *History.* An early critic of the *History* complained that
Hume represented all religion as tending towards superstition or enthusiasm.
The ever vigilant Warburton likewise remarked 'This [the *N.H.R.*] fully
justifies the censure which has been passed upon his *History of Great Britain*;
namely that he owned no Religion but what might be resolved into Superstition or Fanaticism'. Even after Hume's death the row continued: 'We all
know, Sir, what the word SUPERSTITION denoted, in Mr Hume's vocabulary,
and against what Religion his shafts are levelled, under that name'.[5] But
what is it that is so alarming for the religious man, the Christian in particular,
in Hume's identification of vulgar religion with superstition, *provided* he
leaves room for 'true religion'? The quotation marks round 'true religion'
indicate the answer. Such religion, as characterised by Hume, whatever it
ought to have been in history and society, most certainly is not religion as it
has commonly been found in the world. *That* religion, 'vulgar religion',
contains virtually all the religion there actually is, a few saintly stoics like
Marcus Aurelius only excepted. Vulgar religion, described in Hume's

depressingly monochromatic terms, must, for example, comprehend practically the whole history of Christianity. Hume's self-defence in a letter may be disingenuous or it may be that he just does not grasp the implications of what he has done:

> There is no passage in the History which strikes in the least at revelation. But as I run over all the sects successively, and speak of each of them with some mark of disregard, the reader, putting the whole together, concludes that I am of no sect; which to him will appear the same thing as the being of no religion (*Letters*, I, 237).

This remark sounds and probably is sincere. It also sounds like a reasonable and enlightened defence until it is noticed that 'all the sects' constitute pretty well all the religion there actually is. They *are* the 'vulgar religion' of the *N.H.R..* What Hume is doing is to define for himself something called 'true religion' which has none of the distinctive features of actual religions. He himself points out that it will be hard to distinguish such religion from secular morality. He then contrasts true religion with vulgar religion in order both to commend the former and to be able to claim that he has himself some religion. Now I do not wish to suggest that Hume was in the least insincere in this. All I wish to argue is that he cannot conceal his critical analysis of actual religion behind a commendation of something as unreligiously abstract as the 'true religion' which he describes and which he admits (*Dialogues*, 223), will be 'always confined to a very few persons'. Whether Hume's analysis of the causes and origins of religion is true, or near enough true, may be argued one way or the other. That it is intended to apply to religion as it has actually appeared in the world cannot be doubted. This means that his contemporary critics were right. He *is* saying that religion, including Christianity, is subject to the analysis given in the *N.H.R.* and exemplified in the *History*. It *is* caused by fear and fostered by ignorance. It *does* corrupt morality and condone misery.

(iii)   SICK MEN'S DREAMS

Towards the end of the *N.H.R.* Hume generalises his passionate charge against popular religion:

> What a noble privilege it is of human reason to attain the knowledge of the supreme Being; and, from the visible works of nature, be enabled to infer so sublime a principle as its supreme Creator? But turn the reverse of the medal. Survey most nations and most ages. Examine the religious principles, which have, in fact, prevailed in the world. You will scarcely be persuaded, that they are any thing but sick men's dreams . . . What so pure as some of the morals, included in some theological systems? What

so corrupt as some of the practices, to which these systems give rise? (*N.H.R.*, 75f).

But what is it in religion which is detrimental to morality, and inimical to happiness? Hume has two answers to the second part of the question.

In the first place religion is inimical to happiness because the conditions which cause it are also the conditions which religion fosters and in which it thrives. Men turn to religion when they are in some way miserable or afraid:

> It is true; both fear and hope enter into religion; because both these passions at different times, agitate the human mind, and each of them forms a species of divinity, suitable to itself. But when a man is in a cheerful disposition he is fit for business or company or entertainment of any kind; and he naturally applies himself to these, and thinks not of religion. When melancholy, and dejected, he has nothing to do but brood upon the terrors of the invisible world, and to plunge himself still deeper in affliction. . . . But still it must be acknowledged, that, as terror is the primary principle of religion, it is the passion which always predominates in it, and admits but of short intervals of pleasure (*Dialogues*, 225).

This long quotation is the explicit statement of a view which lies behind a great deal of Hume's understanding (and some of his misunderstanding) of religion. As early as the *Treatise* he remarks 'that in matters of religion men take a pleasure in being terrify'd, and that no preachers are so popular, as those who excite the most dismal and gloomy passions' (*Treatise*, 115). As late as his deathbed interview with Boswell he can still talk about religion seeing immortality 'through a gloomy medium'. The pity about this assessment of religion is not that it is wrong, but that it is so excessively one-sided. It is certainly true that a happy and busy people do not readily turn to religion. It is also true that when men are worried, apprehensive or terrified the churches are filled. But this does not mean that religion must foster or increase the terror and gloom. It *may* do so. But then again it may alleviate the terror: religion *might* have delivered Ivan Ilyitch from his fear of death. It cannot be known for certain why Hume had such a distorted and one-sided picture of the psychology of religious practice, but a very obvious possibility would be his study of seventeenth-century history, and the dour and narrow presbyterianism of the Scotland into which he was born. Be that as it may, his picture, though distorted, may be salutary. There is and always has been an aspect of religion which is as Hume describes: morbid, preciously self-pitying, almost pathologically preoccupied with sin and sometimes hypocritical as well — the type is finely portrayed in Scott's *Old Mortality*. Furthermore Hume's observation of the psychology of this sort of religion can sometimes be a great deal more subtle than his general condemnation would lead us to expect: 'The steady attention alone to so important an interest as that of eternal salvation is apt to extinguish the benevolent affections, and beget a narrow, contracted selfishness. And when such a temper is encouraged, it easily eludes all the general precepts of charity and benevolence' (*Dialogues*, 222)[6]

Secondly, religion, particularly monotheism, is detrimental to happiness, according to Hume, because of the bigotry, cruelty and persecuting zeal with which it has been so often accompanied. The charge is put in a circumspect and generalised way in the *N.H.R.*, 48-51. It is exemplified in detail in the *History*. The 'barbarous zeal and theological fervour' of the Scots, 'the dismal fanaticism' of the English parliamentarians, 'the vicious cruelty' of the inquisitions of Madrid and Rome receive frequent mention. And worse — 'The greatest and truest zeal gives us no security against hypocrisy': a generalisation (in *N.H.R.*, 73) which Hume gives particular illustration from the activity of the independent committees which controlled parts of England in 1647:

> The sanctified hypocrites, who called their oppressions the spoiling of the Egyptians, and their rigid severity the dominion of the Elect, interlarded all their iniquities with long and fervent prayers, saved themselves from blushing by their pious grimaces, and exercised, in the name of the Lord, all their cruelty on men (*History*, VII, 94).

As Gibbon observes in the passage quoted as motto to this chapter, the historian must 'discover the inevitable mixture of error and corruption' which disfigures religion. Whether the disfigurement is as extensive as Hume suggests other historians will judge. That it exists no honest man can deny.

It is, however, Hume's charge that religion corrupts morality, rather than his historical analysis of the misery it has produced, which is the more serious. Although the two matters are related, the misery might be argued off as an accidental though frequent aberration. But the immorality, on Hume's understanding, is almost inseparable from popular religion as such. Hume has two charges to put.

In the first place, religion begins in worship (through fear) of capricious amoral power 'But as men farther exalt their idea of their divinity; it is the notion of his power and knowledge only, not of his goodness, which is improved' (*N.H.R.*, 67). As an historical generalisation about world religions this judgement is questionable. As a charge against the sort of God which Christians have traditionally worshipped it has more substance than appears at first sight. The God of St Peter and St Paul embodies curiously discordant elements. He is certainly powerful: the creator and sustainer of all things visible and invisible. He is the God of mercy and love. But he is *also* the God who countenances the everlasting torments of Hell. This last element — now weakened by the liberal draughts with which twentieth-century Christians wash away the taste of traditional teachings — may well be the occasion for the remarks with which Hume follows the generalisation just quoted: 'And while their gloomy apprehensions make them ascribe to him [the god] measures of conduct, which, in human creatures, would be highly blamed, they must still affect to praise and admire that conduct in the object of their devotional addresses'. Two interpretations are, I think, possible. The first is the one already indicated: that Hume is taking seriously the Christian doctrine of Hell, a monstrosity condemned outright in his essay 'Of the Immortality of the Soul' (see above p. 100f). The second (which does not exclude the first) is that he is underlining the moral double-dealing and psychological tensions involved in worship of a God who is capable of inflicting everlasting torments but whom we still feel obliged to think of as good: 'The heart secretly detests such measures of cruel and implacable vengeance; but the judgement dares not but pronounce them perfect and adorable' (*N.H.R.,* 67). But this danger of moral double-talk in the interests of theology is scarcely as serious as Hume's second and fundamental charge: that religion involves the creation of amoral species of merit.

The *Enquiry concerning the Principles of Morals* contains Hume's systematic analysis of 'that complication of mental qualities which form what, in common life, we call PERSONAL MERIT'. The analysis is Aristotelian in tone but with a very strong utilitarian bias. Each of the qualities Hume finds to be admired is *useful* to society. They have a 'tendency to promote the interests of our species, and bestow happiness on human society' and 'the moral obligation holds proportion with the *usefulness*'. But this moral obligation is not difficult or disagreeable or in any way contrary to our nature as normal people. It is an 'interested obligation' and we are inclined to observe it by a combination of many factors: our participation in the feelings of others through sympathy or fellow feeling, our concern to be well thought of in society and live at peace with ourselves and others, our aversion to criminal punishment and disgrace, our calculation of our own greatest happiness etc. In brief, happiness for people and usefulness for society, are the criteria for the morality of an action, and action in accordance with these criteria is both in a man's best interest and in harmony with his normal personality. Morality is social, utilitarian and secular. The will of god and the rewards and punishments of an afterlife play no part in Hume's scheme of morals.

But when Hume examines the observances which are principally associated with religion, he finds not the 'virtue and good morals' which theism appears to enjoin and which would be in accord with a social, utilitarian morality, but always some non-utilitarian, non-moral species of merit:

> It is certain, that, in every religion, however sublime the verbal definition which it gives of its divinity, many of the votaries, perhaps the greatest number, will still seek the divine favour, not by virtue and good morals, which alone can be acceptable to a perfect being, but either by frivolous observances, by intemperate zeal, by rapturous extasies, or by the belief of mysterious and absurd opinions (*N.H.R.,* 70).

The observances of popular religion or 'superstition' are 'frivolous'[7] by contrast with the observances of morality because the former is 'useless, and burdensome; the latter is absolutely requisite to the well-being of mankind and the existence of society' (*Moral Enquiry*, 199: 29). What is more, if men were to judge of things 'by their natural, unprejudiced reason, without the delusive glosses of superstition and false religion' (and, Hume might have added, of political creeds treated like religion) they would never adopt non-utilitarian substitutes for morality:

> Celibacy, fasting, penance, mortification, self-denial, humility, silence, solitude, and the whole train of monkish virtues; for what reason are they every where rejected by men of sense, but because they serve no manner of purpose; neither advance a man's fortune in the world, nor render him a more valuable member of society; neither qualify him for the entertainment of company, nor increase his power of self-enjoyment? We observe, on the contrary, that they cross all these desirable ends; stupify the understanding and harden the heart, obscure the fancy and sour the temper (*Moral Enquiry,* 270:91).

A similar point is made, more sharply, by Philo towards the end of the *Dialogues*. The common people cannot conceive a deity 'pleased with nothing but virtue in human behaviour. The recommendations to the Divinity are generally supposed to be either frivolous observances, or rapturous ecstasies, or a bigoted credulity'. He continues:

> But even though superstition or enthusiasm should not put itself in direct opposition to morality; the very diverting of the attention, the raising up of a new and frivolous species of merit, the preposterous distribution which it makes of praise and blame, must have the most pernicious consequences, and weaken extremely men's attachment to the natural motives of justice and humanity (*Dialogues*, 222).

In the *N.H.R.* a reason is suggested for the raising up of 'new and frivolous species of merit' in religion:

> In restoring a loan, or paying a debt, his divinity is nowise beholden to him; because these acts of justice are what he was bound to perform, and what many would have performed, were there no god in the universe. But if he fast a day ... this has a direct reference ... to the service of God (*N.H.R.* 72) [because it could have no other possible use].

In all this two questions stand out. Do specifically religious observances have the rationale Hume suggests? Do such observances compete with morality?

The peculiarity about the first question is that for practical purposes there is no way of knowing what the answer really is. If a devotee of some religion is asked whether he is fasting rather than doing good works because fasting

is a way in which he can specially commend himself to his god, he may not
be able to answer either yes or no. He could be fasting because that is the
accepted way within his religion of commending himself to god, *or* of
atoning for his sins, *or* of reminding himself of his dependence upon god,
or of separating himself from the cares of the world and the dictates of the
flesh. Any one of these, among other possible answers, could be true, and only
the first invites the repetition of Hume's question: why is fasting supposed to
commend you to god? The answer, 'I don't know. That's just the way we
believe the relationship of god and man to be', is not flagrantly absurd even
if it permits someone like Hume, already persuaded that only virtue and good
morals 'can be acceptable to a perfect being', to reply that the devotee has
misunderstood the relationship. But misunderstanding the relationship is a
somewhat less perversely silly thing than doing something because it is so
useless from every human point of view that it could only be of service to
the deity. After all, the devotee may well retort '*you* have misunderstood
the relationship. Good works are not *alone* acceptable to the supreme being.
We have other information on the subject'. Put in this way the dispute
becomes one between different sects disagreeing about what is pleasing to
god. But this misses the point of what Hume has to say. The strength of his
rationale of religious observances and of the 'monkish virtues' followed for
the sake of the deity alone, is not that his rationale holds for every devotee,
but that to the outsider, the non-participant in religious life, it can be known
to hold in some cases on the admission of the devotee himself, while in
other cases it seems to have a psychological plausibility. How could a thing
so utterly useless as fasting be undertaken for any other than something like
the reason Hume suggests? This is the sort of question which commends
Hume's analysis to the secular outsider, the man of the world, but leaves
the believer unmoved.

The second question — do such observances compete with morality? —
admits of a somewhat more determinate answer. Yes they do. But whether the
competition is or is not an adverse reflection upon religion depends upon the
point of view. From the point of view of the devotee, the 'frivolous species
of merit' introduced into life by his religion, while admittedly not sanctioned
by and possibly even contrary to secular utilitarian morality, is far from
frivolous. It may be amongst the most significant concerns of his life. But
Hume's charge that religion corrupts morality does not pretend to judge
religion from its own point of view. The point of view is that of the world at
large: the world of people who do not share the particular religious beliefs of
the devotee. From *this* point of view the religious observance or 'species of
merit'[8] could be positively evil, as with the inquisitorial hunting out and
burning of heretics; non-moral, as with the habitual Roman Catholic
attendance at mass each Sunday; or positively virtuous, as with any religious
observance which inculcates the precept 'love thy neighbour as thyself'.
Concerning the man-of-the-world condemnation of such religious virtues as
heretic burning Hume has nothing to add. But he has something extra to say

about non-moral religious virtues, namely, that it is very easy for these to become alternatives to morality, diverting the attention of the devotee. The virtue of attending ceremonies can easily become a substitute for loving one's neighbour. Even when religious virtue is identical with secular utilitarian virtue Hume still prefers the latter. Religion too easily gives morality a dismal face and is too easily diverted into observances. If a popular religion were founded

> in which it was expressly declared, that nothing but morality could gain the divine favour; if an order of priests were instituted to inculcate this opinion, in daily sermons, and with all the arts of persuasion; yet so inveterate are the people's prejudices, that, for want of some other superstition, they would make the very attendance on these sermons the essentials of religion, rather than place them in virtue and good morals (*N.H.R.*, 70).

In a letter, Hume once wrote 'I am a Citizen of the World', meaning 'I have not the particular interests and prejudices of a Whig, a Tory, a Christian, a Scotsman, an Englishman or whatever'. This stance, or something like it, is also characteristic of his moral judgement of religion. From the point of view, not simply of an 'outsider' to religion, but of a 'citizen of the world', a point of view concerned with happiness and the good of society, some religious species of merit are frivolous, some are vicious, some are agreeable to the good of mankind. Only the last, consistently and cheerfully pursued, would be 'true religion' in Hume's understanding of that term. It may of course be, as we are continually told in sociology and in trifles culled from Wittgenstein, that there can be no such thing as the view of an impartial citizen of the world. Every view is partial. Every sect has its own species of 'truth' and plays its own verbal 'game'. But this depressing possibility need not keep a man from the admirable and important enterprise of *trying* to see what the moral standards of mankind would be like apart from the 'virtues' preached by particular religious or political sects — 'virtues' which may on occasions seem to the world at large little better than 'sick men's dreams'.

But in all this discussion of the moral effects of religion one cardinal point is missing. The moral precepts of the Christian religion (never mind its practices for the moment) overlap very considerably with the precepts of secular utilitarianism of the type Hume sets out in the *Moral Enquiry,* and the moral precepts of Christianity are guarded by the threat of everlasting punishment and sweetened with the promise of eternal life. As Paley says in his influential *Moral and Political Philosophy,* 'Virtue is, *"the doing good to mankind, in obedience to the will of God, and for the sake of everlasting happiness"* . . . and "everlasting happiness" is the motive of human virtue'.[9] This motive receives not so much as a mention in the *Moral Enquiry.* Why has Hume so ignored it? His own reasons for rejecting doctrines of personal immortality are beside the point here since, *de facto,* very many men accept,

or say they accept, a doctrine of immortality which involves moral
retribution. Even if this belief were demonstrably false (which it is not) Hume
ought to recognise that it is a profitable error and a great advantage on the
side of morality.[10] (He does, but see below).

This omission of Hume's may be criticised in two ways. It may be argued
that the hopes and fears of immortality constitute (as in Paley's definition
of virtue) the *only* motive men have to observe morality, or it may be said
that such hopes and fears constitute one important motive among others.
Either way Hume ignores this potent moral influence of religion — or at least
of Christianity.

Hume's reply to the assertion that the hopes and fears of immortality
constitute the only motive of morality is in the *Moral Enquiry*. If retributive
immortality is indeed a motive to do good, it is, as a matter of common
observation, not the only motive. Our 'interested obligation' to do good has
many facets (see above p. 152) and a normal man is influenced by many of
them. There is no one necessary motive, such as the hope of everlasting
happiness, in the absence of which any normal man will at once rush off into
a life of vicious debauchery. Anyone doing such a thing is a fool or a lunatic,
not an unfortunate victim of an omission in Hume's appraisal of the moral
worth of religion. But surely retributive immortality constitutes *one* of the
most important motives of morality and deserves a mention which it does not
get in the *Moral Enquiry*? The point is well made by Hume himself
(*Enquiry,* 147:155) where, addressing his 'sceptical friend', he says

> You conclude, that religious doctrines and reasonings *can* have no influence
> on life, because they *ought* to have no influence; never considering, that
> men reason not in the same manner you do, but draw many consequences
> from the belief of a divine Existence, and suppose that the *Deity* will
> inflict punishments on vice, and bestow rewards on virtue, beyond what
> appear in the ordinary course of nature. Whether this reasoning of theirs
> be just or not, is no matter. Its influence on their life and conduct must
> still be the same.

The status of this passage is somewhat ambiguous. In the chapter from which
it is taken Hume is at exceptional pains to obscure his own position. The
remarks quoted are in his own first person but I take it that they do *not*
represent his own committed opinion because if they did there would be some
mention of them in the *Moral Enquiry* where men's interests in morality are
discussed at full length. Accordingly I take it that Philo voices Hume's reply
towards the end of the *Dialogues*. His reply is that while the hopes and fears
of immortality *ought* to influence moral conduct *in fact* they do not.
Cleanthes remarks 'For if finite and temporary rewards and punishments
have so great an effect, as we daily find: How much greater must be expected
from such as are infinite and eternal?' To which Philo replies, two paragraphs
later:

Your reasonings are more easily eluded than my facts. The inference is not just: because finite and temporary rewards and punishments have so great influence, that therefore such as are infinite and eternal must have so much greater. Consider — I beseech you, the attachment which we have [if indeed we consider the matter merely in an abstract light: If we compare only the importance of the motives, and then reflect on the natural self-love of mankind; we shall not only look for a great effect from religious considerations; but we must really esteem them absolutely irresistible and infallible in their operation. For what other motive can reasonably counter-balance them even for a moment? But this is not found to hold in reality; and therefore, we may be certain that there is some other principle of human nature, which we have here overlooked, and which diminishes, at least, the force of these motives. This principle is the attachment, which we have] to present things, and the little concern which we discover for objects so remote and uncertain (*Dialogues*, 220: the passage enclosed in square brackets, though a clear development of Hume's point, is deleted in the MS and not usually printed).

A criticism sometimes made of the *Moral Enquiry* is that Hume ignores the hope of everlasting happiness as a motive for morality because he himself rejects such a possibility.[11] He takes it that it does not influence men because it ought not to influence men. But although he himself is aware of this (See *Enquiry*, 147:166) the reverse is his actual position. In the *Dialogues* he admits it ought to influence men but points out that in practice it does not. A parallel observation is afforded by the modern anti-smoking campaign. The smoker is threatened with the probability of heart disease and cancer at some remote but indeterminate time in his future. The threat is exceedingly unpleasant but because of its 'remote and uncertain' character it in fact influences the smoker less than a few pence *now* on a packet of twenty. Likewise the threat of possible eternal punishment *at some time* is less of an influence than the certainty *now* of being expelled from the club for bad behaviour. The point is driven home by Hume in sentences immediately following upon those just quoted from the *Dialogues:*

When divines are declaiming against the common behaviour and conduct of the world, they always represent [the attachment which we have to present things] as the strongest imaginable (which indeed it is) and describe almost all human kind as lying under the influence of it, and sunk in the deepest lethargy and unconcern about their religious interests. Yet these same divines, when they refute their speculative antagonists, suppose the motives of religion to be so powerful, that, without them, it were impossible for civil society to exist (*Dialogues*, 221).

In short, the hope of everlasting happiness and the fear of eternal punish-ment is not regarded by Hume as a significant contribution by popular religion to social morality, and is thus not mentioned by him in the *Moral Enquiry*. These motives do not in fact influence men very much during their lives — Faustian eleventh-hour repentances when the gates of hell are opening are too late to serve the interests of secular society.

*   *   *

At the beginning of this chapter I asked how Hume would answer the argument from general consent. His reply should now be apparent. The explanation why so many men believe in a god, despite the tenuous reasons for doing so, is not that it is a natural belief, but that there are general causes for the belief in human nature. These general causes produce the popular religions of the world. These popular religions or 'superstitions' are distinct from the 'true' religion of the rational and civilised man, but they, not true religion, are the religions whose influence is seen in history and in society. This influence is almost always deplorable from the standpoint of those who seek the general welfare and happiness of mankind. Even the eternal penalties which religion attaches to immoral behaviour do not in reality have the beneficial influence which in theory they should have. At best popular religion is non-moral; at worst it is capable of introducing great misery into the world: 'And the dreadful tribunal of the inquisition, that utmost instance of human depravity, is a durable monument to instruct us what a pitch iniquity and cruelty may rise to, when covered with the sacred mantle of religion'. (*History,* 1st ed. only, Edinburgh 1754, p. 27).

10 The Dispassionate Sceptic

> As to my Opinions, you know I defend none of them positively:
> I only propose my Doubts, where I am so unhappy as not to receive
> the same Conviction with the rest of Mankind.
>
> *Letters*, I, 256

> From accusing me of believing nothing, they now charge me with
> believing every thing. I hope you will be perswaded, that the Truth lyes in
> the middle betwixt these Accusations.
>
> *New Letters*, 231

In any substantial discussion of Hume's critique of religion two questions cannot be entirely ignored. These are: What were Hume's personal beliefs about religion and what are the shortcomings of his critique? The first question, which has attracted a great deal of attention at various times, can, I think, be answered much more completely than most of Hume's commentators seem willing to allow. It is, however, caught up with two tangled and interdependent subsidiary questions both of which have inflamed such protracted controversy as to be in danger of becoming tedious. The first of these subsidiary questions is: who speaks for Hume in the *Dialogues*. The second asks whether the *Dialogues* are concerned with what can be known about god (his nature) or with the existence of god (his being).

(i)   HUME AND PHILO

It has so far been my policy (see p. 13) to treat the two works in which Hume is at pains to conceal his personal position — the *Dialogues* and *Enquiry* Section XI — simply as philosophical arguments in which any point made can be attributed to Hume himself. The only instance in which this policy presented a difficulty was in Chapter 9 (p. 56) where a well-argued point in the *Enquiry* XI flatly contradicted a well-argued point in the *Dialogues*. On that occasion it was necessary to appeal to the *Moral Enquiry* in order to settle, *pro tem.*, which was Hume's own position. I mention this in order to emphasise, what is very well illustrated by the Swinburne/Olding controversy cited in Chapter 2 (and apparently forgotten in some discussion), that it is perfectly possible to carry on a detailed discussion of the philosophical arguments in Hume's works without bothering about who said what and to whom and whether Hume himself would have agreed. But once the interpretation of the *Dialogues* (and to a much lesser extent *Enquiry* XI) is under discussion, it becomes essential to decide which characters speak for Hume himself.

The *Dialogues* are introduced, reported and concluded by one Pamphilius. They take place between Philo, the *careless sceptic*; Cleanthes, the *accurate philosopher*; and the *rigidly orthodox* Demea. (The italics indicate descriptions given by Pamphilius.) Philo criticises the design argument, plays upon the problem of evil and maintains the incomprehensible nature of the divine attributes. Cleanthes defends the design argument, offers solutions to the problem of evil, stresses the need for a comprehensible divine nature and attacks the ontological argument. Demea advocates the ontological argument and maintains that god's nature is a mystery. Lest there should be any premature identification of Hume with Philo, in the final part of the *Dialogues* Philo appears to back out of his opposition to the design argument and Pamphilius sums up: 'I cannot but think that Philo's principles are more probable than Demea's; but that those of Cleanthes approach still nearer the truth'.

Of these four characters Pamphilius (which is as good as to say Cleanthes because of the summing up) has been identified as Hume by Dugald Stewart, Hill Burton (Hume's second biographer), Pringle-Pattison, A. E. Taylor, C. W. Hendel and Andre Leroy among others. Those who have selected Philo include the first reviewer of the *Dialogues* in the *Monthly Review* for 1779[1], Sir Leslie Stephen, T. H. Huxley, N. Kemp Smith in his introduction to the *Dialogues* in 1935[2], and, much more recently, G. Carabelli in *Hume e la Retorica dell'ideologia*.[3] For a short time it appeared as if the scope and thoroughness of Kemp Smith's case, which is argued in minute detail, might have closed the subject. But, in the Joint Session meeting for 1939 (*Hume and Present Day Problems*), Professor Laird shed doubt upon the whole enterprise of identifying Hume in the *Dialogues*: 'the Ciceronian type of dialogue that Hume chose does not permit such canons of interpretation. Each collocutor develops his point of view in successive short speeches and the author has failed if the voice of any one of them is definitely his own'. More recently there have been other rumbles of dissent. For example, James Noxon, in an article since enshrined in V. C. Chappell's useful collection of essays,[4] has objected to Kemp Smith's identification and his objections have been taken up by others: 'Smith has been conclusively refuted by James Noxon', remarks a recent essayist.[5] I shall dispute this later.

Kemp Smith's thesis is 'that Philo, from start to finish, represents Hume; and that Cleanthes can be regarded as Hume's mouthpiece only in those passages in which he is explicitly agreeing with Philo, or in those other passages in which, while refuting Demea, he is also being used to prepare the way for one or other of Philo's independent conclusions' (p. 59). But Smith is careful not to let this general identification tie him down to the absurd rigidity of saying that every word, phrase and sentence in the work is apportioned in this way: *something* of Hume's beliefs can be found in all three speakers. Smith provides a great profusion of evidence. He points out, for example, the dominant position given to Philo both in the extent of what he has to say and in its philosophical importance. He notes that crucial points made by Philo are repeatedly left uncontroverted; that towards the end the dialogue becomes little more than a monologue for Philo with a few bursts of protest from Cleanthes (Demea having departed in disgust); that Philo's final acceptance of the design argument is so hedged and qualified that it seems, much more than is, an agreement with Cleanthes, and so on.

There are a number of additional points which tend to confirm Kemp Smith's thesis. First there is the untutored response of the new reader of the *Dialogues*. Without the prompting of an editorial apparatus I have never yet known any new reader, already familiar with Hume through the *Enquiry*, who did not at once pick out Philo as the hero of the piece. The choice of Philo would have little significance but for the fact that it is exactly what should be expected from the letter in which Hume remarks that he *makes* Cleanthes the hero but could very easily take upon himself the character of Philo (*Letters*, I, 153f). Cleanthes is the contrived hero but Philo, as the naive reader senses, has Hume's favour. Secondly, if Hume does not for the most part identify with Philo's mitigated scepticism, whatever was the point in the first place of all Hume's efforts to cover his tracks? If Hume should really be identified with Cleanthes, he had everything to gain from making this absolutely clear in the text, rather than leaving it to an apparently disingenuous comment from a spectator in the last two lines of the work. The *only* character Hume could not publicly avow in the *Dialogues* is Philo; the only friend he could not admit to being himself is the 'sceptical friend' in *Enquiry* XI. In terms of the politics and prejudices of his day all the cover-up loses its point if Hume is *not*, for the most part, Philo. Thirdly, the scepticism of Philo with regard to theological argument and debate about god's attributes, together with his assent to the propositions that god exists and that his existence is recognisable from the order in nature, and much else in Philo's utterances, are exactly what one finds in the Hume revealed by his private letters and papers: one who doubted, one who believed little, one who disliked religious practices and observances, one who rejected popular religion and all dogmatism and yet retained 'some belief' in a god. It is these similarities which justify speaking of Hume 'covering his tracks' in the *Dialogues* rather than not knowing where he was going or being so uncertain about his position that he communicates his uncertainty to his readers. Much of Philo and much of Hume is so nearly of a piece that it requires a positive effort not to identify Hume and Philo. Finally, Kemp Smith's thesis has been usefully complemented by at least two articles. One is E. C. Mossner's 'The Enigma of Hume'[6] in which the identification of Demea with Samuel Clarke and his less august followers, and of Cleanthes with Butler, is argued in detail. Without going the whole way with Mossner, it is clear that Demea could easily represent the same type of theologian as Clarke and Cleanthes the same type as Butler. This once again leaves Philo as Hume if only on the negative ground that there is no one else he could be: Philo has no matrix outside his creator's mind. The other article is J. V. Price's 'Scepticism in Cicero and Hume'.[7] In this, Price, following up some clues given by Kemp Smith (*Dialogues*, 60f), traces parallels between

Philo in the *Dialogues* and Cotta in Cicero's *De Natura Deorum*. He concludes (p. 106) 'Philo is a skilful blend of Ciceronian structure and Humean philosophy'

Since Kemp Smith's thesis was set out in 1935 no writer known to me has systematically disputed his evidence. What has been done is for a critic to present some general view or hunch which is at variance with Smith's position. An example of this was Laird's contention that the *Dialogues* are Ciceronian in style and as such no speaker is identifiable with the author. This contention seems to be, not so much at variance with Smith, as inviting his conclusions with slightly different emphasis. Thus even in a Ciceronian dialogue one may ask which of the opinions expressed command the author's sympathy and in the case of the *Dialogues* Smith's answer comes again with very little modification: Philo's almost entirely; Cleanthes' in part; Demea's scarcely at all. Another way of attacking Smith's position is that attempted by Noxon in the influential article already cited. There is, as usual, no attempt at reinterpretation or refutation of Smith's actual evidence. What Noxon does is to raise a number of individual points calculated to shed general doubt on Smith's thesis. The points are not numbered by Noxon but I distinguish at least six.[8] They are of enough importance to comment upon in detail in each case.

(1) Cleanthes, Noxon says (p. 366) adopts 'one of Hume's most important principles' when he contends (*Dialogues*, 154) that some beliefs (natural beliefs) are 'neither acquired by rational means nor vulnerable to rational criticism'. The words which Noxon quotes Cleanthes as using when Cleanthes is said to adopt Hume's principle are as follows: 'the arguments for Natural Religion . . . immediately flow in upon you with a force like that of sensation'. But this misrepresents the sense of the original. The subject of Cleanthes' comment is not 'the arguments for natural religion', but, very differently, 'the idea of a contriver'. However the main objection to Noxon's evidence here is that Cleanthes' belief in a designer is *not* parallel, as Noxon seems to imply it is, to a natural belief like belief in an external world. The beliefs are not parallel for a reason already pointed out by Philo and followed up in detail by my argument in Chapter 8. If the philosophical sceptic discovers no rational justification for believing, say in an external world, he still 'must act and live, and converse like other men' (*Dialogues*, 34). The excessive sceptic is under an 'absolute necessity' to do so, and his philosophical scepticism must give way whenever he attends to the ordinary world of his experience. But the religious sceptic is not in this situation. His mitigated scepticism is not rendered academic and unrealistic when he attends to the ordinary world of his experience. Quite the reverse. Such is the remoteness of theological speculation by contrast with our normal experience that 'We must be far removed from the smallest tendency to scepticism not to be apprehensive, that we have here got quite beyond the reach of our faculties' (*Dialogues*, 135; Philo speaking). Thus I would contend that if Cleanthes is adopting 'one of Hume's most important principles' then he is mistaking the application — not a very good ground for identifying Cleanthes with Hume.

(2) Noxon draws attention (p. 368-70) to two passages in Section XI of the *Enquiry* in which Hume appears to voice in his own person opinions which are echoed by Cleanthes in the *Dialogues*. But Noxon also admits the obvious truth that Section XI is so contrived that it is not always possible to isolate Hume's own opinions in it in order to contrast them with opinions which he expresses elsewhere. Moreover one of the passages Noxon cites from the *Enquiry* — to the effect that 'Religion, however corrupted, is still better than no religion at all' (*Dialogues*, 219; cf. *Enquiry*, 147: 155) — is not one of Hume's own opinions: not only because it does not appear in the *Moral Enquiry*, but also because he rejects this view in letters, in his continual depreciation in the *History* of the effects of vulgar religion, and in essays (e.g. the opening remarks in 'Of Superstition and Enthusiasm).

(3) In 1776 Hume wrote to Strahan, his publisher, concerning the *Dialogues*: 'I there introduce a Sceptic, who is indeed refuted, and at last gives up the Argument, nay confesses that he was only amusing himself by all his Cavils; yet before he is silenced, he advances several Topics, which will give Umbrage . . .' (*Letters*, II, 323). Is it likely, asks Noxon, that Hume would refer to his own arguments as 'indeed refuted'? Yes, I would reply, it is likely in the dramatic context of a dialogue of which Hume himself judged 'nothing can be more cautiously and more artfully written' (*Letters*, II, 334). Philo is 'indeed refuted' for the sake of the drama and public opinion; he is not *in fact* refuted in his arguments. If he were *in fact* refuted why do eminent philosophers continue to take his arguments so seriously? The same contrast between Hume's comments on the dramatic setting and his feeling for the actual arguments can be found in an earlier letter already quoted in which on the one hand he remarks that 'I make Cleanthes the Hero of the Dialogue', and that 'the Confusion in which I represent the Sceptic *seems* natural' (*Letters*, I, 153; italics mine), while on the other hand he confesses that he needs help with Cleanthes' arguments and says: 'Had it been my good Fortune to live near you, I shou'd have taken on me the Character of Philo, in the *Dialogue*, which you'll own I could have supported naturally enough'. The inference is clear. Hume's sympathies are with Philo, but he contrives to make Cleanthes the hero (a contrivance which, as already pointed out, even the naive reader is quite likely to see through).

(4) Kemp Smith's judgement is that Philo's final appeal to revealed truth (*Dialogues*, 227, i.e. after his highly qualified acceptance of something in the design argument) is a 'conventionally required proviso'. Noxon asks (presumably to imply the proviso is genuine) 'why Hume would pay such deference to social convention in a work planned for posthumous publication when he has shown so little in books published during his lifetime'. But the implication in this question is just not true. Hume *had* displayed a great deal of concern with social convention in his publications: he withdrew 'Of Miracles' and possibly other items (see p. 102) from the *Treatise*, he modified Section XI of the *Enquiry* into a dialogue in which his own opinions are hard to isolate, he withdrew two of the *Five Dissertations* from publica-

tion, he modified passages in the *History* and he postponed publication of the *Dialogues* for twenty-six years out of deference to the offence they might cause, despite their being 'artfully written'.

(5) The *Dialogues,* says Noxon, furnish one 'vital piece of evidence' namely a single paragraph, 'in which Hume quite clearly speaks for himself' in the dispute between Cleanthes and Philo. The paragraph is a footnote on p.219.

> It seems evident, that the dispute between the sceptics and dogmatists is entirely verbal, or at least regards only the degrees of doubt and assurance, which we ought to indulge with regard to all reasoning: And such disputes are commonly at the bottom, verbal, and admit not of any precise determination. No philosophical dogmatist denies, that there are difficulties both with regard to the senses and to all science; and that these difficulties are in a regular logical method, absolutely insolveable. No sceptic denies, that we lie under an absolute necessity, notwithstanding these difficulties, of thinking, and believing, and reasoning with regard to all kind of subjects, and even of frequently assenting with confidence and security . . .

Unfortunately it is by no means 'quite clear' from the MS (*cf.* edition by J.V. Price, Oxford 1976, p. 250) whether this footnote should stand as a comment by Hume speaking for himself, or whether it is intended as an extension of Philo's long paragraph on scepticism which just precedes it.

But for the sake of Noxon's argument let us presume it is indeed Hume speaking for himself. Noxon interprets the footnote as an affirmation of Hume's mitigated scepticism in contrast to what, in Noxon's estimate, is Philo's excessive scepticism. I cannot accept this interpretation. In Part I of the *Dialogues* Cleanthes has already *mistaken* Philo's position as one of excessive scepticism and has had his mistake corrected:

> *Cleanthes:* Whether your scepticism be as absolute and sincere as you pretend, we shall learn bye and bye, when the company breaks up: We shall then see, whether you go out at the door or the window . . . (p. 132).

> *Philo:* To whatever length any one may push his speculative principles of scepticism, he must act, I own, and live, and converse like other men; . . . But when we look beyond human affairs and the properties of the surrounding bodies: When we carry our speculations into the two eternities, before and after the present state of things; into the creation and formation of the universe; the existence and properties of spirits; the powers and operations of one universal spirit, . . . We must be far removed from the smallest tendency to scepticism not to be apprehensive, that we have here got quite beyond the reach of our faculties (pp. 134-135).

The type of scepticism which Philo here professes is identical in character to the mitigated scepticism which Hume, unequivocally in his own person, defends at the end of the *Enquiry:*

> Another species of *mitigated* skepticism which may be of advantage to mankind, and which may be the natural result of the Pyrrhonian doubts and scruples, is the limitation of our inquiries to such subjects as are best adapted to the narrow capacity of human understanding ... [A correct judgement] ... confines itself to common life ... leaving the more sublime topics to the embellishment of poets and orators or to the arts of priests and politicians (*Enquiry*, 162:170).

Thus whatever construction should be put upon the footnote, the construction which Noxon puts upon it will not do.[9]

(6) 'Another of the difficulties involved in identifying Hume with Philo is raised by the complete reversal of standpoint made by Philo in the twelfth and final dialogue', writes Noxon. 'Some attempts must be made to interpret this admittedly unexpected finale'. Kemp Smith's explanation (which Noxon does not examine) consists in showing in detail that Philo's concessions, when they are carefully examined, fall very far short of a 'complete reversal of standpoint'. They amount to saying, as I have already argued in Chapters 2 and 8, that objections to the design argument do not add up to a total, knockdown, disproof. The *possibility* of interpreting the cause of order in the universe as an intelligent agent survives, and is dramatically overstated by Philo in his apparent reversal of standpoint: 'Here then the existence of a Deity is plainly ascertained by reason' (*Dialogues*, 217). I say 'overstated' because the deity thus ascertained is something exceedingly far short of the god of conventional theism: so far short that, as Philo points out (and he is not controverted by Cleanthes), the atheist and the theist can agree that 'the principle which first arranged, and still maintains, order in this universe, bears ... some remote inconceivable analogy to the other operations of nature, and among the rest to the œconomy of human mind and thought'. Again, in the final paragraph given to Philo (written in 1776, the year of Hume's death), the limitations of the possibility left open by Philo's criticisms of the design argument are stressed:

> If the whole of natural theology, as some people seem to maintain, resolves itself into one simple, though somewhat ambiguous, at least undefined proposition, *that the cause or causes of order in the universe probably bear some remote analogy to human intelligence:* If this proposition be not capable of extension, variation, or more particular explication: If it afford no inference that affects human life, or can be the source of any action or forbearance: And if the analogy, imperfect as it is, can be carried no farther than to human intelligence ... what can [a man] do more than give a plain, philosophical assent to the proposition, as often as it occurs (*Dialogues*, 227).

But it is apparent that in this conclusion the atheist can stress the remoteness and the theist the possibility of the analogy, and this is what Hume allows for in his comments that the dispute is 'merely verbal' and 'incurably ambiguous'.

From these six considerations Noxon arrives at his assessment: 'In one way, Hume was all or two of his characters; in another he was none or neither'.[10] It seems scarcely fair to Noxon to report this conclusion as a 'total' refutation of Kemp Smith. I myself find it difficult to see that Kemp Smith's position has been disturbed in any serious way. Hume is still Philo except when Cleanthes refutes Demea. Not every single sentence fits this formula, but most of the *Dialogues* do, and that is sufficient identification for the sympathies of their author in a Ciceronian dialogue.

The second question of interpretation is whether Hume in the *Dialogues* is concerned with questioning the existence of god, his being, or with questioning what can be said or known about him, his attributes. Now at the commonsense level it seems clear that if we believe in the existence of something, we believe in the existence of a thing with at least one attribute ('existence' itself not counting). If there are no attributes at all — or none which can be known — then nothing exists to believe in. Having said that, the puzzle in the *Dialogues* is supposed to take shape because Pamphilius prefaces the whole discussion with the comment 'What truth so obvious, so certain, as the *being* of a God . . . what obscure questions occur, concerning the *nature* of that divine Being . . .' and this is agreed to by Cleanthes, Demea *and* by Philo: 'the question can never be concerning the *being,* but only the *nature* of the Deity' (p. 142). But Philo (and Demea, somewhat gullibly, but quite in keeping with this theology) also seems to say, what he does not in fact quite say, that the deity is unknowable, that nothing can be said about him, that, in effect, he has no attributes. This appearance has led one group of interpreters to conclude, with various shades of emphasis, that Hume is an essentially irreligious man who does not believe in a god at all, whereas another group says he does; the debate in the *Dialogues* is entirely about god's nature. My own position on this matter is a central thesis in this book and has already been developed in earlier chapters but I shall reiterate it here. It is also the answer to the first and most important question about Hume's personal beliefs — does he believe in a god?

(ii)   A CITIZEN OF THE WORLD

In one of the mottos to this chapter Hume says in effect that the truth about his belief 'lyes in the middle' between the extremes of believing everything and believing nothing. But what does Hume call the middle? Again and again in private and published work Hume gives explicit or implicit assent to the porposition *that there is a god.* This assent is elicited by the recognition that the order to be found in nature *could* (not must) be explained as the

work of an ordering agent. But this ordering agent — and this is the aspect of
the *Dialogues* which easily deceives those in search of Hume's theism or his
atheism — cannot be known to have any attributes other than those just
sufficient to produce the given result; that is to say, the power of an agent
together with 'some remote analogy to human intelligence'. In particular
this god cannot be known to have any *moral* attributes: 'The true conclusion
is, that the original source of all things . . . has no more regard to good above
ill than to heat above cold . . .' (*Dialogues,* 212; see also 211). The alliance
between Philo and Demea over the incomprehensible nature of the deity is
thus a way of showing (as Demea eventually grasps) that the nature of the
deity as allowed by Philo is not a fit subject for adoration as a sacred mystery.
The adorable mystery of god which evokes a religious response is quite different from a possible original source of the order to be found in nature which
might bear some remote analogy 'to the other operations of nature and among
the rest to the œconomy of human mind and thought'. Such an original
source of order could scarcely function even as the start for belief in a
personal God exercising a moral jurisdiction, accessible to prayer, performing
acts of intervention in his creation, and worthy of adoration. In such a God
as this Hume seems to have had no belief at any period in his adult life. But
at the ultimate point of decision in looking for the source of order in nature —
when it could be regarded as an inherent principle in things ('brute fact' is
the more fashionable phrase) *or* as a principle which also warrants very
circumspect use of the word 'intelligent' — at this point of ultimate ambiguity Hume inclines to the latter of the two possibilities. This is Hume's
'some belief'. This is the modest persuasion which caused him to be
shocked at the dogmatic atheism of the *philosophes* and perturbed at the
inconoclastic sneers of Frederick the Great (*Letters,* I, 327). It is not in itself
atheism nor is it defended positively. But it *is* atheism as far as the Christian
God is concerned just as belief in the Christian God was atheism as far as the
classical Roman religion was concerned.[11] This sort of atheism is about as
damaging to Christianity as any atheism could possibly be. For it avoids the
dogmatism, which many people find distasteful, of denying the existence of all
gods whatsoever and yet its diffident affirmation is completely without
religious implications. As Hume points out, by a suitable emphasis and choice
of words both the atheist and theist can agree about it (*Dialogues,* 218)
and the dispute between them becomes 'merely verbal'. But assent to the
existence of god in the sense allowed by Hume is valueless for any theistic
religion. It carries no duties, invites no action, allows no inferences and
involves no devotion. In the light of this the *Dialogues* can be understood as a
discussion of the nature of god, what can be known about him, not a
discussion of the question whether a god exists. But in the course of the
Dialogues it becomes apparent that Hume (Philo) is arguing that we can say
very little about god's nature and what little we can say cannot be said
dogmatically. But the little we can say is neither so little as to invoke the
logical objection that Hume is assenting to the existence of a being with no

attributes at all, nor so much as to arrive at anything like the Christian God. This position is confusing to the reader who consciously or unconsciously looks at the *Dialogues* with Christian preconceptions: Hume's critical discussion of god's nature *does* turn out to be a discussion of the existence of the Christian God because he argues that the god which might exist could not be known to have any of the distinguishing features which the Christian God is supposed to have. Thus from the point of view of assenting to the existence of *some* god the discussion in the *Dialogues* is 'concerning the nature of that divine Being'. But from the point of view of assenting to the existence of the *Christian* God (or anything like him) the question concerns the being of God.

From Hume's fundamental assent to the existence of a god, a belief which, for want of a better name, I shall call 'attenuated deism', certain other of his opinions follow. In each case there is independent evidence that he holds the opinion. The opinions are these four:

(1) That religious observances as such are at best worthless[12] and at worst mischievous with the solitary exception of 'virtue and good morals', which 'alone could be acceptable to a perfect being'. But virtue and good morals are not distinctively religious; prayer and love of god which are, excite Hume's explicit censure. His specific objection to 'loving' god is that in real terms this is not possible:

> A remote Ancestor, who has left us Estates & Honours, acquired with Virtue, is a great Benefactor, & yet 'tis impossible to bear him any Affection, because unknown to us; tho in general we know him to be a Man or a Human Creature, which brings him vastly nearer our Comprehension than an invisible infinite Spirit. A man, therefore . . . from this Circumstance of the Invisibility & Incomprehensibility of the Deity may feel no Affection towards him. And indeed I am afraid, that all Enthusiasts mightily deceive themselves. Hope & Fear perhaps agitate their Breast when they think of the Deity: Or they degrade him into a Resemblance with themselves, & by tha means render him into a Resemblance with themselves, & by that means render him more comprehensible . . . Please to observe, that I not only exclude the turbulent Passions, but the calm Affections. Neither of them can operate without the Assistance of the Senses, & Imagination, or at least a more compleat Knowledge of the Object than we have of the Deity (*New Letters*, 13).

Hence there can be no duty to love god. The remarkable consistency of view between this early letter (1743) and the views expressed in the *N.H.R.* and *Dialogues* can hardly escape notice. In the same letter Hume also provides the only extant explanation of his rejection of prayer. Its rejection is of course a corollary of his attenuated deism but more specifically: our prayers can have no influence on the deity but we can make use of no Expression or even Thought, in Prayers & Entreaties, which does not imply that these Prayers have an Influence . . . This Figure is very dangerous & leads directly & even unavoidably to Impiety & Blasphemy. Tis a natural Infirmity of Men to imagine, that their Prayers have a direct Influence, & this Infirmity must be extremely foster'd & encourag'd by the constant Use of Prayer (ibid).

The objection holds for both Hume's concept of god – how could we suppose the source of order in the universe to be interested in our little wishes – and for the Christian concept of God – if He knows our future as we know our own past how could petitionary prayer move Him to change what is to be? Whether this is or is not a good objection to the Christian use of petitionary prayer has been discussed at length elsewhere and I shall not pursue the matter here. But what cannot be ignored is the exception which Hume makes of virtue and good morals. Why should he suppose that these 'alone could be acceptable to a perfect being'? (*N.H.R.*, 70). There are at least two possibilities. The untidy one is that here we have an odd end of Hume's thought (or lack of it) which refuses to be tied in with the rest. It is an ill-considered vestige of Christianity retained as the absent-minded assumption that if anything is acceptable to the deity, good morals must be. The tidier possibility is that in these contexts (*N.H.R.*, 70; *New Letters*, 12) Hume is not talking about himself. He is saying *if* there were a perfect being as implied in Christianity *then* only good living could be pleasing to him. Hume has an objection to all religion *except* in as far as it is associated with good morality. But this does not entail that he himself practises good morality *because* it would be acceptable to god as he understands that term. Far from it. His social utilitarianism is independent of religion. It is his secular morality which makes him approve of religion if and when it inculcates morality – as 'true religion' would and as 'vulgar superstition' seldom does.

(2) That conventionally required religious observances are of too little real importance to justify making an issue out of disregarding them: 'It is putting too great a respect on the Vulgar, and on their Superstitions, to pique one' self on Sincerity with regard to them . . .' (*New Letters*, 83; see also *Letters*, I, 151f). Hume was not of the scrupulous and dogmatic stuff of which humanist martyrs are made!

(3) That morally contentious issues, for example suicide, and moral distinctions in general, should not be referred to the decision of religious teaching but should be settled by reference to the needs and happiness of people. The most aggressively challenging application of this to a particular case is in the essay 'Of Suicide' but the whole movement of argument in the *Moral Enquiry* is in favour of the independence of utilitarian morality from religion.

(4) That theological argument and dispute is 'sophistry and illusion'. The celebrated final paragraph of the *Enquiry* is the best-known statement of this position but much of the *Dialogues* and considerable areas of the *Enquiry*

itself consist in showing, in particular instances, the futility of attempting to reach reasoned conclusions in theology. The futility is amplified in a letter: 'In Politics & natural Philosophy, whatever Conclusion is contrary to certain Matter of Fact must certainly be wrong, and there must some Error lie somewhere in the Argument, whether we be able to show it or not. But in Metaphysics or Theology, I cannot see how either of these plain & obvious Standards of Truth can have place' (*Letters*, I, 152). There are no basic data in theology — as would be expected if Hume's attenuated deism is the only rational religion.

Other opinions concerning 'the great questions of religion' which Hume certainly held but which do not follow from his attenuated deism are these five:
(1) That the origin of religion is fear of the unknown causes of natural events and that its commonest manifestations are the corrupt forms of superstition and enthusiasm. These *are* religion as it has commonly been found in the world and whose social and moral effects are bad.
(2) That true religion, if any such could be found, would be an inconspicuous personal thing which would enforce morality.
(3) That the priesthood, particularly in institutionalised religion, have an interest in promoting superstition, ignorance, persecution, and, in themselves, hypocrisy. This theme occurs throughout Hume's writings. His earliest and most moderate expression is in the *Treatise*: '. . . in matters of religion men take a pleasure in being terrify'd, and . . . no preachers are so popular, as those who excite the most dismal and gloomy passions' (p. 115). By 1742 he is more explicit

> And the same principles of priestly government continuing, after Christianity became the established religion, they have engendered a spirit of persecution, which has ever since been the poison of human society, and the source of the most inveterate factions in every government (essay 'Of Parties in General').

In the *Three Essays Moral and Political* of 1748 occurs the celebrated note to the essay 'Of National Characters':

> [the clergy] must set a guard over their looks and works and actions: And in order to support the veneration paid them by the multitude, they must not only keep a remarkable reserve, but must promote the spirit of superstition, by a continued grimace and hypocrisy . . . The ambition of the clergy can often be satisfied only by promoting ignorance and superstition and implicit faith and pious frauds. And having got what Archimedes only wanted, (namely, another world, on which he could fix his engines) no wonder they move this world at their pleasure.

Hume's letters are also liberally sprinkled with comments in a similar vein and even in the *History* he remarks '. . . in every religion, except the true, [the diligence of the clergy] is highly pernicious, and it has even a natural tendency to pervert the true, by infusing into it a strong mixture of superstition, folly, and delusion' (*History*, IV, 31). In the late twentieth century these sentiments may appear illiberal and harsh. In eighteenth-century Scotland and to a man born within living memory of the covenanters they might seem little more than indiscreet.

(4) That there has been no particular revelation of the divine nature and purposes which could establish its authenticity to the satisfaction of an impartial, rational man. The evidence for this is 'Of Miracles' together with the total absence of anything to the contrary in any private letter or document. But at certain points in his published discussion of items in the philosophy of religion Hume is in fact apt to refer his readers to revelation. Thus, at the end of the *Dialogues*, Philo advises a person 'seasoned with a just sense of the imperfections of natural reason' to 'fly to revealed truth'. Likewise at the end of the essay 'Of the Immortality of the Soul' he remarks on 'the infinite obligations which mankind have to Divine revelation' for ascertaining 'this great and important truth' and in somewhat similar manner at the beginning and end of the chapter on miracles he talks about being moved by faith or by the Holy Spirit. What should we make of these references? There are a number of possibilities. They could be sincere directions to a source of information about god which is reliable despite its defiance of reason and evidence. But given Hume's other opinions, and his attack upon the authenticity of revelation, the sincerity of such directions is quite excessively improbable. Alternatively they could be mere sarcasms which, in moments of political pressure, allow themselves to be feigned as real. While this could well be the case in 'Of the Immortality of the Soul' the suggestion will not fit the *Dialogues* since the paragraph from which the quotation is taken was written when Hume knew he would not live to see their publication. A third possibility, and one most in keeping with the Calvinism with which Hume was so familiar, is that at these points in his work he is saying that faith in a revelation, possibly arrived at through 'the immediate operation of the Holy Spirit', is the only attitude which is possible for a thinking man who retains a religion more extensive than the possibility of attenuated deism which Philo allows for. But this attitude of faith is not a ground of assent. It is an arbitrary, anti-rational thing which a reasonable man can neither explain nor defend:

> So that, upon the whole, we may conclude, that the *Christian Religion* not only was at first attended with miracles, but even at this day cannot be believed by any reasonable person without one. Mere reason is insufficient to convince us of its veracity: And whoever is moved by *Faith* to assent to it, is conscious of a continued miracle in his own person, which subverts all the principles of his understanding, and gives him a determination to believe what is most contrary to custom and experience (*Enquiry*, 131: 141).

Whoever is moved by faith may well be moved in this way but Hume himself was not of that company: He neither believed in miracles nor was himself the subject of one.

(5) That there is no life after death. I would have thought this so clearly and obviously was Hume's belief that no discussion would be necessary, but in a preliminary attempt to establish his contention that 'Hume has left his readers to wonder about his personal convictions on the great question of religion' Noxon questions it. He dismisses the evidence of Boswell's deathbed interview with Hume: 'Boswell was not persuaded of the philosopher's sincerity nor was Samuel Johnson' (when he heard about the interview). Part of this statement is however contrary to Boswell's explicit report in the passage to which Noxon refers us: 'I had a strong curiosity to be satisfied if he persisted in disbelieving a future state even when he had death before his eyes. I was persuaded from what he now said, and from his manner of saying it, that he did persist'.[13] What is more, Johnson scarcely knew Hume, and *his* refusal to believe that Hume died persuaded of his imminent annihilation is no evidence at all about Hume's beliefs although it may possibly be evidence about Johnson's.[14] But if there were any genuine doubt whether Boswell's deathbed interview revealed Hume's true belief about immortality then there is plenty of evidence elsewhere. His earliest extant note[15] on the subject reveals the scepticism which appeared in full-blown form in 'Of the Immortality of the Soul' and which sufficiently infected the *Treatise* for his disbelief in a future state to be one of the complaints against him in 1745. Indeed his disbelief in this matter formed one of the recurring themes in the complaints of his contemporaries. There is Boswell's report in 1769 (see note 14). There is the calm, Epicurean acceptance of death displayed by Hume in his last letters and recorded in the 'Letter from Adam Smith' (reprinted in *Dialogues,* 243-248) and in Dr Cullen's letter to Dr Hunter (17 Sep. 1776)[16] As late as 1827 Sir Walter Scott remarks in his journal on the dying philosopher's untroubled end[17] — a cause for surprise among the many who knew of his disbelief in immortality. We cannot of course ask him what he believed at the very last moment of consciousness although he was asked that question in a letter which probably never reached him. William Strahan, in a letter headed London, 19 August 1776 (Hume died on 25 August), writes: 'Our soul, or immaterial part of us, some say, is able, when on the brink of dissolution, to take a glimpse of futurity; and for that reason I earnestly wish to have your *last thoughts* on this important subject'.[18] It is almost as if those who knew him waited in apprehensive hope for some dying affirmation of belief from the great sceptic. But none came. That he was TRUE TO THE END, according to his family motto, we may be certain from the lack of any contrary evidence — evidence so eagerly sought by those about him that had any existed it could never have been concealed.

It is always tempting for a biographer or critic to attribute to the object of his study more positive opinions than he had or more consistent beliefs than he at any time possessed. Nevertheless, in Hume's case, as more than one writer has noted, there is a certain unity in his views from start to finish. He was not a man given to different 'periods' of thought. Having had the one colossal re-think which preceded and produced the *Treatise,* much of the rest of his work on philosophy and religion seems to be a consistent working out and application of that one re-think. This, together with the large number of clues and the evidence which Hume has left us, is the justification for attempting to itemise his beliefs and opinions about religion in the way I have done: a basic assent of the understanding to the proposition that a god exists, together with nine other items ranging from immortality to the character of the clergy. But what overall picture do they give us of Hume?

The conventional ascriptions 'atheist', 'agnostic', 'materialist' and even· 'sceptic' catch neither the complexity nor the range of his conclusions about religion.[19] His beliefs, as I have already suggested, are perhaps better described as a highly attenuated deism which is not positively advocated. It is the religion of a 'citizen of the world' who has, after due consideration, rejected the beliefs of all particular sects in favour of a true religion whose sole credo is a diffidently held belief in an intelligent origin of natural order and whose sole observance is the morality which would anyway have been followed for other reasons 'were there no god in the universe'.

(iii) A PUBLIC RELIGION

When one tries to assess Hume's critique of religion as a whole one is immediately struck by its critical aloofness and by Hume's unusual degree of externality to religion. A.E. Taylor made this a cause of complaint and nothing more: 'Criticism is always superficial unless it is inspired by sympathetic insight and an adequate sense of the significance of the issues at stake'.[20] But this is a perverse judgement. That Hume did not have an insider's sympathy with religion and that he was not worried or emotionally involved in the issues which he discusses means, at least in part, that he is the more able to go wherever the argument leads. This treatment of religion as an objective system subject to disinterested discussion was typical of his century. But in Hume's writing one gets very strongly the sense of religion as a public, inspectable phenomenon. Its belief can be examined and its practices observed. There is no hint that he ever views religion from within as a way of life, a metaphysic of existence, a worthwhile thing to which total commitment is possible.

But this limitation, serious as it is, is better in the founder[21] of the philosophy of religion than the obverse: a profound awareness of the possibilities of the religious life without any ability to step back from one's commitment and ask: Is what I believe true? Is my religion a commitment to anything real? In the two centuries which have passed since Hume's death 'total commitment' has proved the easy way out for every anti-rational theology and it is sometimes said that by displaying the barrenness of natural theology Hume opened the way for such developments. He did not. He showed instead what a modest thing a rational man's religion would be and how diffidently it should be held.

*   *   *

There is in the Carlton Cemetery in Edinburgh an austere monument over the tomb of the Great Sceptic. At his own request it records only his name and dates of birth and death, posterity being left to add the rest. Posterity has added a great deal — over eight hundred articles, books and major references in the past quarter-century alone — and it is continually adding more, perhaps at times too much more. No one survives being over estimated, nor is there any surer way of destroying an author's impact than by the wearisome and repetitive over-attention or adulation which can sometimes characterise a bicentenary. Nevertheless, within the limitations of human existence, posterity has already fulfilled the promise of Colonel Edmondstoune in his last letter to the dying philosopher: 'You can't die, you must live in the memory of all your friends and acquaintances, and your works will render you immortal'.

L'envoy

So for the present, gentle reader! and
    Still gentler purchaser! the bard — that's I —
Must, with permission, shake you by the hand,
    And so your humble servant, and good-b'ye!
We meet again, if we should understand
    Each other; and if not, I shall not try
Your patience further than by this short sample —
    'Twere well if others follow'd my example.

Don Juan

Notes

1 Introduction: Hume on Religion

1. See list of abbreviations.
2. E. C. Mossner, 'Hume's Early Memoranda, 1729-1740: The Complete Text'. *Journal of the History of Ideas* (1948).
3. See list of abbreviations.
4. A full discussion of the evidence is contained in E. C. Mossner's 'Hume's Four Dissertations', *Modern Philology* (1950).
5. It contains corrections in Hume's hand which have never been incorporated in any printed edition of the essays. The corrections are noted in my article 'Hume's Suppressed Dissertations – An Authentic Text', *Hermathena* (1968). I adopt these in quotations from the essays in the present work.
6. *English Philosophy since 1900* (Oxford, 1958) p. 164.
7. The considerable bulk of essays – some of them on Hume on religion – which the 1976 bicentenary elicited from Hume scholars seems to further illustrate this generalisation, but at the time of writing not all these essays are available to me.
8. Lincoln, Nebraska, 1965.
9. Stockholm, 1966.
10. The large-scale pre-war study by A. Leroy, *La Critique et la Religion chez David Hume* (Paris, 1930) has always been somewhat inaccessible to English readers and is now almost unobtainable. A recent European work is Giancarlo Carabelli's *Hume e la Retorica dell'ideologia* (Florence, 1972). This is a detailed study of the *Dialogues* in relation to their background in the Scottish and European enlightenment.
11. As already noted in the Preface I write 'God' with a capital letter only when the personal deity of tradition Christianity is specifically intended. In all other or ambiguous usages a small letter is employed. Thus, for example, a small letter will be used when the god referred to could be the non-personal, non-sustaining creator acceptable to the deists. The only exception to this convention is when the reference is to a deity with features common to the Judaic, Christian and Moslem religions (for example, one sustaining, all-powerful, personal God having a moral concern with mankind). In these cases I use a capital letter. I adopt this convention in the hope that it may on occasions prevent ambiguities and not as an accolade to one concept of deity.

2 Order and Design

1. Plato: *Timaeus* 47; Xenophon: *Memorabilia*, 1 iv 4-8; Cicero; *De Natura Deorum*, II xxxiv-xxxv; Aquinas: *Summa Theologica*, 1 Quest, 11 Art. 3; Newton: *Principia Mathematica*, General Scholium; Berkeley: *Alciphron* IV.
2. *The World as I See It* (London, 1935) p. 28.
3. See list of abbreviations.
4. *Analogy of Religion*, chapter 3.
5. J. S. Mill, *Three Essays on Religion*, 4th edition (London, 1875) p.167.
6. R. G. Swinburne, 'The Argument from Design', *Philosophy* (1968) 199-212. I shall subsequently refer to this article as 'Swinburne' followed by the page.
7. Although Hume does not have the theory of natural selection at hand he

does make a suggestion (*Dialogues,* 185) which comes remarkably close to anticipating the theory as an objection to the teleological argument. See below p. 36f.

8. Colin Maclaurin, *An Account of Sir Isaac Newton's Discoveries,* 3rd edition (London, 1775) p.400.

9. See Chapter 3.

10. *Three Essays on Religion,* p.38.

11. *Alciphron,* fourth dialogue, §5.

12. A. Olding, 'The Argument from Design — A Reply to R. G. Swinburne', *Religious Studies* (1971) p.370.

13. McPherson, *The Argument from Design* (London, 1972) p. 73.

14. Antony Flew, *Hume's Philosophy of Belief* (London, 1961) p. 231.

15. For example, L. Pearl, 'Hume's Criticism of the Design Argument', *Monist* (1970) p.275.

16. It is only fair to point out that in a later article Swinburne does retract this judgement ('The Argument from Design — A Defence' *Religious Studies* (1972) p.203). But he does not offer an assessment of the analogy.

17. *Three Essays on Religion,* p.170.

18. Paris, 1970; London, 1972.

19. L. Pearl, op. cit., p. 282.

20. Swinburne, 'The Argument from Design—A Defence', *Religious Studies* (1972) p.199.

21. See Chapter 3.

22. I say 'appears' because the dialogue context of the discussion makes it particularly difficult in this instance to identify exactly Hume's personal conclusions.

23. The answer Hume eventually gives is that sceptics and mystics do not *really* differ: see *Dialogues* Part XII.

24. Whether any worthwhile and possible simplication is achieved in ultimately reducing explanation in terms of laws of nature to explanation in terms of agents is one of the matters explored at some length in the Swinburne-Olding controversy (Swinburne, *Philosophy* (1968) 199-212; Olding, *Religious Studies* (1971) 361-73; Swinburne, *Religious Studies* (1972) 193-205; Olding, *Religious Studies* (1973) 229-232). I shall not follow the argument here since most of the issues lie well beyond those raised by Hume.

25. By 'chaos' Hume probably means something like the 'formless void' of Milton. In the terms I used above, p. 35, this could mean either total mechanical *and* statistical disorder or it could mean matter subject to processes but lacking structures (forms).

26. 'Hume's Immanent God' in *Hume* ed. V. C. Chappell, (New York, 1966)

27. What Jessop actually wrote was 'Hume's *Dialogues,* having the eighteenth century written all over them, are not livingly relevant to an age that has been taught by science and philosophy alike to view the theological problem more vastly and to think about it in ways that Hume did not foresee' *(Aristotelian Society,* Supp. Vol. XVIII (1939) p. 218). In the same symposium A. E. Taylor was even more brisk: 'repeated study of Hume's *Dialogues* leaves me convinced that their permanent worth is commonly over-estimated'. That I disagree with these writers will be apparent; that they were wrong in their estimation is evident from the ever-increasing attention given to the *Dialogues* in recent times.

28. In his book *David Hume: The Newtonian Philosopher* (Boston, 1975), Nicholas Capaldi remarks 'there is no context in which Hume ever challenges the argument from design' (p. 190). While I agree with much of what Capaldi says this particular judgement seems to be at variance with any straightforward reading of the evidence.

3 Evil, Freedom and the Religious Hypothesis

1. M. B. Ahern, *The Problem of Evil* (London, 1971) p. 61.

2. *Evil and the God of Love* (London, 1966) p.341.

3. Nelson Pike, 'Hume on Evil', *Philosophical Review* (1963); reprinted in *God and Evil*, ed. Pike (New Jersey, 1964).

4. For a discussion of this point see R. Puccetti, 'Is Pain Necessary', *Philosophy* (1975).

5. Antony Flew, 'Divine Omnipotence and Human Freedom', in *New Essays in Philosophical Theology*, eds. Flew and MacIntyre (London, 1955); J. L. Mackie, 'Evil and Omnipotence', *Mind* (1955).

6. Flew has reformulated this position in 'Compatibilism, Free Will and God', *Philosophy* (1973)

7. Antony Flew, *Hume's Philosophy of Belief* (London, 1961) p.162.

4   *Being and Necessity*

1. See letter written to Michael Ramsey, 31 August 1737, published in *Archievum Historii Filozofie i Mysli Spolecznej* (1963) (the journal of the Philosophical and Sociological Institute of the Polish Academy of Science). See also *A Letter*, 23.

2. Clarke gave the Boyle Lectures in 1704 and 1705. These were published as *A Discourse concerning the Being and Attributes of God, the obligations of Natural Religion, and the Truth and Certainty of the Christian Revelation.* Page references are to the 9th edition (London, 1738). I say 'appears to be' Clarke's argument. The attribution is suggested by Kemp Smith in his edition of the *Dialogues* (p.115) and is supported by Hume's peculiar combination of what we would now distinguish as the ontological and cosmological arguments — a combination which is characteristic of Clarke. Clarke is also mentioned by name on p.190. But Leibniz' statements of the *a priori* arguments are more familiar to us than Clarke's, and they would presumably have been known to Hume. For example, in the 'Principles of Nature and of Grace, founded on Reason' Leibniz asks 'Why is there something rather than nothing?' — a question Hume echoes. But the echo could also be from Clarke and this, together with the other evidence, leads me to continue speaking of Hume's paraphrase of *Clarke's* argument. But I would certainly not want to maintain that Hume's statement of the *a priori* argument can owe nothing to Leibniz. Note, for example, the similarity between a sentence in *Dialogues* 189 and a sentence in 'On the Ultimate Origination of Things' (see text, p. 69).

3. *De Rerum Natura*, I 215-220, 265-270 *et al.*

4. 'Existence, Predication and the Ontological Argument', *Mind* (1962). Reprinted in *The Many-Faced Argument*, eds. J. Hick and A. McGill (London, 1968). Page references are to this edition.

5. Geach and Anscombe, *Three Philosophers* (Oxford, 1961) p.115.

6. *The Ontological Argument* (London, 1972) p.33.

7. 'Has it been Proved that all Real Existence is Contingent?', *American Philosophical Quarterly* (1971).

8. 'The Existence of God', a debate between Russell and Copleston, broadcast 1948. Reprinted in Russell's *Why I am not a Christian* (London, 1957) and in *The Existence of God*, ed. John Hick (London and New York, 1964) p.169. Page references are to the latter edition.

9. *The Five Ways* (London, 1969) p.66.

10. Lucretius, I, 155.

11. Leibniz, 'On the Ultimate Origination of Things', in *Philosophical Writings*, ed. G.H.R. Parkinson (London, 1973) p.136.

12. *Arguments for the Existence of God* (London, 1970) p.41.

13. Charles Hartshorne, *The Logic of Perfection* (Lasalle, 1962) p.53.

5   *Theology and Meaning*

1. Antony Flew, *Hume's Philosophy of Belief* (London, 1961) p.26.

2. London and New York, 1961.

3. Jonathan Bennett, *Locke, Berkeley, Hume: Central Themes* (Oxford, 1971) p.229.

4. e.g. *Luke* XII, 5-10; *Matthew* XXIII, 33.

6   *The Immortality of a Person*

1. See Chapter 10, Section (ii).

2. See J. Noxon, *Hume's Philosophical Development* (Oxford 1973) p.170.

3. I *Cor.,* XV, 44.

4. I *Cor.,* XV, 53.

5. *City of God,* XIII, 23.

6. The idea is powerfully conveyed by Marcus Aurelius (X,38): 'Bear in mind that what pulls the strings is that Hidden Thing within us: *that* makes our speech, *that* makes our life, *that* one may say, makes the man'.

7. The doctrines of resurrected body and (immaterial) soul combine if it is held that the person survives and has experiences between death and the reconstitution of the body at the general resurrection of the dead in the last day. For the soul as the vehicle of identity of the person in the resurrected body, see Locke, *Essay,* II, xxvii, 15.

8. There is an anecdote (*Lives,* VIII, 4) in Diogenes Laertius which displays the Pythagorean belief in metempsychosis and whimsically anticipates Locke's account of memory as an essential of personal identity: 'Hermes told him he might choose any gift he liked except immortality; so he asked to retain through life and through death a memory of his experiences. Hence in life he could recall everything, and when he died he still kept the same memories'.

9. *God and the Soul* (London, 1969) p.17.

10. See, for example, Antony Flew's 'Is there a Case for Disembodied Survival?', *Journal of the American Society for Psychical Research* (1972), p.131f.

11. *Philosophical Commentaries,* ed. A.A. Luce (London, 1944) p. 301.

12. *Essay,* II, xxvii, 17.

13. I express myself guardedly because of Jonathan Bennett's argument in Chapter 3 of *Locke, Berkeley, Hume: Central Themes* (Oxford, 1971), that what we have is Berkeley's exegetical mistake not Locke's theory of substance. Bennett may well be right, but Berkeley's account of Locke's theory of substance has a life of its own which Hume took over and which I cannot ignore in this chapter.

14. I am obliged to Professor Flew for drawing my attention to this point.

15. I mean immortality in the strong and traditional sense already specified at the start of this chapter and which Flew underlines thus: 'The only use with which we are concerned here — and certainly the only use which would justify Butler's claim that here was "the most important question which can possibly be asked" — is that in which they are intended to support or express . . . the expectation . . . that we shall "Have experiences" after we are dead' ('Can a Man witness his own Funeral?', *Hibbert Journal* (1955-56) p.244).

16. Objections of this type are very elegantly developed by T. Penelhum in 'Hume on Personal Identity' in the *Philosophical Review* (1955) and elsewhere.

17. T. Penelhum, *Survival and Disembodied Existence* (London, 1970) p.97.

18. I should perhaps take the discussion further but to do so would involve a lengthy digression on Penelhum's work and consideration in detail of articles by Bernard Williams, Antony Flew and D.Z. Phillips among others. I do not think this would be justified within the scope of the present work.

19. See *Why I am not a Christian* (London, 1957) p. 72.

20. 'Personal Identity and Individuation', P.A.S. (1957) p. 244.

21. See Luce and Jessop's edition of *The Works of George Berkeley,* vol. VII, p.108 'Nay, I defy any man to produce any parallel to this in any part of the creation, or to assign one single instance wherein God hath given appetite without a possibility of satisfying it' (Sermon VIII). In the *Guardian,* essay no. 27, op.cit., p.181, Berkeley repeats the identical argument.

Notes

22. *Death and Immortality* (London, 1970) p.27.

23. *God and the Soul*, London, 1969 pp. 117-129.

24. See, for example, Samuel Clarke's *Answer to Henry Dodwell* and more particularly Anthony Collins' reply in *Letter to Henry Dodwell* (London, 1709) p. 6f. Hume seems to find common ground with Collins in much of what he has to say.

7 Miracles and Revelation

1. *Discourse concerning Natural Religion and Revelation*, 9th edition (London, 1738) p.388.

2. Ibid., p.372.

3. 'Now what convictions there can be to any sober mind concerning *Divine authority* in any person without such a *power* of *miracles* going along with him, when he is to deliver some *new doctrine* to the world to be believed, I confess I cannot understand'. Stillingfleet, *Origines Sacrae* (London, 1663) p. 143.

4. Locke, *Works*, 10 vols. (London, 1812) vol. ix, pp. 256-65.

5. Toland, for example, alludes to it: a miracle in the New Testament is 'what serv'd to confirm the Authority of those that wrought it, to procure Attention to the Doctrines of the Gospel . . .' *Christianity Not Mysterious* (London, 1696). Leslie, one of his orthodox critics, agrees that 'his [Jesus'] miracles do vouch the truth of what he delivered' *Short Method* (London, 1697) p.6.

6. *Discourse of the Grounds and Reasons of the Christian Religion* (London, 1724).

7. Sir Leslie Stephen's *History of English Thought in the Eighteenth Century*, Chapter IV, Section iv, is still an invaluable guide to the whole controversy.

8. This declaration of his conclusion appears near the beginning of each of the first four *Discourses*.

9. The controversy eventually lost touch with the original issues. The following remarkable heading to a pamphlet illustrates the decline. *The enthusiastic infidel detected being the trial of a Moral Philosopher before the grand senate of bedlam, on a stature of lunacy for publishing a RHAPSODY entitled the Resurrection of Jesus considered in answer to the Tryal of the Witnesses*, by a Brother Lunatic.

10. *The Miracles of Jesus Vindicated* (London, 1729) Part I, p.25.

11. Sherlock, *The Tryal of the Witnesses of the Resurrection of Jesus*, 'London Printed, and Dublin re-printed' (1729). All page references will be to this edition.

12. Annet, *The Resurrection of Jesus considered in Answer to the Tryal of the Witnesses* (London, 1744) 3rd edition, p.3.

13. *Hume's Philosophy of Belief* (London, 1961) Chapter VIII.

14. The account which Sherlock gives (*Tryal*, pp. 62-3) of what would happen 'If one or two were to come into *England,* and report that a Man was raised from the Dead', makes a striking and very specific contrast to Hume's account of the way reports of Queen Elizabeth's resurrection would be received.

15. 'Vindication of the Free Inquiry', in *Miscellaneous Works* (London, 1752) Vol. I, p.351.

16. The points are not easily distinguishable from one another in the way in which Sherlock presents them. They are gathered from the speech of the Counsel for Woolston and from paraphrases offered by the Counsel for the Apostles and Judge.

17. Hume attributes the argument to Tillotson. It is to be found in *Rule of Faith* (London, 1676) 2nd edition, p. 275 and in a more developed form in the *Discourse against Transubstantiation* (1684). But this attribution seems little more than a device which enables Hume to develop his sceptical arguments from the writings of a celebrated churchman.

18. The footnote was added at the end of the 2nd edition (1751), 'The Distance of the Author from the Press is the Cause, why the following Passage arrived not in time to be inserted in its proper Place'. Versions of the Indian Prince Argument occur

in Locke's *Essay,* Butler's *Analogy,* and in several minor authors. Locke's treatment (*Essay,* IV, xv, 5) is concerned with the value of evidence and could have given Hume several useful hints. But Locke does not use the story to substantiate reports of miracles. Butler mentions the argument in the 'Introduction' during the course of some very general remarks concerning probability. Flew (op. cit., p. 176) says that it is Butler's version which Hume follows. I do not think this can be substantiated. It is Sherlock's *use* of the argument, not Butler's reference to it, which provides the butt for Hume's remarks. (The Indian Prince appeared again in 1825 as the Saracen in Scott's *The Talisman,* Chapter 2.)

19. See p. 147f for Hume's use of the word 'superstition'.

20. Newman, *Two Essays on Scripture Miracles;* see also *A Grammar of Assent,* Chapter VIII.

21. *Philosophers and Religious Truth* (London, 1964) p. 35.

22. 'Hume's Theory of the Credibility of Miracles', *P.A.S.,* 1916-17.

23. *Discourse concerning Natural Religion and Revelation,* 9th ed. (London, 1738) p. 384.

24. *The Concept of Miracle* (London, 1970) p. 61.

25. The substance of this paragraph is drawn from my 'Miracles and the Religiously Significant Coincidence', *Ratio* (1975).

26. I am indebted to Professor Flew for suggesting both these difficulties to me.

27. C.S. Peirce, *Values in a Universe of Chance,* ed. P.P. Wiener, (New York, 1958) p. 292f. Quoted in Flew, op. cit., p. 179.

28 For Hume's use of the term 'popular religion' see below p. 148.

29. 'Hume, Flew, and the Miraculous', *Philosophical Quarterly* (1970) p. 235.

8 *Scepticism and Natural Belief*

1. The similarity of thought to an item in Diogenes Laertius' Life of Pyrrho might be noted in view of Hume's addiction to the phrase 'Pyrrhonian doubt': 'With regard to the things about which our opponents argue so positively, claiming to have definitely apprehended them, we suspend our judgement because they are not certain, and confine our knowledge to our experience (*Lives,* IX, 103). This is of course a very modified statement of the sort of extreme scepticism normally associated with Pyrrho and rejected by Hume.

2. I say 'final' theory because it is evident from *Treatise,* 96, and other early passages that Hume hesitates at first between belief being 'A lively idea related to or associated with a present impression' and belief being 'a particular manner of forming an idea'.

3. It is interesting to note that in some chapters devoted to attacking Hume's account of belief, Thomas Reid comes to an almost identical conclusion concerning its indefinability: 'In like manner, every man that has any belief — and he must be a curiosity that has none — knows perfectly what belief is, but can never define or explain it' *(Inquiry into the Human Mind,* Chapter II, Section V).

4. Hendel has 'demanded'. Hume's final corrected edition of 1777 has 'commanded' which seems to make better sense.

5. Flew, *Hume's Philosophy of Belief,* p. 98.

6. Since Hume muffs his account of personal identity and then continues as if nothing had gone wrong (e.g. *Treatise,* 329) it could be argued that belief in my own identity as a person going beyond the limitations of my memory should be added as a fourth. But I am not convinced this belief could be conclusively evidenced from within Hume's own writings. The other three can.

7. R.J. Butler, 'Natural Belief and the Enigma of Hume', *Archiv fur Gescicte der Philosophie* (1960), pp. 73—100. This article contains much with which I am in agreement, the argument which I refer to as 'Butler's thesis' being only a part of it. I shall refer to it subsequently as 'Butler' followed by the page.

8. *An Abstract of a Treatise of Human Nature* (1740) ed. J.M. Keynes and
P. Sraffa (Cambridge, 1938) p. 24.

9. Examples can be found in *Treatise*, 633; the essay 'The Platonist' (1742);
Enquiry, 135: 145; *N.H.R.*, 22; *Dialogues*, 214.

10. Who speaks for Hume in the *Dialogues* is a vexed question which has always
drawn the attention of critics and scholars. An impressive list of authorities may be
assembled to support Philo and an almost equally impressive list for Cleanthes. Demea
and Pamphilius have been suggested and one commentator has even found Hume's sole
personal contribution in a passage which Kemp Smith places as a footnote on p. 219.
So far in this book I have taken the philosophical arguments in the *Dialogues* on their
own merits and given as little attention as possible to the speakers. In Chapter 10 I
shall have more to say about Hume's own beliefs and the interpretation of the
Dialogues but at this stage I accept what I shall later have little occasion to amend, namely,
Kemp Smith's thesis that, although something of Hume's own beliefs is put into the
mouths of all three characters, nevertheless, Philo represents Hume in all he says and
Cleanthes can be regarded as Hume's mouthpiece only in those passages in which he is
either agreeing with Philo or refuting Demea. This is much the same as the opinion of
the first reviewer of the *Dialogues* when he writes: 'Philo is the hero of the piece; and
it must be acknowledged that he urges his objections with no inconsiderable degree of
acuteness and subtlety' (*Monthly Review*, July to December 1779, vol. LXI, p. 343).

11. Even Demea's profession 'that each man feels, in a manner, the truth of
religion within his own breast' (*Dialogues*, 193) does not claim for belief in god the
universality and *unavoidability* which would be required to make it a natural belief.

12. In *Alciphron* IV, 16—17, the sceptic Lysicles argues 'you must know then
that at bottom the being of God is a point in itself of small consequence, and a man
may make this concession without yielding much. The great point is what sense the
word *God* is to be taken in'. He concludes 'Since, therefore, nothing can be inferred
from such an account of God, about conscience, or worship, or religion, you may even
make the best of it. And, not to be singular, we will use the name too, and so at once
there is an end of atheism'.

13. My position is not the same as that advocated by Nelson Pike in his edition
of the *Dialogues* (New York, 1970). Pike contends that although Philo totally rejects
any 'scientific' version of the design argument he accepts the 'irregular' version which
Cleanthes tries to develop in his bizarre suppositions in Part III — suppositions which
had there, unsurprisingly I would have thought, left Philo 'a little embarrassed and
confounded' (*Dialogues*, 155). The detailed reasons for *not* accepting Pike's interpretation are set out in a forthcoming article by P.S. Wadia and I shall not anticipate them
here.

9 *The Causes and Corruptions of Religion*

1. This may seem a gratuitous undertaking. Surely his account of the causes of
religious belief is well enough known already? I would have thought so myself but for
an astounding comment in a relatively recent book on Hume: 'Judging by the methods
employed in the *Treatise,* we should have expected him first to have considered the
meaning of the word "God". . . . Then we should have expected Hume to give some
account of the origin of our belief in the existence of God, independently of the truth
of that belief. In short, we should have expected his treatment of God to follow the
lines laid down in his treatment of causation, the material world, and the self. But he
does not attempt this. All he does is to consider some ancient arguments for the
existence of God, and expose their weakness, and conclude that belief in God is not
rationally founded' (A.H. Basson, *David Hume*, London, 1958, p. 107-8). It may of
course be that Hume's contribution to the philosophy of religion should be brushed off
as 'disappointing' (loc. cit.). But disappointment need not be compounded by gross
disregard of what Hume actually wrote on the subject.

2. *Prospect for Metaphysics,* ed. Ian Ramsey (London, 1961) p. 84.

3. Charles Blount, *Oracles of Reason* (London, 1696) p. 195.

4. *De Veritate,* trans. M.H. Carre (Bristol, 1937) Chapter IX.

5. The three items referred to are, in order, *An Analysis of the Moral and Religious Sentiments of David Hume* (Edinburgh, 1755); *Remarks on Mr D. Hume's Essay on the Natural History of Religion* (London 1757) p. 15; *A Letter to Adam Smith on the Life, Death and Philosophy of his friend David Hume, by one of the people called Christians* (Oxford, 1777) p. 13.

6. Cf. J. Kahl, *The Misery of Christianity* (London, 1971) Chapter 1.

7. The word 'frivolous' is used by Hume with reference to religious observances, and/or virtues in the *Dialogues,* the *N.H.R.* and the *Moral Enquiry.*

8. In a discussion of this subject it might seem desirable to distinguish between what Hume has to say about religious observances and ceremonies on the one hand and frivolous species of merit or 'monkish virtues' on the other. But the subjects are not consistently separated by Hume and any attempted distinction by another on his behalf would be tenuous and of questionable value.

9. 2nd edition (London, 1786) p. 36.

10. The corollary of this point, which regards Hume as destroying expectations of immortality rather than simply ignoring a vital moral influence of relgion, has never been put better than it was by the first reviewer of the *Dialogues.* It is worth recalling his comment at length: 'But suppose Mr Hume's principles are let loose among mankind, and generally adopted, what will then be the consequence? Will those who think they are to die like brutes, ever act like men? Their language will be, *let us eat and drink, for to-morrow we die.* When men are once led to believe that death puts a final period to their existence, and are set free from the idea of their being accountable creatures, what is left to restrain them from the gratification of their passions but the authority of the laws? But the best system of laws that can be formed by human wisdom, is far from being sufficient to prevent many of those evils which break in upon the peace, order and welfare of society. A man may be a cruel husband, a cruel father, a domestic tyrant; he may seduce his neighbour's wife or his daughter, without having any thing to fear from the law; and if he takes pleasure in the gratification of his irregular appetites, is it to be supposed that he will not gratify them? What, indeed, is to restrain him?' (*Monthly Review* (July—Dec 1779) vol. LXI, p. 347). The substance of this protest is answered by Hume's remarks (*Dialogues,* 220) quoted below.

11. One of the reasons why he rejects the possibility is a moral reason: everlasting reward and punishment suppose two sorts of men, the good and the bad, and men do not fit into these exclusive categories. See Chapter 6.

10 The Dispassionate Sceptic

1. His opinion is the more interesting because he gives a hint that he knew Hume personally — 'Hume was a very benevolent and amiable man . . . we *know* he was' (italics in original).

2. Kemp Smith lists earlier protagonists in the interpretation dispute in full detail, p. 58f. His argument that Hume is Philo etc. is on pp. 58-75 and 97-123.

3. Florence, 1972.

4. James Noxon 'Hume's Agnosticism', *The Philosophical Review* (1964) reprinted in *Hume, a Collection of Critical Essays,* ed. V.C. Chappell (New York, 1966) pp. 361—83. I shall refer to this article as 'Noxon' with, where necessary, the page of the Chappell reprint.

5. Nicholas Capaldi, 'Hume's Philosophy of Religion', *International Journal for Philosophy of Religion* (1970) p. 238n.

6. *Mind* (1936)

7. *Journal of the History of Ideas* (1964).

8. What follows is substantially the same as part of an article of mine in *Journal of the History of Philosophy*, July 1976. I am indebted to the directors of the Journal for permission to reproduce the material here. I reproduce it, not in order to underline my disagreement with Professor Noxon whose good-tempered and generous reply appears in the *Journal* for October 1976, but because his thesis is the most important statement of a position with which the whole tenor of my argument is at variance. What is more, Professor Noxon's thesis has acquired something of the character of an orthodoxy. See Nicholas Capaldi's judgement in his *David Hume* (Boston 1975) p. 194n.

9. A somewhat similar objection to Noxon's point is made by Forrest Wood, 'Hume's Philosophy of Religion as Reflected in the Dialogues', *Southwestern Journal of Philosophy* (1971). I also agree with much of what Wood says on other matters. In particular he offers a shorter version (with transatlantic reference) of my argument that belief in god is not a natural belief (see Chapter 8).

10. It seems appropriate to recall Hume's own reply to a critic of the dialogue which concludes the *Moral Enquiry:* 'But you impute to me both the sentiments of the Sceptic and the sentiments of his antagonist, which I can never admit of. In every Dialogue, no more than one person can be supposed to represent the author' (*Letters*, I, 173).

11. See, for example, Apuleius, *Metamorphoses* IX, 14 and Marcus Aurelius, *Meditations* III, 16.

12. Note, for example, the tone of a letter written in 1750 at a time of alarm about an earthquake in London: 'I see only a Pastoral Letter of the Bishop of London, where, indeed, he recommends certain pills, such as fasting, prayer, repentance, mortification and other drugs, which are entirely to come from his own shop' (*Letters*, I, 141).

13. From *Private Papers of James Boswell*, eds. Scott and Pottle, vol XII. Quoted in full in *Dialogues*, 76.

14. Some years earlier Boswell had greatly upset Johnson by insisting that Hume was not afraid of death: 'I told him that David Hume said he was no more uneasy to think he should *not be* after this life than that he *had not been* before he began to exist . . .' *Boswell in Search of a Wife*, eds. Brady and Pottle (London, 1957; limited edition) p. 353.

15. 'Hume's Early *Memoranda* 1729—1740: The Complete Text' by E.C. Mossner, *Journal of the History of Ideas* (1948). Entry 27: 'It seems to be a kind of Objection against the Immortality of the Soul to consider the trifling Accidents of Marriage. Copulation etc. that bring Men into Life.' Even this earliest extant note on the subject seems to display the scepticism which was to be confirmed by all Hume's later remarks.

16. J. Hill Burton, *Life and Correspondence of David Hume* (Edinburgh, 1846) vol. II, p. 516.

17. *The Journal*, ed. W.E.K. Anderson (Oxford, 1972) p. 326.

18. Hill Burton, *Life*, vol. II, p. 512n.

19. In a somewhat diffuse article in *Religious Studies* (1976), P.G. Kuntz offers the astounding summary 'Thus he was led to theistic conclusions' (p. 428). This judgement is on the face of things, and using 'theistic' in any accepted sence, simply false; nor do Kuntz's arguments justify it.

20. *Aristotelian Society*, Supp. Vol. XVIII (1939), p. 179.

21. The judgement is my own. Others may demur. But when 'philosophy of religion' is understood in its usual modern sense — as analysis of the truth and meaning of religious beliefs — it is difficult to think of anyone other than David Hume as its founder. I notice that in his book *The Emergence of Philosophy of Religion* (New Haven, 1967) J. Collins begins his account with Hume and T. Penelhum remarks, rightly I believe, that the *Dialogues* 'is beyond any question the greatest work on philosophy of religion in the English language' (*Hume*, London 1975, p. 171). Hume is of course not the first

exponent of 'philosophies' of religion: those characteristically nineteenth-century views which treat the *phenomenon* of religion without much reference to its claims to substantial truth. The first philosophy of religion in *that* sense may well have been provided by Hegel. (Cf. B.M.G. Reardon, *Hegel's Philosophy of Religion*, London 1977, p. 77f.).

Index